MONTANA, WYOMING & IDAHO

TRAVEL✦SMART™

MONTANA

Wyoming Tourism

Old Faithful, Yellowstone National Park

MONTANA, WYOMING & IDAHO

TRAVEL ★ SMART™

C. J. Box

John Muir Publications
Santa Fe, New Mexico

Acknowledgments
Nobody knows a state or a town better than the people who live there and love it, and I'm extremely grateful for the good folks who have generously provided ideas, updates, information, and opinions. Those special friends include Gene Bryan and Chuck Coon, Victor Bjornberg, Karen Ballard, Georgia Smith, Stephenie Anderson, Karen Connelly, Claudia Wade, Kim Wimmler, Kiersten Holland, Carol Waller, Carrie Schiller, Laurie Soehner, Linda Semrow, Rhonda Olson, Mike Labriola, Patti Benner, Norma Tirrell, Racine Friede, Patty Kiderlen, John Brewer, Susan Harmala, Karen Chase, Carole Perkins, Jennie Hutchinson, Hillary Hammer, Marlyn Black, and *especially* Melissa Zorko.

Dedication
This book is dedicated to my family: wife, pal, and partner Laurie; and daughters Becky, Molly, and Roxanne, who have to put up with (and can sometimes join me in) my travels.

John Muir Publications, P.O. Box 613, Santa Fe, New Mexico 87504

Printed in the United States of America.
First edition. First printing February 1998.

ISSN 1096-4460
ISBN 1-56261-319-7

Editors: Sarah Baldwin, Heidi Utz
Graphics Editor: Stephen Dietz
Production: Marie J. T. Vigil, Nikki Rooker
Design: Janine Lehmann, Linda Braun
Typesetting: Cowgirls Design
Map Illustration: Kathleen Sparkes White Hart Design
Map Style Development: American Custom Maps—Albuquerque, NM USA
Printing: Publishers Press
Front Cover Photos: *small*—© Andre Jenny/Unicorn Stock Photos
                    large—© Kevin Syms Photography
Back Cover Photo: Grand Teton Lodge Co.

Distributed to the book trade by
Publishers Group West
Emeryville, California

HOW TO USE THIS BOOK

The *Montana, Wyoming & Idaho Travel•Smart* guidebook is organized in 22 destination chapters, each covering the best sights and activities, restaurants, and lodging available in that specific destination. Thanks to thorough research and experience, the author is able to bring you only the best options, saving you time and money in your travels. The chapters are presented in logical sequence so you can follow an easy route from one place to the next. If you were to visit each destination in chapter order, you'd enjoy a complete tour of the best of Montana, Wyoming, and Idaho.

Each chapter contains:

• User-friendly maps of the area, showing all recommended sights, restaurants, and accommodations.
• "A Perfect Day" description—how the author would spend his time if he had just one day in that destination.
• Sightseeing highlights, each rated by degree of importance: ★★★ Don't miss; ★★ Try hard to see; ★ See if you have time; and No stars—Worth knowing about.
• Selected restaurant, lodging, and camping recommendations to suit a variety of budgets.
• Helpful hints, fitness and recreation ideas, insights, and random tidbits of information to enhance your trip.

The Importance of Planning. Developing an itinerary is the best way to get the most satisfaction from your travels, and this guidebook makes it easy. First, read through the book and choose the places you'd most like to visit. Then, study the color map on the inside cover flap and the mileage chart (page 12) to determine which you can realistically see in the time you have available and at the travel pace you prefer. Using the Planning Map (pages 10–11), map out your route. Finally, use the lodging recommendations to determine your accommodations.

Some Suggested Itineraries. To get you started, six itineraries of varying lengths and based on specific interests follow. Mix and match according to your interests and time constraints, or follow a given itinerary from start to finish. The possibilities are endless. *Happy travels!*

SUGGESTED ITINERARIES

With the *Montana, Wyoming & Idaho Travel•Smart* guidebook, you can plan a trip of any length—a one-day excursion, a getaway weekend, or a three-week vacation—around any special interest. To get you started, the following pages contain six suggested itineraries geared toward a variety of interests. For more information, refer to the chapters listed—chapter names are bolded and chapter numbers appear inside black bullets. You can follow a suggested itinerary in its entirety, or shorten, lengthen, or combine parts of each, depending on your starting and ending points.

Discuss alternative routes and schedules with your travel companions—it's a great way to have fun, even before you leave home. And remember: don't hesitate to change your itinerary once you're on the road. Careful study and planning ahead will help you make informed decisions as you go, but spontaneity is the extra ingredient that will make your trip memorable.

© C. Calovich/Idaho Department of Commerce

Craters of the Moon National Park, Idaho

Best of the Region Tour

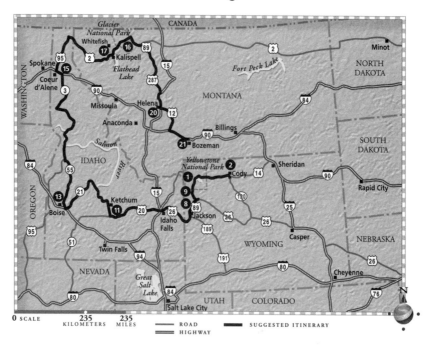

This "greatest hits" extravaganza could leave you gasping and thoroughly satiated with spectacular Rocky Mountain scenery. With Yellowstone as a centerpiece, this tour can be explored again and again.

- **② Cody** (Buffalo Bill's hometown)
- **① Yellowstone National Park** (America's first and best)
- **⑨ Grand Teton National Park** (America's most spectacular mountains)
- **⑧ Jackson Hole** (Wyoming's premier resort town)
- **⑪ Sun Valley/Ketchum** (maybe Bruce Willis will buy you a drink)
- **⑬ Boise** (largest city in the three-state region)
- **⑮ Coeur d'Alene/North Idaho** (golf course's floating green)
- **⑰ Flathead Valley** (Kalispell and Whitefish)
- **⑯ Glacier National Park** (Going-to-the-Sun Road)
- **⑳ Helena** (Montana's capital)
- **㉑ Bozeman** (location for *A River Runs Through It*)

Time needed: 2 to 3 weeks

Nature Lover's Tour

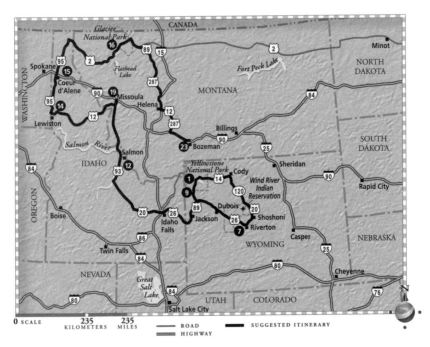

There's a real possibility that a visitor could see nearly every big game species in North America on this route, from grizzlies in Glacier to wolves in Yellowstone and elk in Grand Teton.

- ❶ **Yellowstone National Park** (grizzlies, black bears, moose, bison, elk, coyotes, deer, antelope, eagles, wolves, and 10,000 thermal features)
- ❼ **Wind River Country** (National Bighorn Sheep Interpretive Center, Wind River Mountain Range)
- ❾ **Grand Teton National Park** (all of the Yellowstone creatures except wolves, with the mind-numbing backdrop of the Teton Range)
- ⑫ **River of No Return Country** (elk, mountain goats, waterfowl, salmon)
- ⑲ **Missoula** (Rocky Mountain Elk Foundation)
- ⑭ **Hells Canyon Country/Lewiston** (sturgeon, mountain goats)
- ⑮ **Coeur d'Alene/North Idaho** (steelhead)
- ⑯ **Glacier National Park** (bear grass, grizzlies, black bears, wolves)
- ㉓ **Bozeman** (big trout)

Time needed: 10 to 14 days

Western Heritage Tour

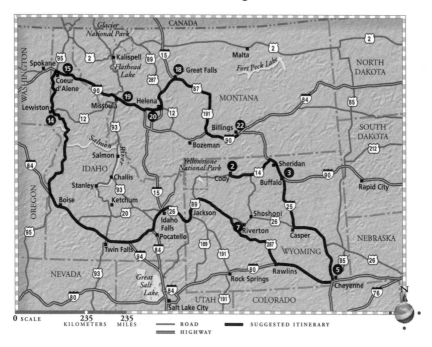

This is where it all happened—range wars, American Indian wars, historic trails—the actual Wild West.

- **❷ Cody** (Buffalo Bill Historical Center, Old Trail Town)
- **❸ Bighorn Country** (Bradford Brinton Memorial, Trails End State Historic Site, Fort Phil Kearney)
- **❺ Cheyenne** (Cheyenne Frontier Days Old West Museum)
- **❼ Wind River Country** (Wind River Indian Reservation, South Pass City State Historic Park)
- **⑭ Hells Canyon Country/Lewiston** (Nez Percé Park and Museum)
- **⑮ Coeur d'Alene/North Idaho** (Cataldo Mission)
- **⑲ Missoula** (Fort Missoula)
- **⑳ Helena** (Gates of the Mountains)
- **⑱ Great Falls** (Lewis & Clark sites)
- **㉒ Billings** (Little Bighorn Battlefield National Monument)

Time needed: 10 to 14 days

Family Fun/National Parks and Monuments Tour

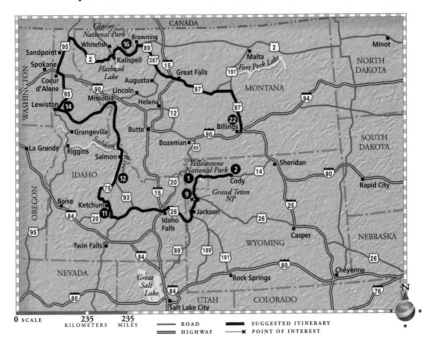

It was the outstanding scenery and natural wonders in the region that created the national park system, including the world's first national park (Yellowstone), the first national monument (Devils Tower, in Wyoming), and the nation's first national forest (Shoshone, in Wyoming).

- ❷ **Cody** (Shoshone National Forest)
- ❶ **Yellowstone National Park** (the United States' first and best park)
- ❾ **Grand Teton National Park** (river trips and cruises)
- ⓫ **Sun Valley/Ketchum** (Craters of the Moon National Monument)
- ⓬ **River of No Return Country** (Sawtooth National Recreation Area)
- ⓮ **Hells Canyon Country/Lewiston** (Hells Canyon National Recreation Area)
- ⓰ **Glacier National Park** (great hiking trails)
- ㉒ **Billings** (Little Bighorn Battlefield National Monument)

Time needed: 10 to 14 days

Winter Tour

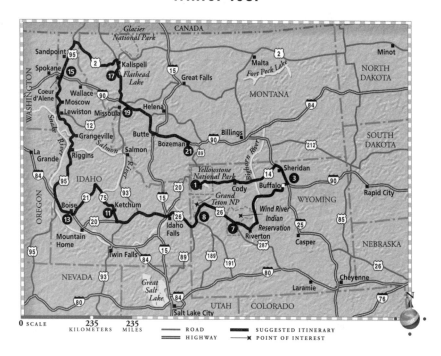

Yes, magnificent skiing is possible north of Colorado and Utah—as is some of the best snowmobiling in the country.

- ❶ **Yellowstone National Park** (snowcoach, snowmobile from West Yellowstone)
- ❸ **Bighorn Country** (snowmobiling in the Bighorns)
- ❼ **Wind River Country** (snowmobiling in the Wind Rivers)
- ❽ **Jackson Hole** (Jackson Hole Ski Area, Grand Targhee, Snow King)
- ⓫ **Sun Valley/Ketchum** (Sun Valley Ski Area)
- ⓭ **Boise** (Bogus Basin)
- ⓯ **Coeur d'Alene/North Idaho** (Schweitzer Mountain Ski Area, Silver Mountain)
- ⓱ **Flathead Valley** (Big Mountain Ski and Summer Resort)
- ⓳ **Missoula** (Snowbowl)
- ㉑ **Bozeman** (Big Sky Ski and Summer Resort, Bridger Bowl, cross-country skiing)

Time needed: 2 to 3 weeks

Adventure Tour

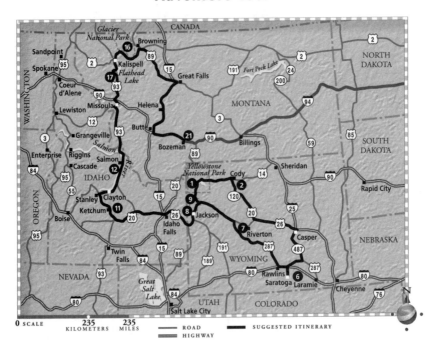

- **❶ Yellowstone National Park** (hiking, camping)
- **❷ Cody** (white-water rafting, horsepacking, hiking, trekking)
- **❻ Saratoga/Platte Valley** (white-water rafting, wilderness horsepacking trips, hiking, camping, trekking)
- **❼ Wind River Country** (white-water rafting, wilderness horsepacking trips, mountain climbing, hiking, trekking, llama treks, goat treks)
- **❾ Grand Teton National Park** (hiking, camping, mountain climbing)
- **❽ Jackson Hole** (white-water rafting, wilderness horsepacking trips, mountain climbing, hiking, trekking)
- **⓫ Sun Valley/Ketchum** (horsepacking, hiking, trekking)
- **⓬ River of No Return Country** (white-water rafting, wilderness horsepacking trips, mountain climbing, hiking, trekking)
- **⓱ Flathead Valley** (white-water rafting, horsepacking, hiking, trekking)
- **⓰ Glacier National Park** (hiking, camping)
- **㉑ Bozeman** (white-water rafting, horsepacking, hiking, trekking)

Time needed: 21 to 30 days

USING THE PLANNING MAP

A major aspect of itinerary planning is determining your mode of transportation and the route you will follow as you travel from destination to destination. The Planning Map on the following pages will allow you to do just that.

First, read through the destination chapters carefully and note the sights that intrigue you. Then, photocopy the Planning Map so you can try out several different routes that will take you to these destinations. (The mileage chart that follows will help you to calculate your travel distances.) Decide where you will be starting your tour of the region. Will you fly into Billings, Boise, or Jackson, or will you access the region from major hubs like Denver or Salt Lake City? Will you be driving from place to place or flying from place to place and renting a car for day trips? The answers to these questions will form the basis for your travel route design.

Once you have a firm idea of where your travels will take you, copy your route onto one of the additional Planning Maps in the Appendix. You won't have to worry about where your map is, and the information you need on each destination will always be close at hand.

Cheyenne Frontier Days

Planning Map: Montana, Wyoming & Idaho

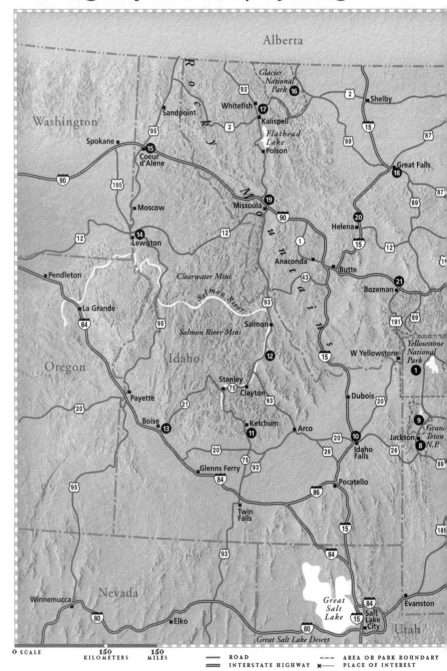

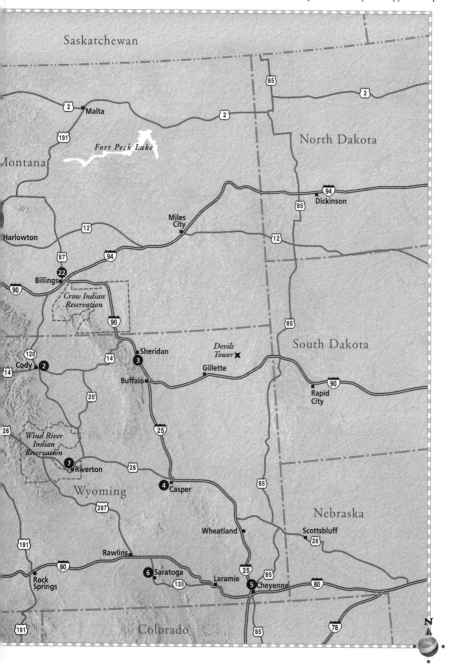

MONTANA, WYOMING, AND IDAHO MILEAGE CHART

	Billings, MT	Boise, ID	Bozeman, MT	Casper, WY	Cheyenne, WY	Coeur d'Alene, ID	Cody, WY	Glacier NP, MT	Great Falls, MT	Helena, MT	Idaho Falls, ID	Jackson Hole, WY	Lewiston, ID	Missoula, MT	Salmon, ID	Saratoga, WY	Sheridan, WY	Sun Valley, ID
Boise, ID	407																	
Bozeman, MT	123	290																
Casper, WY	229	505	305															
Cheyenne, WY	370	607	444	142														
Coeur d'Alene, ID	414	281	305	609	743													
Cody, WY	92	359	125	180	319	428												
Glacier NP, MT	321	355	241	539	681	142	363											
Helena, MT	180	360	127	404	546	255	234	142										
Idaho Falls, ID	179	291	81	383	523	235	204	160	89									
Jackson Hole, WY	236	209	159	292	404	370	163	362	280	219								
Lewiston, ID	191	272	148	283	348	407	107	378	276	222	64							
Missoula, MT	409	194	289	578	707	91	404	203	277	236	313	362						
Salmon, ID	274	251	164	468	606	142	289	113	132	95	148	192	170					
Saratoga, WY	324	519	377	106	90	670	256	618	489	458	318	266	628	535				
Sheridan, WY	101	469	208	137	275	511	106	422	281	276	267	207	496	369	340			
Sun Valley, ID	322	93	212	409	519	299	267	335	302	232	117	180	227	223	106	432		
Yellowstone NP, WY	120	288	98	263	399	345	101	291	178	131	123	99	319	207	157	374	183	201

WHY VISIT MONTANA, WYOMING, AND IDAHO?

The average visitor to Montana, Idaho, and Wyoming has a short laundry list of places to see: Yellowstone National Park is undoubtedly at the top of the list, then Glacier and Grand Teton National Parks, Devils Tower, Sun Valley, Coeur d'Alene, Jackson Hole, and so on. But as spectacular as these individual destinations are, the region as a whole is more than the sum of its parts; perhaps its most powerful pull is the deep pleasure it offers in seeing that such a place *still exists*.

This region of vast spaces filled with muscular rivers, epic mountain ranges, and herds of wildlife grazing under massive skies figures prominently in the real and mythic story of America itself. Today's visitors can see the same mountains and plains seen by the first white Americans to explore the continent, Lewis and Clark and the Corps of Discovery. Here Buffalo Bill Cody built a town and named it after himself, and Lieutenant Colonel George Armstrong Custer lost both his army and his life. The very names of many places here evoke the legends of the American West: Yellowstone, Medicine Bow, Ketchum, Last Chance Gulch, Wind River, the Oregon Trail, Chief Joseph, Cheyenne, Sitting Bull, Bozeman, and the River of No Return.

You can still feel something young, fresh, and hopeful about the Northern Rockies. Maybe that feeling has to do with how sparsely populated the region is and how much the land itself still dominates day-to-day life. Or maybe it's the fact that much of the area's "history" is still so new that you can practically reach out and touch it.

HISTORY

When President Thomas Jefferson doubled the size of the United States with the Louisiana Purchase in 1803, no one knew exactly what the territory contained—how big, how diverse, and how virtually impenetrable it was. Jefferson hoped the new country had a route—a Northwest Passage—that would connect the Mississippi with the Pacific Ocean and open up the new country to travel by watercraft. The president assigned his trusted secretary, Meriwether Lewis, to lead an expedition to explore the new land, and Lewis immediately asked his old friend William Clark to become

co-captain. The expedition left St. Louis, Missouri, in 1804. The
route was to take them through what is now North and South
Dakota, Montana, Idaho, and Oregon to the Pacific Ocean. No one
heard from them for more than two years.

Lewis and Clark didn't find the hoped-for water route, but they
did return with news of a spectacular land of endless mountain ranges
and plains, where millions of bison grazed thick grass. The curiosity of
a young nation was piqued. Oh yes, Lewis and Clark reported, there
were beaver, too. Lots of them. Big fat ones swarming the high
mountain streams and creeks. The kinds of beaver whose pelts could
be sold to trendy hat makers in Europe.

Expedition member John Colter was immediately hired to turn
around and lead a small commercial scouting party back to the Rocky
Mountains in search of those beaver, thus staking out the parameters of
a brand-new industry. In addition to finding beaver, Colter was, in
1807, the first white man to venture into what is now Yellowstone
National Park. Colter's Eastern friends later doubted his sanity when
he told them he had seen a place where water shot out of the ground,
mountains hissed and roared, and canyons slashed through the
countryside like stab wounds. They called it Colter's Hell.

Streams of trappers coursed through the Northern Rockies for
the next 20 years. Jim Bridger discovered South Pass in Wyoming—
later to become the land bridge across the Rocky Mountains for the
Oregon Trail in the 1840s and after. The Oregon Trail hosted one of
the greatest mass migrations the world had ever seen. Thousands died
along the trail. Regional populations of Sioux, Crow, Blackfoot, Nez
Percé, and a dozen other Native American tribes occupying lands rich
in accessible resources were the first to confront either negotiated
settlements, relocation, or violence.

Although the bitter feelings that resulted from the "winning of
the West" still resonate in the region more than a hundred years since
the last battles, those feelings are beginning to dissipate. White settlers
have begun to recognize and celebrate the culture and history of the
people who first occupied the land, while American Indians have
survived with varying degrees of success. Unemployment and
alcoholism are still higher on reservations than they are outside.
However, tourism has boosted some tribes' economies. "We've been
hosting tourists on our land for 200 years," a tribal council member in
Montana recently said. "We might as well recognize it." In recent years
American Indians of the region are reaffirming their unique and

separate cultures in different ways, in many cases relearning their original languages and religions.

Much of the mythology of the American West occurred in the three-state area. It truly was, and to some extent still is, the Wild West. Sitting Bull and Crazy Horse whipped Custer on the Little Bighorn River in southern Montana, just a couple of hours north of Buffalo, Wyoming, where "nesters" later fought the Johnson County Range War, against the hired gunmen sent by cattle barons. Chief Joseph led his band of Nez Percé against the United States government across Idaho, Wyoming, and Montana in what has come to be known as one of the greatest military campaigns in American history. Butch Cassidy and the Sundance Kid hung out at the Hole in the Wall in central Wyoming, C. M. Russell painted cowboys and Indians the way they really looked in Montana, and gold and silver miners went big or went home in the rain-lashed mountains of north Idaho.

Yellowstone became a park (originally called—ahem—"The National Park") in 1872, well before Montana, Idaho, and Wyoming attained statehood (in 1889, 1890, and 1890, respectively). The first national forest, Shoshone, and the first national monument, Devils Tower, were both established by President Theodore Roosevelt in northern Wyoming.

The region's economy has traditionally capitalized on its resources: mining, minerals, agriculture, timber, and recreation. However, political and economic changes have seen declines in logging, mining, and mineral extraction in recent years. The beauty and quality of life available here have brought an influx of newcomers to places like Paradise Valley and Flathead Valley in Montana, Sun Valley and Coeur d'Alene in Idaho, and Jackson Hole and Cody in Wyoming—and with those newcomers, a clash of cultures and expectations. It is just the latest in the continuing cycle of old versus new, of boom followed by bust. Tourism is now the second or third largest industry in each state.

THIS LAND IS YOUR LAND, THIS LAND IS MY LAND

Much of the land in all three states is owned by the federal government. In Idaho, for example, more than half of the total land mass is public land. It's easy to get confused by which federal agency—the National Park Service, the United States Forest Service, the Bureau of Land Management—owns what. Rules and regulations vary from national parks to national forests to designated wilderness areas, scenic byways, national grasslands, national monuments, and massive BLM tracts. Hunting, for example, is allowed on all federal lands except national parks, but it is also regulated by the states themselves. Motorized vehicles are allowed on backroads of most BLM and Forest Service lands (with some exceptions) but rarely in national wilderness areas and national parks. A "let-it-burn" fire policy often exists in national parks like Yellowstone, while a "put-it-out" policy exists in the national forests bordering the park. Puzzled? Join the club.

Residents sometimes develop a love-hate relationship with the local federal land managers, who have so much say-so in the use and regulation of the land. Sometimes the people who live in the midst of thousands of miles of federal land claim they feel like colonists. The "proper" use of the land, whether for cattle grazing, mining, timbering, or recreation, is endlessly discussed, and there are heated discussions about exactly who owns the land. Land management decisions spark controversy. Everyone, it seems, has an opinion—the environmentalists, the ranchers, the loggers, the miners, the backpackers, the anglers, the politicians, and the federal land managers.

CULTURE

The land mass of Montana, Wyoming, and Idaho is 328,609 square miles, and the combined population of the states is 2,465,000. To put that in perspective, the region is a little larger in size than the total square mileage of Albania, Austria, Belgium, Bosnia and Herzegovina, Brunei, Bulgaria, the Czech Republic, Denmark, El Salvador, Germany, Israel, Luxembourg, Monaco, Singapore, Trinidad and Tobago, and Wales combined . . . *with the total population of Pittsburgh.* That works out to about seven people per square mile—plenty of room to ride your horse . . . or to get lost.

With so few people in it, the land has always dominated the culture as well as day-to-day life in these states. Tough winters beget tough natives, and the distances between places sometimes result in a sense of isolation. Coping with the weather and the isolation often creates a sense of community as well as a wry, "we're-all-in-this-together" sense of humor. Visitors are almost always treated warmly; by and large, folks want to say hello, help you out, and find out what brought you to the region.

Most of the residents of these three states are down-to-earth, friendly, independent as all get-out, very Republican, and pretty well convinced that they won't be moving soon. They will likely be insulted if you don't seem to like their state as well as they do. And while locals are usually warm, they're not naive; they welcome visitors, but they don't necessarily embrace the newcomer who buys a 10-acre ranchette on what used to be the McKenna place and is suddenly wandering around town in $500 ostrich-skin boots looking for a perfect latte and preaching about how to improve the community.

A place that celebrates independence, freedom, and the right to voluntary solitude is bound to attract those from the farthest ends of the spectrum, such as the Freemen of Montana, the white supremacists of north Idaho, and even individuals like the alleged Unabomber, who was finally found in a remote shack in the Montana mountains. For sure, they exist. But these extremists are few in number and pose little threat to residents and travelers. After all, they've settled in the most distant crannies of the region to get away from people, not to engage them.

We would be remiss not to mention the number of celebrities who have, in some cases, made well-publicized relocations to the Northern Rockies in the past few years. Although some of these stardust-flecked types last just a winter or two before running back to California like crazed rabbits, many have chosen to stick it out and make the area their home, or one of them. The list of "stickers" includes well-known folks like Ted Turner, Jane Fonda, Michael Keaton, Brooke Shields, Meg Ryan, Dennis Quaid, and Andie McDowell in Montana; Bruce Willis, Demi Moore, and Clint Eastwood in Idaho; and Harrison Ford and James Baker in Wyoming. Celebrity watching, though, is not encouraged. Most of these people have chosen to relocate here to get away from all of that, at least part of the year. Their wishes are generally respected by locals, and in most cases very little fuss is made over them except by visiting journalists.

Overall, though, the region of Montana, Wyoming, and Idaho is a big piece of America that hasn't changed much. A writer in Montana coined a phrase for it. He called it "the last best place."

THE ARTS

Although there are brilliant exceptions, the fine arts are not as predominant in the Northern Rockies as in other regions of the United States. However, much of the best Western art in the country can be found within the region, in places like the spectacular five museums of the Buffalo Bill Historical Center in Cody, Wyoming, and the C. M. Russell Museum in Great Falls, Montana, which houses that seminal cowboy artist's life work.

In addition to the traditional Western art and other specialized museums, such as the magnificent National Museum of Wildlife Art in Wyoming, the Museum of the Rockies in Montana, and the Basque Museum and Cultural Center in Idaho, the area is flecked with a growing number of galleries specializing in regional art. American Indian arts and crafts can be seen and purchased in shops and on reservations. Other artwork currently shown within the region ranges from high-end lodgepole pine furniture, leather "Western" clothing, and antler chandeliers to funky retro cowboy items that more closely recall Roy Rodgers' Hollywood than C. M. Russell's Montana.

CUISINE

*B*eef! Lots of beef! Cut off its horns, wave it over a fire, and drag it on out here because we're mighty hungry! Next topic, please. Actually, although just a few years ago the above statement would have pretty much summed up the area's cuisine, we're happy to report that it is no longer completely true. Not that there is anything wrong with beef, mind you. Unlike many parts of the United States, the Northern Rockies suffer from short growing seasons as well as a tradition of eating food that keeps you going, though it's not necessarily food to linger over and discuss. Cowboy meals were the original fast food— large slabs of beef roasted and sliced, a mound of beans thrown on a plate, a slice or two of bread, and lots of hot coffee. The idea was simple: squat, eat, and get back to work.

Although the Beef Thing is loosening its grip on the region's menus, and new restaurants are serving a variety of cuisines, the best places—the places locals recommend—are still steakhouses and restaurants where they serve lots of beef. And why not? For the people who live here, heaven is a big, range-fed, T-bone steak cooked medium rare over a flame, with a big, baked Idaho potato or fries. Even the so-called "oysters"—usually called "Rocky Mountain Oysters" or "Prairie Oysters"—are actually the testicles of young bulls or rams. The newest addition to the basic menu is locally brewed beer.

Many restaurants that cater to the tourist trade list items like "medallions of elk" and "fresh Rocky Mountain trout" on their menus. Although the dishes can be wonderful, the "medallions" are likely from farm-raised red deer of Montana or New Zealand, and the trout are raised on farms, probably in Idaho. Federal regulations prohibit fresh game and fish from being served in commercial establishments. Because of this, those who are seeking authentic regional cuisine beyond beef must get acquainted with locals and wrangle an invitation to someone's home or to a game dinner. You might also find the subtle tastes and textures of Dutch-oven cooking in the backcountry with a cowboy outfitter, or "milk-can" or "cream-can" cooking in small communities.

However, you can find some surprisingly good restaurants scattered throughout the area, including those that specialize in Chinese, Mexican, Italian, Greek, Thai, and other ethnic and local food. Some wonderful specialty foods exists in some unlikely places; along the route of the original transcontinental railroad (now I-80 in southern Wyoming), for example, nearly every community has an outstanding Chinese restaurant—Chinese laborers built the railroad, and a few stayed. In north-central Montana the Hutterite Colonies community prepare fresh, homemade foods much as the Amish do. And in Idaho you can find potato bars, with spuds the size of NFL footballs and toppings like chili, cheese, and vegetables.

Though they are rare in these parts, vegetarians have been known to survive and live a healthy existence in Montana, Idaho, and Wyoming. (Actually, vegans not only survive but thrive these days, since it's rare to find a menu that doesn't include at least a few delicious nonmeat dishes.)

FLORA AND FAUNA

The states of Montana, Idaho, and Wyoming contain huge tracts of country inhabited by animal herds and carpeted with grasses and plants. The region is among the most undeveloped (or best-preserved—take your pick) in the lower 48 states. With the possible exception of Alaska and the Serengeti Plain in Africa, there are more species running free in this area than anywhere else on earth. Almost every big-game species known to North America exists in the wild in the three-state region. Because of the diversity of terrain, vastly different ecosystems support vastly different animals and plants.

The very high mountain peaks in all three states are home to mountain goats, bighorn sheep, chukar partridge, peregrine falcons, and whitefish and golden trout in alpine lakes and ponds. The slopes range from heavily wooded evergreen forests with treeless parks carpeted by high-mountain flowers like purple columbines to stark rocky outcrops with dozens of brands of lichen and scrub.

Mid-mountain we find elk, grizzly, and brown bear, moose, bald and golden eagles, mountain lions, pine grouse, wolves (existing in Montana, newly reintroduced in Idaho and Wyoming), rainbow, brook, lake, and cutthroat trout in the streams and lakes, salmon and steelhead runs in the big Idaho rivers, trumpeter swans, red-tail hawks, and an overlap of the plains' species that follow. These creatures thrive within lodgepole pine forests and amidst bear grass, berries, and wildflowers in such profusion that from a distance they resemble fireworks.

In the foothills and on the open plains are herds of pronghorn antelope (the second fastest animal on earth), mule and white-tail deer, bison, coyotes, fox, rainbow and brown trout in the rivers, ducks, Canada geese, sandhill cranes, rabbits, squirrels, prairie dogs, badgers, prairie falcons and hawks, pheasants, prairie chickens (sage grouse), and skunks. Cottonwood trees and willows hug the banks of streams and rivers, but on the plains beyond the watersheds, trees can be rare. If you see a grove of trees out in the middle of the prairie it's likely a sodbuster or farmer planted them, then gave up and left. Sagebrush and hardy grasses hold the earth in place on the arid plains and provide shelter and food for the herds of animals.

I would recommend taking a drive with a local who knows his or her wildlife or else hiring a guide to accompany you on a river or into a national park or wilderness area. Going with someone who knows the country can open it up for you in ways you couldn't have imagined.

THE LAY OF THE LAND

The diversity of the terrain in the three states is astonishing—from Pacific Northwest rain country in north Idaho and northwest Montana, to the spectacular Rocky Mountains that run like a spine through all three states, to Wyoming's high desert steppe plateau, to the deepest river gorge in North America (Hells Canyon) at the Idaho/Oregon border. In a single day you can drive from lush, high alpine lakes to arid sand dunes with no water for miles.

The geography has such bold variations and moods that explorers, geologists, scientists, biologists, surveyors, and residents armed with measuring devices have scrambled throughout it for many years. What they have discovered is an amazing array of superlatives: "highest," "biggest," "deepest," etc. Geologists touring the three states experience sensory overload. Because of the massive upthrusts in the earth's crust and the mountains growing out of it, literally all of the earth's geologic periods are visible within the region. On a single drive across I-80 in Wyoming or through Wind River Canyon in Central Wyoming, you can whiz by geologic strata (Jurassic, Triassic, Pre-Cambrian, etc.) that span the entire history of the earth.

OUTDOOR ACTIVITIES

If your favorite activities are shopping, lying on the beach, going to the opera, or eating gourmet food night after night, don't bother visiting Montana, Wyoming, and Idaho. But if you long to experience the great outdoors, this is certainly the place to be. Many of the most popular activities started out as ways to access the land, but they've since become industries—and passions—all their own, from mountain hiking and trekking to fly fishing on the greatest blue-ribbon trout fisheries in North America to mountain biking, horseback riding, river rafting, and camping.

Activities can be as rigorous or easy as your level of fitness and interest. National parks, national forests, state parks, and BLM lands all offer multiple forms of recreation. Many hiking trails require no more than a good map and proper clothing. To truly experience the best in the area, though, go with a professional, at least the first time. Guides and outfitters in all three states can take you wherever you want to go, using whatever means you wish to get there. Obtain a listing of bonded and certified outfitters and their specialties from the state or community in which you plan to base your adventures, and ask for references (see the Resources list at the end of the next chapter). Count on spending a minimum of $150 per day per person for the serious stuff like horsepacking and multiday guided river trips.

Although the majority of visitors treat it as such, there is really no reason to think of the region as only a summer destination. Yes, it's cold, but it's a *dry* cold. You may have heard that before, but in this case it's true. The lack of humidity in the Northern Rockies results in unusual winter conditions—deep powder snow and the feeling that it's not nearly as cold as it should be at ten below zero.

Downhill skiers are discovering that the Rocky Mountains actually do extend north of Colorado and that several unique and challenging resorts are "off the beaten path." Places like Jackson Hole and Grand Targhee in Wyoming, Big Sky, Red Lodge, Bridger Bowl, and Big Mountain in Montana, and Sun Valley, Brundage, Schweitzer, and Silver Mountain in Idaho offer world-class snow, runs, and hospitality, without the cookie-cutter feeling of the more popular resorts to the south.

Snowmobiling is a great way to access wonderful places like Yellowstone Park and lesser-known mountain ranges. An experienced outfitter can teach you the basics of operating a modern snowmobile. Some ranches and lodges specialize in snowmobiling, cross-country skiing, and even snowshoeing and winter camping.

PRACTICAL TIPS

HOW MUCH WILL IT COST?

You can find great values in Montana, Wyoming, and Idaho. With the exception of a few months a year in resort towns adjacent to national parks, across-the-board rates are most similar to those in the rural Midwest. For $90 to $125 a day, you can access the region very comfortably. By budgeting that much you'll be able to spend a little more on excursions such as river trips, horseback rides, and maybe even a day or two on a guest ranch. It's certainly possible to spend less ($60 to $80 per day) and still have a good trip, especially if you can mix camping a few nights a week with budget accommodations.

Most of the lodgings I've recommended are of the Best Western variety because they provide a certain standard of quality and economy. I've also tried to suggest offbeat ranches, lodges, and bed and breakfasts in each destination chapter. Rates for ranches and lodges range from as low as $50 to as high as $200 a night, depending on the establishment's location, amenities, and overall quality as well as on the number of meals included. The rule-of-thumb price for a fully inclusive stay (room, at least two meals, horseback riding, hiking, and other ranch activities included) is around $125 a night per person. In general, bed and breakfasts run $60 to $80 per night (less, in many cases) and range from traditional, if not exactly elegant, "bunk and beans" houses to literally the best places in town.

Like the states that surround them, the region's national parks offer a healthy mix of economical and resort accommodations. Admission to Yellowstone, Glacier, and Grand Teton National Parks has recently increased from $10 per car to $20 per car—still one of the greatest travel bargains in America. Anglers hang out en masse in the bare-bones rustic cabins ($40 a night) in the Roosevelt area of Yellowstone for quick access to great fishing. State park fees for camping range from $5 to $10 per night, depending on amenities. Commercial campgrounds average $14 to $18 per night, and public campgrounds range from $4 to $8 per night.

You'll rarely complain of too-small portions at local cafés or diners. In these rugged states, quantity rules, and meals are usually cheap. International visitors are often awestruck by the region's huge meals offered at small prices. When I travel through the three states with my family, we save money and spend less time sitting in restaurants by eating larger than normal meals at the beginning and end of the day and having snacks and drinks in the car for lunch. Breakfasts in the region are almost always ample and can easily sustain even teenagers beyond lunch. (Figure $5 to $8 each for big breakfasts and $12 to $20 for large dinners.)

More than 90 percent of all visitors travel by car, and it's not unusual for locals to travel 40 miles for dinner—or to recommend that you do so. Fortunately, gasoline prices are lower (approximately $1.10 to $1.30 per gallon) than they are nearly anywhere else in the country. Retail prices are also lower; you can expect to pay 10 to 20 percent less than average for many goods and services, except in resort towns during high season. Montana doesn't even have a sales tax.

CLIMATE

Weather across these states is, in a word, changeable. Because most of the region is higher than 5,000 feet, temperatures vary tremendously, especially in early summer and fall. In the mountains, be prepared for anything—every month of the year has seen snow at one time or another. I remember shivering in a tent in the Bighorn Mountains of Wyoming, eating hot dogs and beans on the Fourth of July while it snowed outside. Yellowstone Park seems to have a climate system all its own. You can't judge what the weather in the park will be like by the weather at gateway communities such as West Yellowstone, Cody, or Jackson. If you camp in Yellowstone in mid-September, for example, you might hike into the backwoods on an 80-degree afternoon and wake up the next morning with a skim of ice on your cooking pots. That's a temperature swing of about 50 degrees in one day, and it calls for careful planning.

Dressing in layers (usually a light T-shirt covered by a heavier cotton shirt covered by a windbreaker or fleece jacket; more, of course, in winter months) is the best way to control your body temperature. I overheard an expression for this method of dressing from a German tour guide: "Dress like an onion," she advised her group. And there's a good reason why nearly everyone is wearing a hat, fashionable or otherwise: to prevent high-altitude sunburn, which can happen remarkably quickly. Pack sunblock as well as sunglasses. Take plenty of water along with you and drink more of it than you normally would to avoid dehydration. Be careful not to overexert yourself in the thin mountain air. But don't let the mountains intimidate you—I've been with visitors who experienced

1

YELLOWSTONE NATIONAL PARK

Yellowstone is the world's first national park—a place so unusual, so spectacular, and so awe-inspiring that writer Wallace Stegner once dubbed it "America's best idea." We'll start our journey here because Yellowstone is the center of the three-state region both geographically and spiritually.

The park itself contains 2.2 million acres of wild and diverse terrain. Over 10,000 thermal features are within the borders, ranging from fumeroles (steam vents) to mud pots (best not viewed with a hangover) to geysers. Even without the thermal features, this is an amazing place. The Yellowstone River has cut 1,200 feet through the yellow rock (hence the name) and has produced the Grand Canyon of the Yellowstone and Lower Falls, twice the height of Niagara Falls. The Hayden Valley is without question one of the most picturesque places on earth—a rolling green saddle dotted with bison, elk, coyotes, eagles, and the occasional black or grizzly bear. Yup, the bears are still there, though harder to find than in the bad old days when they would beg from car to car. The National Park Service has been relocating "problem" bears into the backcountry for years.

To have a legitimate "Yellowstone Experience" (meaning you explore more than the figure-eight road system), give yourself at least three days. There's a lot more to Yellowstone than the roadside attractions. I recommend four to five days if you can afford the time. ◼

YELLOWSTONE NATIONAL PARK

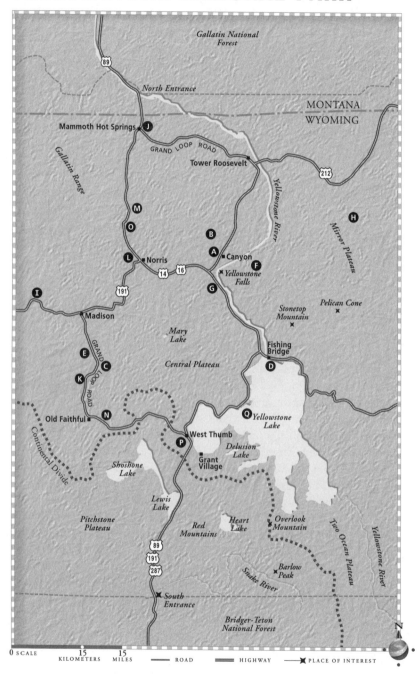

Sights

- Ⓐ Canyon Village
- Ⓑ Dunraven Pass
- Ⓒ The Firehole River
- Ⓓ Fishing Bridge
- Ⓔ Fountain Paint Pots
- Ⓕ Grand Canyon of Yellowstone
- Ⓖ Hayden Valley
- Ⓗ Lamar River Valley
- Ⓘ The Madison River
- Ⓙ Mammoth Hot Springs
- Ⓚ Midway Geyser Basin
- Ⓛ Norris Geyser Basin
- Ⓜ Obsidian Cliff
- Ⓝ Old Faithful
- Ⓞ Roaring Mountain
- Ⓟ West Thumb
- Ⓠ Yellowstone Lake

A PERFECT DAY IN YELLOWSTONE NATIONAL PARK

A brisk walk along the wooden walkway that meanders through the Old Faithful Geyser Basin will jump-start the morning and whet your appetite. Time the walk so that you arrive at Old Faithful Geyser in time for an eruption (they occur approximately every 72 minutes), then enjoy a leisurely breakfast in the historic and cavernous Old Faithful Inn. Ask the hotel to pack a lunch for you and take it along on a two-hour Lake Yellowstone guided fishing trip. Keep a couple of the perfect Yellowstone cutthroat trout for dinner. Spend the afternoon exploring Fountain Paint Pots and Norris Geyser Basin. Have a cold Black Dog Ale in the sunroom of Lake Hotel, while you listen to a string quartet and the hotel cooks up your trout for dinner. Go to bed earlier than you have in years.

YELLOWSTONE 101

Aside from the wildlife, thermal features, and geography, there is considerable human history within the park, from the wondrous log Old Faithful Inn and the massive wood-framed Lake Yellowstone Hotel to the simple and rustic Roosevelt Lodge Cabins.

Please keep in mind that only 2 percent of Yellowstone (primarily the road system and accommodations) has been developed. That means that once you get off the road, sometimes just a few hundred feet along one of the many well-marked and -maintained hiking trails, you can plunge into a whole different world than that seen through the windshield. Very few of the park's 3 million visitors ever venture off the road.

The cost for entering Yellowstone Park doubled in 1997, from $10 per car to $20 per car, but it's still one of America's greatest bargains. Much of the fee increase will be allocated toward park maintenance. However, the backlog of repairs is daunting, and stretches of the road system remain atrocious.

OPENINGS AND CLOSINGS

Yellowstone Park sets no strict seasonal opening and closing times because of unpredictable road and weather conditions. For exact dates call the National Park Service ahead at (307) 344-2015. Dates for the upcoming summer are usually announced the preceding December. However, here are a few general guidelines for summer openings:

April 18—West side roads open to motor vehicles. Mammoth to Madison to Old Faithful; Madison to West; and Norris to Canyon.
May 2—East and south roads open. Canyon to Fishing Bridge to East Entrance; Fishing Bridge to West Thumb to South Entrance; West Thumb to Old Faithful; Cooke City via Colter Pass to the Chief Joseph Scenic Highway intersection.
May 23—Tower to Canyon; and Long Lake gate via Beartooth Pass to the Montana state line.
The following are general guidelines for closing dates:
October 14—Tower to Canyon; and Long Lake gate via Beartooth Pass to the Montana state line.
November 3—All park roads.

(Note: The road from the North Entrance to Upper Mammoth Terrace and Mammoth via Tower Junction to the Northeast Entrance remains open to wheeled vehicles year-round.)

YELLOWSTONE IN WINTER

In the summer as many as 3 million people visit Yellowstone Park. In the winter months, the number drops to about one-tenth of that. The roads are not plowed in winter, and access is by snowmobile, cross-country skis, or snowcoach (a tracked passenger vehicle) only. During the winter, Yellowstone is buried in snow, and the park becomes a wholly different and, many feel, an even more fascinating place. Lodging is available only at Old Faithful Snow Lodge (a dormitory-type structure located behind the famous inn) and Mammoth Hotel at the North Entrance. Many winter visitors access the park via West Yellowstone, Montana (the "Snowmobile Capital of the World"), as well as Jackson, Wyoming, or Gardiner, Montana. These entrances have scheduled snowcoach service provided by AmFac Parks and Resorts. Private snowmobile access via the East Gate is primarily for guests of Pahaska Teepee (see Cody chapter). Thermal features that look spectacular in the summer appear even bigger and steamier in the dead of winter, and animals (bison and elk in particular) share the roadways and geyser basins with human visitors.

STUPID HUMAN TRICKS

Even though they may appear "tame," all Yellowstone Park animals are wild. Each has developed a kind of comfort zone regarding humans. Don't even try to find out what that comfort zone is. Keep your distance. Take photos from a comfortable distance with a telephoto lens, even while the fools around you rush in. Tourists who act stupidly toward wild animals (especially bison) get hurt, and even killed, every year. We don't want that to happen to you.

SIGHTSEEING HIGHLIGHTS

All activities mentioned below are run by the authorized concessionaire of Yellowstone Park, AmFac Parks and Resorts. To make advance activities reservations, call (307) 344-7311. For TDD (Telephone Device for the Deaf), call (307) 344-5395. Within the park, visitors can make activities reservations at their hotel lobby's Front Desk/Activity Desk.

★★★ **Fountain Paint Pots**—Not as massive as many of the other geyser basins in Yellowstone, Fountain Paint Pots is unique in that it contains all four forms of thermal activity seen in Yellowstone Park along one short walkway. Fumeroles, burbling mudpots, hot springs, and erupting geysers are all within a few hundred feet of one another. Fountain Paint Pots is an excellent place for children to experience a microcosm of geothermal activity in a brief time. (30 minutes)

★★★ **Grand Canyon of Yellowstone**—Even without the animals and the thermal activities, Yellowstone Canyon, with its spectacular colorful views and two huge waterfalls, probably merits the designation of a national park unto itself. Lower Falls plunges 308 feet and is most accessible via Artists Point and Inspiration Point. Upper Falls is easier to get to from the road and, although considered less awesome than Lower Falls, is certainly worth the short walk. (1 hour)

★★★ **Hayden Valley**—After what sometimes seem like too many miles of pine trees (some still burned from the 1988 fires) along the road, the Hayden Valley provides one of the grand, epic views in Yellowstone. A huge park of gently rolling hills with the Yellowstone River meandering through it, Hayden Valley looks like one of those places where someone is in charge of perfectly choreographed bison herd and waterfowl placement. There are turnoffs throughout the valley to stop and view the bison, elk, deer, coyotes, Canada geese, and even the occasional black bear. Drive carefully, though. Many more people are injured in Yellowstone by car accidents than animal incidents. (30 minutes)

★★★ **Lamar River Valley**—I like the Lamar River Valley for what it isn't. The valley doesn't have geysers, canyons, or waterfalls, and much of the area is covered with sagebrush and dotted with just a few trees. The valley contains the best fishing in Yellowstone Park, as well as wildly rugged natural scenery and terrain often ignored by visitors hightailing it to the geysers. Wolf enthusiasts may happen upon the Canadian wolf packs that were recently introduced by the National Park Service. The valley's Roosevelt area is also the place for stagecoach rides ($5.90 adults, $4.90 children) and terrific steak cookouts ($28 adults, $16.95 children) via wagon. (1 hour)

★★★ **Mammoth Hot Springs**—Mammoth Hot Springs grows on you with a subtle, quiet beauty unlike anything else within the park. There are no flashy erupting geysers here, but thousands of years of mineral-rich water flow have created massive terraces and pools, a testament to the ever-changing stream of nature. The springs are not as colorful or full as in previous years and the flow constantly changes along the terraces, giving the area a haunting beauty, especially in the bone-white sections where elk frequently rest. The Mammoth area also contains Yellowstone headquarters, the National Park Service, the concessionaire (AmFac), and a place from which to rent horses for trail rides (one-hour ride, $17, two-hour ride, $27). (1 hour)

★★★ **Norris Geyser Basin**—As the "Geyser Gazers" (folks particularly interested in geyser activities who sometimes hang out all summer in Yellowstone) will tell you, Norris Geyser Basin is one of the ornery areas that just keep surprising you with new and furious thermal activity. Check out the information posted at the entrance to find out which geysers may erupt during your visit. (2 hours)

★★★ **Old Faithful**—Old Faithful geyser may not be quite as faithful as it used to be (100- to 140-foot eruptions occur every 60 to 90 minutes, with an average wait of 72 minutes), but the fact is that the geyser is still, deservedly, the most famous thing in Yellowstone Park. Even the most cynical of visitors will "oooh" and "ahhh" when the geyser blasts. I've seen Old Faithful erupt more than 50 times, and I still don't want to miss it. A chalkboard at the activity desk inside the Old Faithful Inn predicts the next geyser's eruption, so stop by and plan your time around it. The inn (built in 1903) is a structural marvel, and Old Faithful is just one of many geysers the basin offers. (3 hours)

Norris Geyser Basin

★★★ **Yellowstone Lake**—The largest lake at this elevation (7,731 feet) in North America, Yellowstone Lake is the hub within Yellowstone Park. It is also one of the deepest lakes known, and scientists are now discovering underwater geysers and canyons that rival anything on the surface. The Fishing Bridge area near the lake is considered prime grizzly bear habitat and is thus off-limits to hikers and campers. Further down the shore, though, Bridge Bay Marina offers fishing trips, scenic cruises, and boat rentals. It's best to go out on the lake in the morning; afternoon squalls are common and come quickly. (2 hours)

★★ **Fishing Bridge**—Once lined on both sides of the road with anglers dropping baited hooks into the water, Fishing Bridge has long been closed to fishing to avoid potential human and grizzly bear encounters as well as to maintain a healthy Yellowstone cutthroat trout population. The bridge is still a fun place to visit to watch wild trout cruise the crystal-clear Yellowstone River and rise for insects. (30 minutes)

★★ **Midway Geyser Basin**—Located between Madison Junction and Old Faithful, Midway offers a nice boardwalk bridge over the Firehole River and access to two beauties, the Grand Prismatic Spring and Excelsior Spring. Grand Prismatic is known for its range and variety of colors, and Excelsior is unique for the large volume of water (4,000 gallons per minute) it angrily pumps out of the ground and into the Firehole. (30 minutes)

★★ **West Thumb**—If Yellowstone Lake indeed looks like a hand (I've never quite agreed), then you can understand how the West Thumb geyser basin got its name. West Thumb is the first geyser basin a visitor entering Yellowstone from the south (Grand Teton Park) will encounter. Unlike Norris, West Thumb may have seen its best days as a spectacular area, but it offers a good thumbnail sketch (pun intended) of a once-great geyser basin as well as a beautiful first view of Yellowstone Lake. (30 minutes)

★ **Canyon Village**—A sprawling area located less than a mile from the Grand Canyon of the Yellowstone, Canyon Village features a large concentration of cabin accommodations and an early 1960s cafeteria that looks like it was designed by George Jetson. (30 minutes)

★ **Dunraven Pass**—Drivers who aren't sure they like high mountain roads may get sweaty palms approaching Dunraven Pass (8,859 feet) between Canyon and Tower, but the views and vistas between the road and Specimen Ridge are breathtaking. (1 hour)

★ **The Firehole River**—Although the National Park Service does not encourage swimming or bathing in the waters of Yellowstone Park (and I certainly wouldn't want to challenge them), if one *were* to go swimming or bathing in soothing bathtub temperature water with the occasional view of a bison, elk, or bald eagle, then one *might* consider the Firehole River just south of Madison Junction. (30 minutes)

★ **The Madison River**—The Madison River is to fly fishers what Yankee Stadium is to baseball fanatics—a holy shrine of the sport. The road from Madison Junction to West Yellowstone follows the crystal-clear Madison. Stop at the turnouts and just look at this river. If you were a trout, wouldn't you want to live here? (15 minutes)

★ **Obsidian Cliff**—Obsidian is the black stone that was a favorite of American Indian tool- and arrowhead-makers, and this site was the source of projectile points found as far away as Ohio. Obsidian Cliff is the site of the legendary "Glass Mountain" that explorer and trapper Jim Bridger once found. According to Bridger, he could see an elk through the glass on the other side of the mountain and wasted several shots at it to no avail. (15 minutes)

★ **Roaring Mountain**—To appreciate this feature and understand how it got its name, you'll need to turn off your car engine, get out, and listen. You'll hear the sound of dozens of hissing steam vents along the face of the mountain. Although purportedly not as loud as it once was, it's still worth a stop. (15 minutes)

FITNESS AND RECREATION

The choice and quality of activities within Yellowstone are almost boundless. Activities range from short easy walks to vigorous trekking. With the exception of Glacier National Park, no other place in the region offers hikers and backpackers as many trails and opportunities as Yellowstone. For easy to moderate walking and hiking, there are well-established routes through the **Old Faithful Geyser Basin**, the

Midway Geyser Basin, the **Biscuit Basin**, the **Fountain Paint Pot Nature Trail**, and the **Terrace Walk at Mammoth Hot Springs**, as well as dozens of other lesser-known trails. Hikers who want more challenging trails and backcountry experiences should contact the National Park Service at (307) 344-2114 or stop by a park ranger station or visitor's center up to 48 hours before departing for permits, guidelines, and regulations.

Other activities include the following: Horseback rides are available at **Mammoth Hot Springs**, May 18 to 21; **Roosevelt Lodge**, June 8 to August 25; and **Canyon Village**, June 14 to September 7. A one-hour ride costs $17; two-hour ride, $27. Guided fishing trips can be had at **Bridge Bay Marina**, June 15 to September 15. One to six people can rent a 22-foot cabin cruiser for $40 per hour or a 34-foot boat for $54 per hour. Rowboats can be leased for as little as $22.75 per day. Outboards and dock rentals are also available. All of the above activities can be reserved in advance by calling (307) 344-7311. Activities can be arranged within the park, at the Front Desk/Activities Desk in all Yellowstone lodges.

FOOD

There was a time when national park food was not unlike the food found in your average junior high school cafeteria or airplane. I can't tell you to expect gourmet experiences at every turn, but I will say that the food is good, and in some cases excellent, in Yellowstone Park. And even though some sameness exists on menus throughout the park, there are a few secrets for exceptional dining and joyous gluttony.

Dining rooms can be found at **Mammoth Hot Springs Hotel, Old Faithful Inn, Grant Village**, and **Lake Yellowstone Hotel**. To make reservations (essential during high season) at any of the four dining rooms, call (307) 344-7901 or contact the front desk. The menu is the same at these places and includes steak, seafood, chicken, and vegetarian and daily specials. Prices are moderate—$14 to $25 per person. Service is generally slow but friendly, if at times a bit frazzled. It's best not to be in a hurry. For atmosphere, the best places to eat are the Old Faithful Inn—ask for the old house section near the piano and etched glass—and the Victorian Lake Yellowstone Hotel. One of my favorite meals is grilled trout (even better if you caught it yourself), rice, and dry white wine.

Some of the best barbecued ribs and beans I've ever had can be found in the rustic log setting of **Roosevelt Lodge**. After dinner you can sit back in a rocker on the front porch, put your feet up, and watch the sun go down. Setting out from the same location is the "Old West Dinner Cookout" via horseback or stagecoach to Yancey's Hotel site. Dinner is large and good, including steak, corn, coleslaw, cornbread, and those excellent Roosevelt beans.

Cafeterias are located at **Lake Lodge**, **Old Faithful Lodge**, and **Canyon Lodge**. If you want something simple, fast, and sit-down, do the cafeteria thing. Hamilton Stores are located throughout the park, each with a small kitchen and fast food. Breakfasts are especially good and can often be better and cheaper than the dining rooms. The best fast food in the park is probably the Hamilton Store at Canyon, with basic burgers and hot dogs followed by the Canyon specialty, ice cream.

Be forewarned: Throughout the park, you're bound to encounter "Yellowstone Time," a term used to describe the particular lack of urgency that comes over park employees, particularly waitstaff. Most are well-scrubbed, well-meaning, and extremely helpful and friendly. They have generally come from all over the globe for the privilege of working in Yellowstone. But most are not professional waitpeople and therefore aren't as quick and adept as the pros. In dealing with "Yellowstone Time," you can either lose your cool and get frustrated and angry, or sit back and remember that you are on vacation in a gorgeous setting and that there's no rush. I recommend the latter.

LODGING

As in all national parks, the federal bureaucratic philosophy that oversees services and accommodations within park borders is both fair-minded and mind-numbingly complex. Therefore, even though the following information is detailed, I would still recommend contacting either the National Park Service, (307) 344-2015, or AmFac Parks and Resorts, (307) 344-7311, to obtain lengthy written information about rules, regulations, and latest opening and closing dates for hotel accommodations and campgrounds. *Reservations are strongly recommended for all Yellowstone accommodations.* To reserve, call (307) 344-7311.

Please keep in mind that there are no televisions and very few telephones in the rooms in the park. If you are traveling with children who must watch Nickelodeon in the morning, they're out of luck. If you do need the amenities of the average hotel or motel, consider staying outside the park in one of the gateway communities (see below) and day-tripping into the park for the length of your stay.

YELLOWSTONE NATIONAL PARK

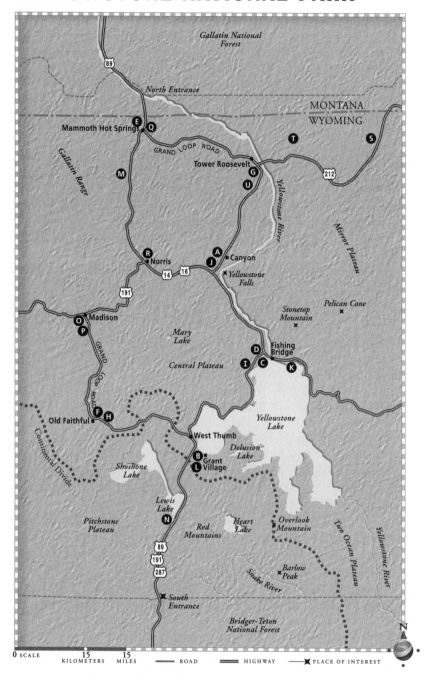

Gallatin National Forest

89

North Entrance

MONTANA
WYOMING

E Q
Mammoth Hot Springs

GRAND LOOP ROAD

Gallatin Range

M

Tower Roosevelt

G

U

Yellowstone River

T

S

212

Mirror Plateau

R
Norris

14   16

A
J   Canyon

Yellowstone Falls

191

Stonetop Mountain

Pelican Cone

Mary Lake

Central Plateau

D
I   C   Fishing Bridge

K

GRAND LOOP ROAD

F H
Old Faithful

Yellowstone Lake

West Thumb

Delusion Lake

B
L   Grant Village

Continental Divide

Shoshone Lake

Lewis Lake

N

Pitchstone Plateau

Red Mountains

Heart Lake

Overlook Mountain

Two Ocean Plateau

Yellowstone River

89
191
287

Barlow Peak

Snake River

South Entrance

Bridger-Teton National Forest

N

0 SCALE

15   15
KILOMETERS   MILES   ROAD   HIGHWAY   PLACE OF INTEREST

Food

- Ⓐ Canyon Lodge
- Ⓑ Grant Village
- Ⓒ Lake Lodge
- Ⓓ Lake Yellowstone Hotel
- Ⓔ Mammoth Hot Springs Hotel
- Ⓕ Old Faithful Lodge
- Ⓖ Roosevelt Lodge

Lodging

- Ⓐ Canyon Lodge and Cabins
- Ⓑ Grant Village
- Ⓓ Lake Yellowstone Hotel and Cabins
- Ⓔ Mammoth Hot Springs Hotel and Cabins
- Ⓕ Old Faithful Inn
- Ⓗ Old Faithful Snow Lodge
- Ⓖ Roosevelt Lodge and Cabins

Camping

- Ⓘ Bridge Bay
- Ⓙ Canyon Campground
- Ⓚ Fishing Bridge RV Park
- Ⓛ Grant Village Campground
- Ⓜ Indian Creek
- Ⓝ Lewis Lake
- Ⓞ Madison
- Ⓟ Madison Campground
- Ⓠ Mammoth
- Ⓡ Norris
- Ⓢ Pebble Creek
- Ⓣ Slough Creek
- Ⓤ Tower Fall

Note: Items with the same letter are located in the same town or area.

Yellowstone accommodations consist of nine distinct "properties" within the park. Prices range from a $24 "rustic shelter" in Roosevelt to a $342 parlor-and-bedroom suite at Lake Yellowstone Hotel. Here are the ones I recommend: The **Old Faithful Inn** (May 3 to October 20) is by far the most popular lodging in Yellowstone Park, and even if you aren't staying there, you need to visit. It's the coolest log cabin I've ever seen, and even more amazing when you learn that it was built in 1903—during the winter. Rooms with bath run from $68 to $92, $47 without bath. Cabin units (May 17 to September 15 and always a good deal for families or friends who are very close) are also available from $22 to $38 per night. The **Old Faithful Snow Lodge** (May 10 to October 6) is a dormitory-type structure that's cozy and intimate in the winter but . . . dormitory-like in the summer. Rooms range from $47 to $53, cabins from $63 to $84.

Lake Yellowstone Hotel and Cabins (May 11 to September 29) was completed in 1891 and recently renovated to a beautiful 1920s look. This is truly the elegant place to stay here. Rooms with bath run from $84 to $125 per night. Cabins are $63.

I've always liked creaky old **Mammoth Hot Springs Hotel and Cabins** (May 17 to October 6) even though the hotel hallways evoke some of the scariest scenes in *The Shining*. It was once Fort Yellowstone, headquarters of the U.S. Army, which ran the park before the advent of the U.S. Park Service. Renovations are planned. Hotel rooms are $64 with bath and $47 without. Cabins are $34.

Canyon Lodge and Cabins (June 1 to September 8) is a sprawling complex cabin city that's good for families; its suburban feel has been copied by Disney theme parks in their "wilderness" accommodations. Lodge rooms go for $93 a night and are worth it. Cabins are $48 to $84. **Roosevelt Lodge and Cabins** (June 8 to August 26) is a sentimental favorite, even though you've got to be pretty rough-and-tumble (or a fly fisher) to enjoy the "rustic" cabins. Units with bath are $63, followed by "economy" cabins with a toilet and sink. The lowest level "rustic shelters" (no facilities) are $24.

Oops, I nearly forgot **Grant Village** (May 24 to September 22). Yellowstone's own "Mistake by the Lake" is the newest of all of the accommodations, built in 1984 and modeled, I think, on those roadside motels that got famous for charging $8 a night.

The following accommodations are wheelchair accessible: Old Faithful Inn, Old Faithful Snow Lodge, Lake Yellowstone Hotel, Canyon Lodge and Cabins, and Grant Village.

It makes a lot of sense (especially in the busiest season, from mid-June through mid-August) to stay in one of the Yellowstone gateway communities instead of in Yellowstone itself. You'll find more information on each of these communities later in this book, but you can contact the following chambers of commerce to obtain accommodations information:

Wyoming: **Cody**—(307) 587-2297
Dubois—(307) 455-2556
Jackson—(307) 733-3316

Idaho: **Idaho Falls**—(208) 523-1010

Montana: **Cooke City/Silver Gate**—(406) 838-2272
Gardiner—(406) 848-7971
Red Lodge—(406) 446-1718
West Yellowstone—(406) 646-7701

CAMPING

There are more than 2,500 individual campsites in 13 public and private campgrounds within Yellowstone National Park, ranging from the largest (420 sites) at Bridge Bay to the smallest (29 sites) at Slough Creek. For hard-sided recreational vehicles the only option is **Fishing Bridge RV Park**, ($23/night, reservations required). Campgrounds have drinking water, flush or pit toilets, fire grills, picnic tables, and limited parking space. Pets are permitted on a leash. Only one motorized vehicle and/or trailer is allowed per campsite. Individual sites are limited to one family (parents with dependent children) or a party under seven people. All campgrounds have a 14-day stay limit. If you don't have a reservation, be sure to arrive as early in the day as possible and check out the campground availability boards at each entrance. If sites are available, grab them before touring the rest of the day.

AmFac Parks and Resorts operates four campgrounds and the RV park. Reservations are strongly recommended; call (307) 344-7311.

Private campgrounds include the following: **Bridge Bay**, May 24 to September 23, 3 miles south of Lake Village, 420 sites, $12.50 per night; **Canyon Campground**, June 7 to September 8, east of Canyon Junction, 280 sites, $12.50 per night; **Grant Village Campground**,

June 21 to October 8, 2 miles south of West Thumb, 346 sites, $12.50 per night; and **Madison Campground**, May 1 to November 3, 292 sites, $12.50 per night. Fishing Bridge RV Park is $23 per night and reservations are a must.

National Park Service–maintained campgrounds that don't accept reservations include: **Indian Creek**, June 9 to September 11, 75 sites, $8 per night; **Lewis Lake**, June 9 to October 31, 85 sites, $8 per night; **Madison**, May 1 to October 30, 85 sites, $12.50 per night; **Mammoth**, open all year, 85 sites, $10 per night; **Norris**, May 19 to September 18, 118 sites, $10 per night; **Pebble Creek**, June 9 to September 5, 36 sites, $8 per night; **Slough Creek**, May 26 to October 31, 29 sites, $8 per night; and **Tower Fall**, May 26 to September 11, 32 sites, $8 per night.

Just as gateway communities offer accommodations right outside of Yellowstone, area forests offer quality camping sites without the crush of high-season traffic. To find out more about surrounding national forest campgrounds, call the following:

> **Bridger-Teton National Forest** (South Gate)—(307) 733-2752
> **Gallatin National Forest** (North Gate)—(406) 587-6701
> **Shoshone National Forest** (East Gate)—(307) 527-6241
> **Targhee National Forest** (West Gate)—(208) 624-3151

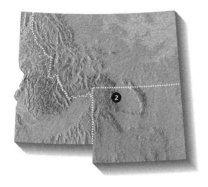

2
CODY

When a group of entrepreneurs formed to create a town to the east of Yellowstone Park in 1895, they turned to their well-known friend and asked him if he would not only be president of the company but also help name and promote a new community. The friend was Colonel William F. "Buffalo Bill" Cody of Wild West Show fame. A little over 100 years later, Cody has a population of 8,600 people and is a thriving community still proud of its Western character and cowboy roots. Buffalo Bill himself built the most impressive hotel, naming it after his daughter, Irma. The town's biggest attraction is the Buffalo Bill Historical Center, a vast complex housing four unique museums; it has been referred to as "the Smithsonian of the West."

The Shoshone National Forest, which lies east of Cody, was the first national forest in the United States. It was so designated by President Teddy Roosevelt, a frequent visitor, who dubbed the drive from Cody to the east gate of Yellowstone as "the most scenic 52 miles in America." Those 52 miles, also known as the Wapiti Valley, feature the scenic Shoshone River, beautiful and complex rock formations, and a series of tucked-away dude and guest ranches. ◼

CODY

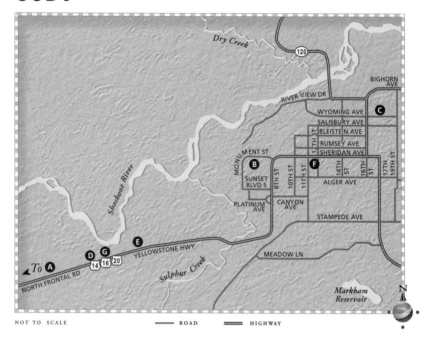

NOT TO SCALE   ━━ ROAD   ══ HIGHWAY

Sights

- **A** Buffalo Bill Dam and Visitor Center
- **B** Buffalo Bill Historical Center
- **C** Cody Chapel Murals
- **D** Cody Nite Rodeo
- **E** Historic Wyoming Territory Old West Miniature Village
- **F** Irma Hotel
- **G** Old Trail Town

A PERFECT DAY IN CODY

Start the morning with a big breakfast at the Irma Hotel, then step out onto Main Street wearing your cowboy hat and squinting into the sun. Drive west to the main lodge of one of the historic guest ranches in the Wapiti Valley to meet the wrangler who will match you with the right horse and gear; then lead the way into the mountains. In the afternoon, head back to Cody and the four museums of the Buffalo Bill Historical Center. Have an early dinner at the Proud Cut before heading out to Old Trail and the Cody Nite Rodeo to whoop it up.

SIGHTSEEING HIGHLIGHTS

★★★ **Buffalo Bill Historical Center**—You'll realize why the admission ticket you purchase is good for two days when you enter this 230,000-square-foot complex housing four museums. The BBHC is quite simply the nation's greatest museum dedicated to the American West. And like other great museums, the complex is constantly improving, initiating, and hosting major exhibitions.

The **Whitney Gallery of Western Art**, completed in 1959, showcases paintings and sculpture depicting the historical, contemporary, and mythic West. Artists represented include Albert Bierstadt, George Catlin, Charles Miller, Charlie Russell, Thomas Moran, Frederic Remington, and Dallas Sharp.

The **Buffalo Bill Museum**, completed in 1969, is dedicated to the man who provided the town, the dam, the scenic byway, the museum, the . . . (you get the drift) with their very *names*. This museum gives an honest portrait of the life of Buffalo Bill Cody, the scout, hunter, guide, showman, and entrepreneur.

The **Plains Indian Museum**, completed in 1979, examines the artifacts, dress, and culture of the region's Plains Indians, including the Sioux, Blackfeet, Cheyenne, Crow, Shoshone, and Nez Percé. This is a fascinating, illuminating display.

The **Cody Firearms Museum** (formerly the Winchester Museum but rededicated in 1991 with the opening of the new wing) traces the development of firearms through human history, emphasizing early American design and engineering. There are more than 5,000 firearms on display, from European blunderbusses to Gatling Guns to modern rifles. Details: 720 Sheridan Avenue; (307) 587-4771; open daily May 8 a.m. to 8 p.m., June through September 7 a.m. to 8 p.m., October

8 a.m. to 5 p.m.; November through April Thursday through Monday 10 a.m. to 2 p.m. Admission: $8 adults, $6.50 seniors, $4 students (ages 13 to 21), $2 youth (ages 6 to 12), free under 6. (4 hours)

★★ **Cody Nite Rodeo**—It's said that there's a rodeo going on someplace in Wyoming, Montana, and Idaho every night of the summer, but timing is the key. In Cody timing's no problem because it really does have a rodeo every single night of the summer—and a pretty good one at that. Cody likes to call itself the "Rodeo Capital of the World," and the Nite Rodeo, going since 1938, is the primary reason. Details: Yellowstone Highway; (307) 587-5155. Admission: $10 adults, $4 children in the grandstand; $12 and $6 in the "Buzzard's Roost" (behind the chutes). (2 hours)

★★ **Irma Hotel**—Buffalo Bill Cody built the elegant Irma Hotel at the turn of the century and named it for his daughter. Decorated with Frederick Remington paintings, the building's focal point is the magnificent cherrywood bar claimed to have been a gift from Queen Victoria to Buffalo Bill. Details: 1192 Sheridan Avenue; (307) 587-4221. Free. (30 minutes)

★★ **Old Trail Town**—About 15 years ago, a local man named Bob Edgar went up in the mountains and out on the plains, gathering historic cabins, homes, and buildings, bringing them back to Cody, then reconstructing them. Included is the grave of "Jeremiah" Johnson and hideouts used by Butch Cassidy and the Sundance Kid. Inside are good collections of artifacts. Bob or Terry Edgar will probably be there to say hello and answer any questions. Details: Yellowstone Highway; (307) 587-5302; open May 20 through September 15 8 a.m. to 7 p.m. Admission: $4 adults, children under 12 free. (30 minutes)

★ **Buffalo Bill Dam and Visitor Center**—Buffalo Bill knew that water fueled growth and prosperity in the arid mountain West. He also knew that in order to make Cody and the surrounding area prosper, irrigation was necessary. The Buffalo Bill Dam was completed by the Bureau of Reclamation in 1910. At a height of 325 feet, it was the highest dam in the world. In 1993 an extra 25 feet were added. Because of its significance, the dam was placed on the National Register of Historic Places in 1973. The Buffalo Bill Dam Visitor Center provides a commanding view of Shoshone Canyon and

offers natural history displays. Details: 6 miles east of Cody on
Yellowstone Highway; (307) 587-5714; open daily May 8 a.m. to
6 p.m.; June to Labor Day 8 a.m. to 8 p.m.; Labor Day through
September 8 a.m. to 6 p.m. Free. (30 minutes)

Cody Chapel Murals—These murals illustrate historic scenes from
the first 70 years of the Church of Jesus Christ of Latter Day Saints
(the Mormons). The exhibit tells the story of the colonization of
Wyoming's Big Horn Basin. Details: Wyoming Avenue and 17th
Street; (307) 587-3290; open June through mid-September; call for
hours. Free. (20 minutes)

Historic Wyoming Territory Old West Miniature Village—This
miniature village has dioramas of Western and Wyoming history as
well as American Indian and other artifacts. Details: 142 West
Yellowstone Highway; (307) 587-5362; open daily June to August
8 a.m. to 10 p.m.; May and September 10 a.m. to 6 p.m. Admission:
$3 adults, $1 children. (20 minutes)

FITNESS AND RECREATION

River trips from two hours to a half-day are run through **Shoshone
River Canyon**. Trips include both white-water and scenic stretches
and are available May through September. Most trips cost $18 for
adults and $15 for children for a 6-mile trip (approximately two hours);
$24 adults and $20 children for a 13-mile trip (approximately three
hours); and $45 per person for half-day or gourmet trips. Check out
Wyoming River Trips, (307) 587-6661, and **River Runners**, (307)
527-RAFT. The Cody area also offers great trout-fishing waters
including the Yellowstone Park drainages. For guided trips, call **Tim
Wade's North Fork Anglers**, (307) 527-7274, or **Yellowstone
Troutfitters**, (307) 587-8240.

Opportunities abound for beginner to experienced equestrians in
and around Cody. Trail rides are available at nearly all Wapiti Valley
and Sunlight Basin lodges and are too numerous to list here. For
available in-town rides, contact **Cedar Mountain Trail Rides**, (307)
527-4966, or the **Gateway Motel and Campground**, (307) 587-6507.
Golfers will enjoy the **Olive Glenn Golf and Country Club**, 802
Meadow Lane, (307) 587-5551, an 18-hole PGA championship golf
course open to the public.

FOOD

I don't know whether it's the atmosphere or the breakfasts of steak and eggs or beer-batter pancakes at the **Irma Hotel**, 1192 Sheridan Avenue, (307) 587-4221, that makes me go back time and again. **La Comida**, 1385 Sheridan Avenue, (307) 587-9556, offers decent Mexican food at affordable prices. **Maxwell's**, 937 Sheridan Avenue, (307) 527-7749, serves good salads, sandwiches, pastas, and daily specials. The **Proud Cut**, 1227 Sheridan Avenue, (307) 527-6905, is what Cody is all about with its "Kickass Cowboy Cuisine," including thick steaks and Rocky Mountain Oysters (bull testicles). **Cassie's Supper Club**, 214 Yellowstone Avenue, (307) 527-5500, offers some of the same attitude and is located in a former house of prostitution. Very fine Northern Italian dining can be had at **Franca's Italian Dining**, 1421 Rumsey Avenue, (307) 587-5354, with excellent food and service at very affordable prices.

LODGING

The largest lodging complex in town is the Cody Holiday Inn and Buffalo Bill Village Resort. The **Holiday Inn**, 1701 Sheridan Avenue, (307) 587-5555, is standard and hosts a large percentage of international customers en route to Yellowstone, at rates of $50 to $120 for a single. The **Buffalo Bill Village Resort**, 1701 Sheridan Avenue, (307) 587-5544, is adjacent to the Holiday Inn and consists of refurbished small historic cabins built in the 1920s, with rates of $60 to $85. The **Comfort Inn at Buffalo Bill Village Resort**, 1601 Sheridan Avenue, (307) 587-5556, offers budget accommodations and, like the cabins, guests can use all the resort facilities; rates are $40 to $120.

The **Best Western Sunset**, 1601 Eighth Street, (307) 587-4265, is a popular 120-room facility, with rates from $44 to $99. The new **Burl Inn**, 1213 17th Street, (307) 587-2084, features burl wood decor. Rates are $55 to $95. The **Irma Hotel**, 1192 Sheridan Avenue, (307) 587-4221, is still charming if you request the old rooms. Rates run from $45 to $95.

Located at the east gate to Yellowstone Park, **Pahaska Tepee Resort**, 183-CCC Yellowstone Highway, (307) 527-7701, occupies the site of Buffalo Bill's original hunting lodge. This unusual property has 50 units from $65 to $95 including activities.

CODY

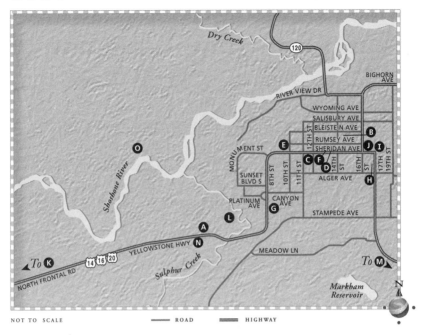

NOT TO SCALE   ━━━ ROAD   ═══ HIGHWAY

Food

- **A** Cassie's Supper Club
- **B** Franca's Italian Dining
- **C** Irma Hotel
- **D** La Comida
- **E** Maxwell's
- **F** Proud Cut

Lodging

- **G** Best Western Sunset
- **H** Burl Inn
- **I** Cody Holiday Inn and Buffalo Bill Village Resort

Lodging (continued)

- **J** Comfort Inn at Buffalo Bill Village Resort
- **C** Irma Hotel
- **K** Pahaska Tepee Resort

Camping

- **L** Camp Cody
- **M** Cody KOA Campground
- **N** Ponderosa Campground
- **O** Shoshone Forest

Note: Items with the same letter are located in the same town or area.

Guest ranches and lodges vary tremendously in amenities, activities, and price. The best way to choose a ranch is to contact the **Park County Travel Council**, 836 Sheridan Avenue, P.O. Box 2777, Cody, WY 82414; (307) 587-2297.

CAMPING

Cody features three good private campgrounds within town. All offer hookups, activities, and facilities and range from $12 to $20 per night. **Cody KOA Campground**, 5561 Greybull Highway, (307) 587-2369, open May through September, provides free breakfast and entertainment. The **Ponderosa Campground**, 1815 Yellowstone, (307) 587-9203, is large and within walking distance of the BBHC. **Camp Cody**, open all year is a mile from the Buffalo Bill Historical Center, at 415 Yellowstone Avenue, (307) 587-9730.

There are many public sites in the surrounding **Shoshone Forest**, ranging from the free Dead Indian Campground to $5 per night. Contact the National Forest Service at (307) 527-6921.

NIGHTLIFE

If you like your nightlife wild and Western, you'll like Cody after dark. If you prefer cool jazz or rap, you'll need to drive a thousand miles away. **Cassie's**, 214 Yellowstone Avenue, (307) 527-5500, features live C&W bands, dancing, and an active bar. **Angie's Silver Dollar Saloon**, 1313 Sheridan Avenue, (307) 587-3554, offers live entertainment including rock 'n' roll and comedy shows. Call ahead to see who and what is on. The **Bronze Boot**, 525 West Yellowstone, (307) 587-6595, has easy listening music and sometimes a dinner theater. And you'll need to take a look at the painting that inspired the name of the **Bottoms-Up Lounge** in the Holiday Inn, 1701 Sheridan Avenue, (307) 587-5555.

Scenic Routes: The Wapiti Valley and the Sunlight Basin

Two of the most scenic drives in Wyoming are based out of Cody and can even be combined into one magnificent day-long trip that begins and ends in town.

Reached by driving north from Cody on Highway 120 to Highway 296, the **Chief Joseph Scenic Highway** meanders through the Sunlight Basin, one of the most beautiful places on earth, en route to Cooke City, Montana, and the northeastern entrance to Yellowstone National Park. The drive affords spectacular mountain vistas and access to a dozen excellent guest and dude ranches, many of which are in the basin itself.

In 1877 Nez Percé Chief Joseph guided 200 of his people through this area to escape U.S. Army persecution. They continued through Montana until they were exhausted and defeated just south of the Canadian border. The rugged and spectacular canyons, mountains, and gorges viewable from the recently paved road will take your breath away, and you'll wonder just how Chief Joseph was

THE WAPITI VALLEY AND THE SUNLIGHT BASIN

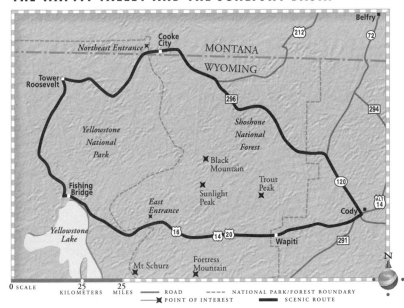

able to move through them so efficiently with his entire band of men, women, and children. Around 23 miles into the trip, after descending the unfortunately named **Dead Indian Hill**, the traveler will come to a bridge that crosses the **Sunlight Creek Canyon**. The junction of Highways 296 and 212 is a very popular rock climbing area. Ample camping opportunities are available along this scenic route.

The other route, U.S. Highway 14-16-20 West, goes through the Wapiti Valley and covers 101 miles of varied and spectacular scenery en route to the east entrance of Yellowstone. Recently widened and improved, the road takes you to some of the finest, oldest, and most interesting guest and dude ranches in the country as well as the first ranger station (**Wapiti**) in the first national forest (**Shoshone**). The haunting rock formations known as the **Holy City** are best viewed at dusk. Teddy Roosevelt called the second half of the route "the most scenic 50 miles in America." ◼

3

BIGHORN MOUNTAIN COUNTRY— SHERIDAN/BUFFALO

If you were to pick one place to be the subject of a mini-series about the real Wild West—encompassing the epic of western expansion, large-scale fights with American Indians, violent range wars between cattlemen and sheepmen, gripping cultural struggles between Old World noblemen and New World sodbusters—you would probably choose the Bighorn Mountain area in northern Wyoming. Important and violent events happened here in the midst of the beautiful mountains, lush valleys, and gorgeous Western sunsets.

Native Cheyenne, Sioux, and Arapaho Indians hated the encroachment of the Bozeman Trail across their lands in the 1870s. So many battles resulted that the trail became known as the "Bloody Bozeman." After settlement, Buffalo and Sheridan were established. Sheridan attracted English blue-blood nobility, who established a cattle-baron empire. Buffalo attracted independent sodbusters and a rakish element who claimed parcels of the cattle barons' land as their own. It was only a matter of time before the two would clash. When they did, in the 1890s, the battle became known as the Johnson County Range War, which is the subject of countless books and movies about the West.

Today both Sheridan (population 13,400) and Buffalo (population 3,300) proudly retain their Western heritage, and they wear it well. Both boast attractive and authentic downtown areas, and both have escaped (so far, anyway) the urban gentrification that is transforming traditional communities all over the West. ◪

SHERIDAN

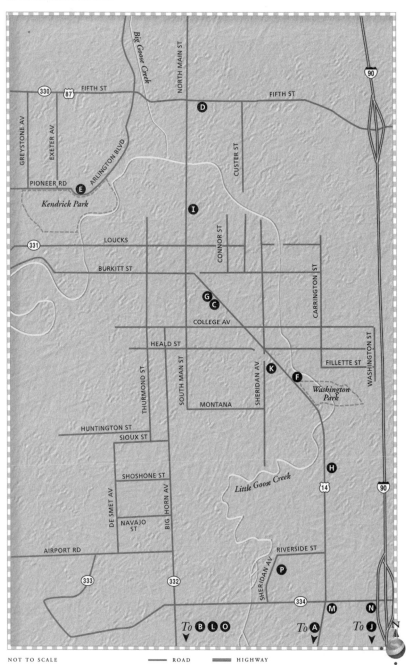

NOT TO SCALE   ━━ ROAD   ▭▭ HIGHWAY

Sights

Ⓐ Big Horn Equestrian Center

Ⓑ Bradford Brinton Memorial

Ⓒ King's Saddlery

Ⓓ Sheridan Inn

Ⓔ Trail End State Historic Site

Food

Ⓕ Cattleman's Cut

Ⓖ Ciao

Ⓗ Golden Steer

Ⓘ Sanford's Grub, Pub, & Brewery

Ⓙ Wagon Box Supper Club

Lodging

Ⓚ Best Western Sheridan Center Motor Inn

Ⓛ Blue Barn Bed and Breakfast

Ⓜ Mill Inn

Ⓝ Sheridan Holiday Inn

Ⓞ Spahn's Big Horn Mountain Bed and Breakfast

Camping

Ⓟ Big Horn Mountain KOA

A PERFECT DAY IN BIGHORN MOUNTAIN COUNTRY

It's Western history day, and after a big steak-and-eggs breakfast (pick any place) in Sheridan, go to King's Saddlery and buy a King Ropes baseball cap. Then proceed to Buffalo via Fort Phil Kearney to learn how wild the West sometimes got. Relive the Johnson County Range War at the Jim Gatchell Museum. Now that you know how the squatters and poor cowboys fared, visit the Bradford Brinton Memorial to see how the other side—the cattle barons— lived. Wind up the day sipping lemonade on the covered porch of the Sheridan Inn before heading to the Mint Bar to spend the evening drinking beer and swapping lies with cowboys.

SIGHTSEEING HIGHLIGHTS

★★★ **Bighorn National Forest**—OK, this gets confusing. Is it "Bighorn," one word, or "Big Horn," two words? Well, it just depends. The national forest is the Bighorn National Forest. The town is Big

Horn, Wyoming, and the river is also the Big Horn. The animal is a bighorn sheep. Got that?

Wyoming is blessed with five national forests covering a wide variety of terrain. The Bighorn National Forest turned 100 years old in 1997. The Bighorns are Wyoming's most underrated mountains, containing hundreds of miles of excellent byways, camping, fishing, hunting, and exploring opportunities. The 189,000-acre **Cloud Peak Wilderness Area** is one of Wyoming's great backpacking and horse-packing areas, with elevations ranging from 8,500 to 13,165 feet. There are 19 managed campgrounds in the Bighorns, many located on prime fly-fishing and spin-casting lakes and streams.

Highways 16, 14, and 14A are designated as National Scenic Byways. A short distance off Highway 14A is the **Medicine Wheel**, a mysterious remnant of Native American culture so ancient that no one knows which tribe created it. Made of stones forming 28 spokes with a circumference of 245 feet, the wheel sits high on a remote mountain top. Scientists estimate that it's at least 7,500 years old, and today's American Indians still revere it as a powerful spiritual site. For more information on the Medicine Wheel in the Bighorn National Forest, call (307) 548-6541. Details: Buffalo Ranger District, National Forest Service, 1425 Fort Street, Buffalo; (307) 684-1100. (30 minutes)

★★ **Bradford Brinton Memorial**—Tucked away on a cottonwood-lined, paved road, the memorial is the former site of Brinton's Quarter Circle A Ranch. The spacious, 20-room ranch house is the main attraction, with its charming antique furnishings, monogrammed linens, handmade quilts, silver, and outstanding collection of Western art and rare books. The artwork is by the likes of Charles Russell, Frederick Remington, and John James Audubon. Details: 239 Brinton Road, Big Horn; (307) 672-3173; open May 15 through Labor Day 9:30 a.m. to 5 p.m. Admission: $3 adults, $2 seniors and children. (1 hour)

★★ **Fort Phil Kearney**—This state historic site has the bloodiest history of any fort in the West. Thousands of American Indians, including the Sioux, Arapaho, and Cheyenne, clashed repeatedly with the 250 U.S. Cavalrymen stationed there to protect the Bozeman Trail. Fort Phil Kearney was the focal point of siege after siege by Chief Red Cloud, until the Army finally gave up and retreated, ceding it to the natives. It was also the site of the Wagon Box fight, a battle in which soldiers tipped over their wagons to use as barricades and staved off a

Sioux onslaught by the use of rapid-fire rifles. The visitor's center and state museum are staffed during the summer only. Details: 17 miles north of Buffalo off I-90 and U.S. 87; (307) 684-7629; open daily May 15 through September 8 a.m. to 6 p.m., April through May 14 and October and November Wednesday through Sunday noon to 4 p.m. Admission: $1 adults, under 18 free. (1 hour)

★★ **Jim Gatchell Museum**—This four-level museum in two buildings features one of the largest collections of America Indian artifacts in Wyoming, along with memorabilia from the Johnson County Range War of 1892 and the Bozeman Trail. Detailed dioramas depict scenes from the Wagon Box fight, the Range War, and Buffalo's Main Street as it appeared in the 1880s. A collection of saddles and pioneer items fills the lower portion of the main building. This fine museum is a treasure trove for Western history buffs. Details: 100 Fort Street, Buffalo; (307) 684-9331; open daily May through October 9 a.m. to 8 p.m. Admission: $2 adults, children free. (1 hour)

★★ **King's Saddlery**—The King family of Sheridan has been making saddles for kings, queens (including Elizabeth, who visited in the 1980s), Arab sheiks, rodeo champions and rodeo queens, and people from all walks of life for more than 30 years. Because of the superior quality of their workmanship in saddles and, later, ropes (a fixture on the heads of thousands of cowboys and cowboys-to-be across the West is the King Ropes baseball cap), the operation moved out of a Sheridan garage and onto Main Street. It continues to grow, and so does the Kings' reputation. The family has added a museum to the manufacturing facility, but the walls of working ropes and beautiful saddles are the prime attraction. Details: 184 North Main, Sheridan; (307) 672-2702 or (800) 443-8919; open Monday through Saturday 10 a.m. to 6 p.m. Free. (30 minutes)

★★ **Sheridan Inn**—Only six years after Lt. Col. George Custer was wiped out less than 120 miles to the north, the Sheridan Inn opened its doors. Now a National Historic Landmark, the Inn was considered the finest hotel between Chicago and San Francisco at the time, lodging such famous people as Buffalo Bill, Calamity Jane, Teddy Roosevelt, Will Rogers, Charlie Russell, General Blackjack Pershing, and Ernest Hemingway. Buffalo Bill even auditioned performers for his Wild West Show from the inn's front porch. The unique construction, including

69 gables and a pleasant shaded porch on a beautifully landscaped lawn, has always attracted attention. The historic building was saved from destruction by a local philanthropist and has been lovingly restored by a group of volunteers. Details: Fifth and Broadway, Sheridan; (307) 674-5440; open Memorial Day to Labor Day Monday through Saturday 9 a.m. to 8 p.m., Sunday 10 a.m. to 4 p.m.; rest of the year 9 a.m. to 3 p.m. Admission: $3 adults, $2 children, and $10 families. (1 hour)

★ **Trail End State Historic Site**—The Flemish Revival home of former Wyoming Governor and U.S. Senator John B. Kendrick (called "The Cowboy Senator") was completed in 1913. It is fully furnished with original artifacts and period reproductions. Along with the Bradford Brinton Memorial, it's a glimpse into how the "other half"— the moneyed cattle barons—lived in the early twentieth century. Guided tours are available. Details: 400 Clarendon Avenue, Sheridan; (307) 674-4589; open daily June through August 9 a.m. to 6 p.m.; rest of the year 1 p.m. to 4 p.m. Free, but donations appreciated. (1 hour)

Big Horn Equestrian Center—The first polo field and the Big Horn Polo Club were established in Wyoming in the 1880s, as entertainment for the blue-bloods who had moved west and north to establish Wyoming as cattle country. Both the field and the club still exist, and the game is played every Sunday afternoon from May through September. The Equestrian Center is also the place to be for dressage competitions, steeplechase races, steer-roping events, soccer tournaments, and more. Details: City of Sheridan Convention and Visitors Bureau, P.O. Box 7155, Sheridan, WY 82801; (800) 453-3650, ext. 22. (20 minutes)

FITNESS AND RECREATION

Miles of hiking, backpacking, horsepacking, llama trekking, and mountain biking are available within the **Bighorn National Forest**. Many of the trailheads are located adjacent to campgrounds and lead visitors to some of the best fishing and scenery in the area. Excellent trails include **Hunter, Circle Park, Elgin Park, West Tensleep Lake**, and **Battle Park**. For maps, permits, and good information, contact the Buffalo Ranger District, National Forest Service, 1425 Fort Street, Buffalo, WY 82834; (307) 684-1100. Buffalo offers a fine local trail system, the **Clear Creek Trail System**, which includes 11 short stages through historic Buffalo and along Clear Creek. The system is well-marked, and maps are available at the Buffalo Chamber of Commerce, 55 North Main Street, (307) 684-5544. For pack trips and guided fishing trips in the Bighorns, I recommend **Fly Shop of the Big Horns**, 227 North Main Street, Sheridan, (307) 672-5866, or Pete Dube's **Bear Track, Inc.**, 8885 U.S. 16 West, Buffalo, (307) 684-2528, for trips lasting from an hour to several days. The **Buffalo Golf Course**, West Hart Street, Buffalo, (307) 684-5266, is considered to be one of Wyoming's great secrets, and the **Kendrick Golf Course**, Loucks Street, Sheridan, (307) 674-8148, has been rated one of Wyoming's five best golf courses by *Golf Digest*. **Antelope Butte** is a small ski area in the Bighorns near Dayton, with 18 runs and three lifts. Lift tickets are a very affordable $20. For details, call (307) 655-9530.

FOOD

Ahem. The steaks are very good tonight. Talk about cattle country. The base of the Bighorns, including Sheridan and Buffalo, literally exist because of cattle. Therefore, they know a little something about beef.

In Sheridan, the **Golden Steer**, 2071 North Main, (307) 674-9334, and the **Cattleman's Cut**, 927 Coffeen Avenue, (307) 672-2811, are famous for huge and affordable steaks in a family-style atmosphere. There's a debate over which serves the best steak, but I think it's a toss-up. **Sanford's Grub, Pub, & Brewery**, 1 East Alger Avenue, (307) 674-1722, is a new addition, offering microbrews (try the Big Horn Wheat), burgers, steaks, pasta, and a raucous college-type atmosphere. **Ciao**, 120 North Main, (307) 672-2838, is a new fine-dining restaurant that's getting high marks for its romantic atmosphere and excellent food.

In Buffalo, the **Busy Bee Diner**, 2 North Main, (307) 684-7544, is an icon, a classic burger-slinging diner that's faded through the years but still worth a stop. **Colonel Bozeman's**, 655 East Hart Street, (307) 684-5555, serves traditional American favorites (meaning steaks and burgers) amid Old West displays. Between Sheridan and Buffalo in Story, the **Wagon Box Supper Club**, 108 North Piney Road, (307) 683-2444, offers wonderful steaks and seafood in a 1907 log building.

BUFFALO

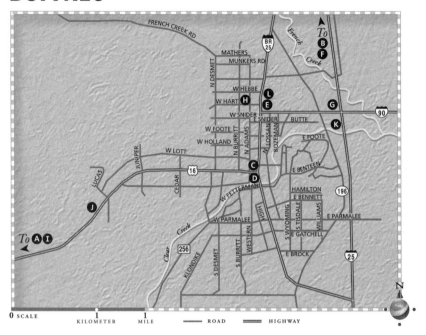

Sights

- **A** Bighorn National Forest
- **B** Fort Phil Kearney
- **C** Jim Gatchell Museum

Food

- **D** Busy Bee Diner
- **E** Colonel Bozeman's
- **F** Wagon Box Supper Club

Lodging

- **G** Crossroads Inn
- **H** Cloud Peak Bed and Breakfast

Camping

- **I** Big Horn Mountains Campground
- **A** Bighorn National Forest
- **J** Buffalo KOA
- **K** Deer Park Campground
- **L** Indian Campground

Note: Items with the same letter are located in the same town or area.

LODGING

In Sheridan, the **Sheridan Holiday Inn**, 1809 Sugarland Drive, (307) 672-8931, is the largest property (212 rooms) offering the most amenities (including an elevator, which is big-time stuff in Wyoming). Rates are $48 to $125 depending on season. The **Mill Inn**, 2161 Coffeen Avenue, (307) 672-6401, is a former flour mill that's been recently refurbished. Big rooms and good value at $29 to $52. The **Best Western Sheridan Center Motor Inn**, 612 North Main, (307) 674-7421, has an excellent location in the heart of downtown, within walking distance of King's Saddlery and The Mint, at rates from $35 to $58.

Big Horn boasts two excellent bed and breakfasts, the **Blue Barn Bed and Breakfast**, Highway 335, (307) 672-2381, offering three beautiful rooms in a 75-year-old dairy barn for $75 to $85; and **Spahn's Big Horn Mountain Bed and Breakfast**, 5 miles west of Big Horn, (307) 674-8150, providing four rooms in scenic surroundings and binoculars with breakfast for $65 to $115.

In Buffalo, kids will enjoy the **Crossroads Inn**, 75 North By-Pass, (307) 684-2256, for its nice outdoor pool. Rates range from $28 to $67. The **Cloud Peak Bed and Breakfast**, located at West Hart and Burritt Streets, (307) 684-5794, has five distinct rooms and $40 to $70 rates.

CAMPING

As noted above, **Bighorn National Forest** contains dozens of good campsites at rates ranging from free to $8 per night. In Buffalo, the **Big Horn Mountains Campground**, Highway 16 East, (307) 684-2307, has 83 sites with hookups on 12 acres for $13 to $15 per night. The **Buffalo KOA**, Highway 16 East, (307) 684-5423, offers 82 sites on 13 acres with activities for $19 to $20 per night. **Deer Park Campground**, U.S. 16, (307) 684-7981, has 100 sites with hookups and some pull-throughs for $15 to $19 per night. **Indian Campground**, 660 East Hart Street, (307) 684-9601, is the biggest of all, with 100 sites, activities and amenities, hookups and some pull-through sites for $15 per night. Sheridan's **Big Horn Mountain KOA**, 63 Decker Road, (307) 674-8766, has 115 sites in a shady location with hookups, pull-throughs, activities, and chuckwagon barbecue for $15 per night.

NIGHTLIFE

In Sheridan the art deco–style **WYO Theater**, 38 North Main, (307) 672-9084, is the oldest operating vaudeville theater in the state. Live performances include summer melodramas, musicals, dance productions, and musicians ranging from top country performers to jazz to blues and classical performers. Call to see what's on. The **Mint Bar**, 157 North Main, (307) 674-9696, is a Wyoming monument that has been serving up shots and beers to thirsty cowboys and other residents for generations. It's worth a look even if you order sarsaparilla because it's as skinny and long as any bar anywhere and sports authentic Old West atmosphere.

SIDE TRIP: DEVILS TOWER

A very worthwhile day trip (approximately 200 miles) from Sheridan or Buffalo is a visit to Devils Tower, the country's first national monument. Devils Tower is accessible via I-90 east from Sheridan through Gillette, then north from Moorcroft on U.S. 14. The U.S. 14 portion of the drive is a beauty as well, as the visitor begins to enter Wyoming's wooded Black Hills country. The monument became a star in the 1980s after Steven Spielberg used it as the site of an alien landing in *Close Encounters of the Third Kind*, but American Indians have long considered it a sacred place. Devils Tower rises 1,280 feet from the valley to form a conical, fluted, flat-topped cone visible for miles in any direction.

The tower is 1,000 feet across at the bottom and 275 feet across the top. Indian legends about the tower describe its rising from the earth to save seven sisters from a great bear who, in trying to climb to them, created the scratches, or flutes, that run vertically from the base to the top. Modern geologists have determined that the tower forms the core of a volcanic passage that cooled and was later exposed through centuries of erosion. Devils Tower National Monument, (307) 467-5283, is administered by the National Park Service. The visitor's center and campground are open daily June through August from 8 a.m. to 7:45 p.m., April/May and September/October from 8 a.m. to 4:45 p.m. Admission is $4 per vehicle.

Scenic Route: Medicine Wheel Passage

Meandering through the northern section of the Bighorn Mountain Range and Bighorn National Forest on Highway 14-A from Dayton, you'll come across many steep grades and winding roads. If you've got children or companions who tend to get carsick on mountain roads, this may not be the route to take, unless you plan to pull over frequently and simply drink in the mountain vistas, which is highly recommended. Also recommended are good brakes on the car for the steep grades and switchback turns. Along the route there are wonderful views of limestone cliffs and patches of alpine meadows between the mountains. Pull over at the many pullouts that offer great views of the geological formations, including the **Garden of the Gods Pinnacles**.

From **Burgess Junction** you'll pass the **Medicine Wheel** and descend the west face of the Bighorn Mountain Range. Because of some vandalism and the sacred nature of the site, the Medicine Wheel road has been re-engineered so that visitors can no longer simply drive up beside it but must hike up the mountain. It takes about

MEDICINE WHEEL PASSAGE

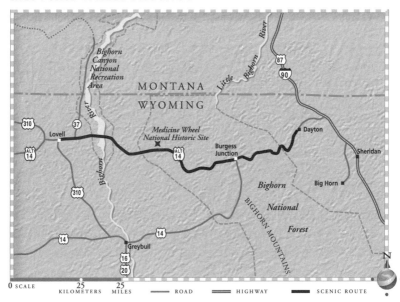

ten minutes to get up there, and it's worth it. Further on in the distance one can see the **Absaroka Mountains** as well as the **Yellowstone Plateau**. Just before reaching **Lovell**, the highway crosses the part of Bighorn Canyon National Recreation Area known as Bighorn Lake. Lovell (population 2,000) is an immaculate small community located at the southern entrance to Bighorn Canyon Recreation Area. The **Pryor Mountain Wild Horse Range**, a refuge for wild horses as well as big game animals, is also accessed via Lovell. This route, along with many in the region, is closed during the winter. ◣

4

CASPER

Casper, the second largest city in Wyoming, with 48,000 residents, has always had that . . . attitude. It's an aggressive, cocky, "in-your-face" persona that, quite frankly, makes the more genteel sorts from places like Cheyenne and Jackson just a little bit nervous. Casper is Wyoming's go-go city, the only town with a big city feel that probably comes from being the epicenter of energy (and population) booms and busts for years. Petroleum, coal, uranium, and bentonite are or have been extracted here.

Casper is fun—a raucous place sparkling at the foot of Casper Mountain. At one time Casper boasted more pickup trucks per capita than any other city in the United States. But the community is not all blue-collar. Many of Wyoming's most successful politicians (recently Secretary of Defense Dick Cheney) and entrepreneurs (cable television was invented here) come from Casper. So do most of Wyoming's professional athletes (baseball players, mostly). It's been a tough and interesting place ever since Lieutenant Colonel Caspar Collins, the town's namesake, charged across the North Platte River with his cavalry troops to circumvent an Indian attack on a wagon train and ended up with an arrow sticking out of his head.

Casper has always been a crossroads place, a logical overnight stop on most trips through the region. The Oregon, Mormon, California, Pony Express, Jim Bridger, and Bozeman Trails all met at Casper. The Oregon Trail landmarks of Independence Rock, Fort Caspar, Devils Gate, and Natural Bridge are all within striking distance. ◨

CASPER

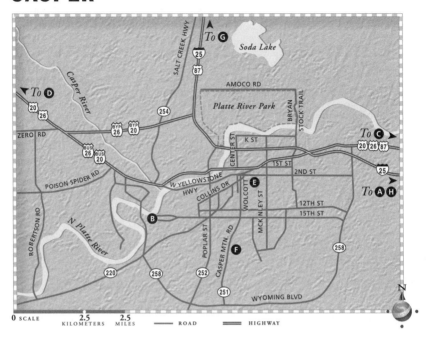

Sights

Ⓐ Ayres Natural Bridge

Ⓑ Fort Caspar Museum and Restored Cavalry Fort

Ⓒ Glenrock Paleontological Museum and Education Center

Ⓓ Hell's Half Acre

Ⓔ Nicolaysen Art Museum

Ⓕ Tate Mineralogical Museum

Ⓖ Willow Creek Ranch

Ⓗ Wyoming Pioneer Memorial Museum

A PERFECT DAY IN CASPER

Start the day at the Chef's Coop, drinking coffee and sharing stories with the locals, then wander downtown. Among the specialty shops and boutiques is the hint of money and ambition that still burbles just beneath the surface of the town. Lou Taubert's Ranch Outfitters has been selling Stetsons to ranchers and local businessmen for decades. Drive to Douglas and check out the Oregon Trail displays at the Wyoming Pioneer Museum; then return to Casper for the dinosaur exhibits at the Tate. Go for a big steak and a couple of cold beers at Benhams or the Goose Egg before pulling on your tightest jeans and biggest hat and go "sneakin' to the Beacon" for live, and loud, music and dancing.

SIGHTSEEING HIGHLIGHTS

★★★ **Wyoming Pioneer Memorial Museum**—Located in Douglas within the Wyoming State Fairgrounds complex, the museum offers a suprisingly warm and intimate look at the pioneer lifestyle through well-arranged displays of relics. Special emphasis is placed on travelers heading west along the Oregon Trail and those few who settled in rugged Central Wyoming. Other displays include American Indian and military artifacts. Details: Wyoming State Fairgrounds, Douglas; (307) 358-9288; open June through August Monday through Friday 8 a.m. to 5 p.m., Saturday 1 p.m. to 5 p.m. By appointment the rest of the year. Free, but donations appreciated. (1½ hours).

★★ **Ayres Natural Bridge**—Known as a landmark by the pioneers along the Oregon Trail, Ayres Natural Bridge is a huge stone formation 50 feet high and 150 feet long that arches over LaPrele Creek. Part of the appeal of the landmark is the lack of development or commercialization of the site, although there is an attractive park with picnic tables and campground amenities. Details: located 5 miles off of I-25 west of Douglas. Free, but there is a fee for overnight camping. (30 minutes).

★★ **Fort Caspar Museum and Restored Cavalry Fort**—Originally named Platte Bridge Station in 1862, the U.S. Army outpost was created to guard against American Indian raids on pioneers traveling the Oregon Trail. The name was changed to Fort Caspar when, on a mission to escort a wagon train, Caspar Collins and his detachment were overwhelmed by Red Cloud's Sioux Indians in 1865. The growing city also took his name, although the story goes that a postal clerk changed the spelling from "Caspar" to "Casper." The museum and interpretive center offer exhibits on Indians, the military, and local history. Details: 4001 Ft. Caspar Road; (307) 235-8462; open mid-May to mid-September Monday through Saturday 8 a.m. to 7 p.m., Sunday 12 p.m. to 7 p.m.; Fort closed rest of the year but museum open Monday through Friday 8 a.m. to 5 p.m., Sunday 1 p.m. to 4 p.m. Free. (1 hour)

★★ **Nicolaysen Art Museum**—A massive building housed in a renovated power plant, the "Nic" is especially notable for the **Discover Center**, an interactive arts and crafts area for children. Changing art exhibits range from the predictable (Western art) to the daring and eclectic. Details: 400 East Collins Drive; (307) 235-5247; open Tuesday through Saturday 10 a.m. to 5 p.m., to 8 p.m. on Thursday, Sunday noon to 4 p.m. Admission: $2 adults, $1 children. (1 hour).

★★ **Tate Mineralogical Museum**—Central Wyoming is dinosaur country, and the fossil and mineral displays at the Tate are exceptional. Local paleontologists have displayed parts of "Bertha," a 30-ton Brontosaurus, and "Sniffles," a newly-identified dinosaur. Details: 125 Casper College Mountain Road; (307) 268-2514; open Monday through Friday 9 a.m. to 5 p.m., Saturday 10 a.m. to 3 p.m. (1 hour).

★ **Glenrock Paleontological Museum and Education Center**— Imagine how that local rancher felt when it was pointed out to him that the big rock that he cleaned his boots on every day was a partially buried Stegosaurus skull? That skull and other local fossil finds are displayed here. Details: 20 miles east of Casper on Wyoming Highway 20/87; (307) 436-5652; open summer months Monday through Saturday 10 a.m. to 4 p.m., rest of the year Saturday 10 a.m. to 4 p.m. or by appointment. Free. (30 minutes).

★ **Hell's Half Acre**—Located 40 miles west of Casper on Highway 20-26, this bizarre and haunting geological moonscape has attracted passers-by for years. Erosion caused by water and wind has molded the sandstone landscape into a frozen froth of pinnacles, buttes, and caves. The site was "otherworldly" enough to be chosen as the movie location for big-budget *Starship Troopers*, released in 1997. A restaurant, bar, motel, and campground adjoin the site. Details: Highway 20-26; (307) 235-9235. Free. (20 minutes)

✶ **Willow Creek Ranch**—Located in the northern part of Natrona County near the infamous "Hole in the Wall" country that served as hide-out for Butch Cassidy and the Sundance Kid (among others), the Willow Creek Ranch is crisscrossed with trails used by American Indians, outlaws, and early army wagon trains. The trails are virtually untouched since the days of their use, and the country is rugged. Working ranch stays or day-trip explorations can be arranged. Calling ahead is essential. Details: P.O. Box 10, Willow Creek Road, Kaycee, WY 82639; (307) 738-2294. Open May through October, weather permitting. (minimum 1 day)

FITNESS AND RECREATION

Edness Kimball Wilkins State Park, located east of Casper on Highway 20-26, offers wildlife watching, swimming, picnicking, fishing, and a pleasant 3-mile biking and jogging trail. The **Alcova-Pathfiner Recreation Areas**, 29 miles southwest of Casper on Highway 220, offer a Dinosaur Nature Trail, a marina with boat and jet-ski rentals, excellent fishing (big fish), camping, and bird watching. Birding is a big-time activity in and near Casper, in fact, and **Casper Mountain** is considered a premier birding area. The local **Audubon Club** offers a hotline at (307) 265-BIRD as well as guides for 13 local bird-watching areas. Bird lists are also available at the Casper Area Visitor Center at 500 North Center.

Historic Trails Expeditions, (307) 266-4868, offers excellent wagon rides and overnight stays on the historic pioneer trails that surround Casper.

Multiday trips are also available on the Continental Divide, as well as horseback riding. Float trips are available on the North Platte River from **Wyoming's Choice River Runners**, (307) 234-3870, for scenic wildlife viewing.

FOOD

A local favorite for breakfast and lunch is the **Chef's Coop**, 1040 North Center, (307) 237-1132, offering an extensive menu, daily

CASPER

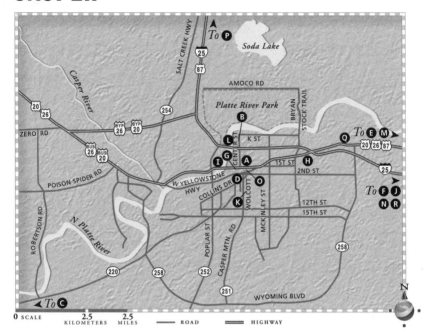

Food

Ⓐ Benhams

Ⓑ Chef's Coop

Ⓒ Goose Egg Inn

Ⓓ Ivy and Lace

Ⓔ Paisley Shawl Restaurant

Ⓕ Plains Trading Post Restaurant

Ⓖ Poor Boys Steak House and Restaurant

Lodging

Ⓗ Best Western East Casper

Ⓘ Casper Hilton Inn

Lodging (continued)

Ⓙ Cheyenne River Ranch

Ⓚ Durbin Street Inn Bed and Breakfast

Ⓛ Holiday Inn Casper

Ⓜ Hotel Higgins

Ⓝ LaBonte Inn

Ⓞ Parkway Plaza Hotel & Conference Center

Camping

Ⓟ Antelope Run Campground

Ⓠ Casper KOA

Ⓡ Douglas Jackalope KOA

specials, and a pleasant family atmosphere. **Ivy and Lace**, 236 South Center, (307) 265-0858, is open for lunch and features a tea room atmosphere and eclectic menu.

Big steaks are a specialty in the heart of ranch country, and they can be found at the **Goose Egg Inn**, 5 miles southwest of Casper on Highway 220, (307) 473-8838, named for the Goose Egg Ranch from Owen Wister's *The Virginian*. **Poor Boys Steak House and Restaurant**, I-25 and Center Street, (307) 473-8838, has been the recipient of the Wyoming Stock Growers "Beef Backer of the Year" award for its quality beef. **Benhams**, 739 North Center, (307) 234-4531, is an old favorite that recently went through some hard times but is back to being the elegant dining experience it once was—you know, the place to take your date on prom night. The steaks, salmon, and chicken are all well prepared . . . and if the walls of the adjoining Pump Room could talk!

Residents of Casper often travel down the road to Glenrock and Douglas for dining. One of Wyoming's best, the **Paisley Shawl Restaurant**, 416 West Birch, Glenrock, (307) 436-9212, is a three-star establishment located in the historic Hotel Higgins. In Douglas, the **Plains Trading Post Restaurant**, 628 Richards, (307) 358-4489, decorated with furnishings from old bank buildings, offers an extensive menu and huge portions.

LODGING

Because of its mid-state and interstate highway location, Casper offers plenty of rooms and good rates for travelers. The **Parkway Plaza Hotel & Conference Center**, I-25 and Center Street, (307) 235-1777, is the largest hotel property in the state, with 275 rooms, convention space, and $42 rates.

The **Casper Hilton Inn**, 800 North Poplar, (307) 266-6000, has 226 rooms, a popular lounge, and convention hotel amenities with $42 to $62 rates. Rounding out the "big three" is the **Holiday Inn Casper**, 300 West "F", (307) 235-2531, with 200 oversized rooms, plenty of amenities, and $65 to $71 rates. The **Best Western East Casper**, 2325 East Yellowstone, (307) 234-3541, is cozy and quiet, with 40 rooms and $40 to $69 rates.

The **Durbin Street Inn Bed and Breakfast**, 843 South Durbin, (307) 577-5774, has four well-appointed rooms in a historic downtown Casper home for $45 to $60 per night. Visitors who prefer historic hotels will like both the **Hotel Higgins**, 416 West Birch, Glenrock, (307) 436-9212, with eight rustic guest rooms for $46 to $70, and the **LaBonte Inn**, 206 Walnut, Douglas, (307) 358-2380, with 22 rooms, a historic and lively saloon, and $40 to $60 rates.

For an authentic working ranch experience with friendly hosts, try the **Cheyenne River Ranch** north of Douglas, (307) 358-2380. Betty and Don Pellatz host overnight bed-and-breakfast guests and offer multiday stays and real cattle drives. Call for reservations and directions.

CAMPING

Antelope Run Campground, 1101 Prairie Lane, Bar Nunn, Casper, (307) 577-1664, offers 65 RV sites as well as tent areas for $10 to $16; it's open from April through October 1. **Casper KOA**, 2800 East Yellowstone, (307) 237-5155, has 65 RV sites and 20 tent sites over 8 acres and includes a seasonal nightly buffalo barbecue, a whirlpool, and a small heated pool for $10 to $18 rates. The **Douglas Jackalope KOA**, 168 Cold Springs Road, Douglas, (307) 358-2174, has 54 RV sites, hookups, and pull-throughs, and KOA amenities for $15 to $20; it's open March 15 through November 1.

NIGHTLIFE

Things can get wild and western in Casper with its after-hours mix of cowboys, oilfield workers, and travelers. But if you're up to it, the thing to do is to go "sneakin' to the Beacon," meaning the **Beacon Club** in Mills, 4100 West Yellowstone Highway, (307) 577-1503, for live country music and classic rock bands.

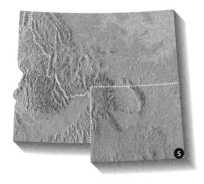

5

CHEYENNE

As you ascend toward Cheyenne from the south, the first thing you'll see as you cross the Colorado border is a massive metal bison silhouette on the eastern horizon, followed soon after by real bison herds near Interstate 25. It's a good introduction to Wyoming.

The capital of "The Cowboy State" is blessed with one of the best names in the West as well as the best rodeo. Despite its initial flat and windy appearance, Cheyenne is actually a mountain town over 6,000 feet in elevation—much higher than the "Mile High" city of Denver, only two hours to the south. Once a rowdy railroad town nicknamed "Hell on Wheels" unofficially and "Shey an'nah" (after a local nomadic American Indian band) semi-officially, the name "Cheyenne" stuck. In the 1880s Cheyenne was one of the wealthiest per capita cities in America, home to dozens of cattle barons who built stately Victorian mansions and whose massive ranches dotted Wyoming.

Today Cheyenne is the largest city, with a little over 50,000 people, in the state with the fewest people (Wyoming's population is 480,000). The governor's home phone is in the telephone book. Cheyenne has survived the mineral boom-and-bust cycle of the West better than many communities because of its government, transportation, retail, healthcare, tourism, and manufacturing economy. The Victorian core of the city is well-preserved, with Cheyenne's "Hell-on-Wheels'" history just beneath the veneer. The town is a good place to "cowboy up" and buy Western and outdoor wear, thanks to the legacy of Cheyenne Frontier Days. ◼

CHEYENNE

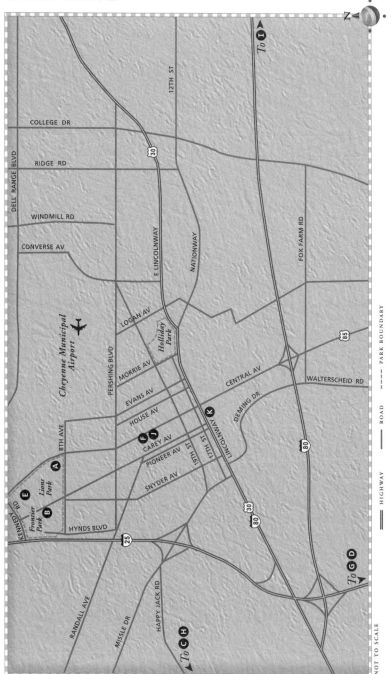

Sights

- **Ⓐ** Cheyenne Botanic Gardens
- **Ⓑ** Cheyenne Frontier Days Old West Museum
- **Ⓒ** Curt Gowdy State Park
- **Ⓓ** Hell on Wheels Rodeo
- **Ⓔ** Lion's Park
- **Ⓕ** State Capitol
- **Ⓖ** Terry Bison Ranch
- **Ⓗ** Veedauwoo
- **Ⓘ** Wyoming Hereford Ranch
- **Ⓙ** Wyoming State Museum
- **Ⓚ** Wyoming Transportation Museum

A PERFECT DAY IN CHEYENNE

After a large, leisurely breakfast downtown at Lexie's, work your way on foot through the Victorian section of downtown Cheyenne. Imagine that you were one of those cattle barons who built the homes, sending Texas gunfighters north toward the Bighorn Mountains to chase out nesters. At Lions Park, stroll around Sloan's Lake, followed by a visit to the Botanic Garden. From there, walk across the street to Frontier Park and the Old West Museum. Later in the afternoon, drive up Old Happy Jack Road beyond Curt Gowdy Park to the haunted rock formations that make up Veedauwoo. Return at dusk for a big sirloin at Little Bear or a buffalo steak at the Senator's Steak House on the Terry Bison Ranch, followed by an evening of outdoor excitement at the local Hell on Wheels Rodeo.

SIGHTSEEING HIGHLIGHTS

☆☆☆ **Cheyenne Frontier Days Old West Museum**—Renovated, retooled, and recently improved to better capture and interpret Cheyenne Frontier Days and other historic events, the Old West Museum has extensive collections of horse-drawn carriages, railroad memorabilia, Old West history, Western art, and CFD memorabilia. It now has a good children's section and gift shop (note: I'll rarely say *any* place has a good gift shop). Details: 4501 North Carey Avenue; (307) 778-7290; open summer weekdays 8 p.m. to 6 p.m., weekends 10 a.m. to 5 p.m.; winter weekdays 9 a.m. to 5 p.m., weekends 11 a.m. to 4 p.m. Admission: $2. (1 hour)

★★★ **State Capitol**—Built in 1886 for $131,000, including the real gold leaf covering the dome, the Wyoming State Capitol is widely considered one of the more charming capitols in the United States. With stained-glass ceilings, Corinthian balconies, and Wild West murals, the building is small, comfortable, and so laid-back that it's not unusual to discover that the man standing next to you is the governor. Details: Capitol Avenue and 24th Street; (307) 777-7220; open Monday through Friday 8:30 a.m. to 4:30 p.m. Free, but if you want to join a tour, call ahead. (30 minutes)

★★ **Lion's Park**—The center of Cheyenne is Lion's Park, a large municipal park filled with tall trees and plenty of room. Within the park are boating, fishing, bike paths, miniature golf, picnic areas, playgrounds, a wildlife exhibit with bison and elk, a swimming pool, and the Botanic Gardens (see below). The park is adjacent to Frontier Park, home of Cheyenne Frontier Days. For further information, contact Cheyenne Parks and Recreation, (307) 636-6423. (30 minutes)

★★ **Cheyenne Botanic Gardens**—This 6,800-square-foot solar-powered and -heated greenhouse conservatory displays perennials, annuals, wildflowers, rose gardens, a community vegetable garden, lily pond, sensory garden, and cactus garden. Details: 710 South Lions Park Drive; (307) 637-6548; open weekdays 8 a.m. to 4:30 p.m., weekends 11 a.m. to 3:30 p.m. Free, but donations are appreciated. (1 hour)

★★ **Hell on Wheels Rodeo**—Not everyone can make it to Cheyenne during Frontier Days, but that doesn't mean they can't see something the city is famous for: rodeo. Although tiny compared to Cheyenne Frontier Days, the Hell on Wheels Rodeo is closer to what some of the locals have been doing nightly throughout the region since they settled it—riding, roping, whooping it up, and getting bucked off and falling on their heads. The rodeo is outdoors, so it can get cool even in summer. Details: Terry Bison Ranch, 51 I-25 Service Road East; (307) 634-4171. The rodeo starts at 6:30 p.m. Tuesday and Wednesday nights June through August (except during Cheyenne Frontier Days). Admission: $5 adults, $4 seniors, and $1 children. (2–3 hours)

★★ **Veedauwoo**—Pronounced "VEE-duh-voo," this National Forest Recreation Area is located 30 miles west of Cheyenne along

I-80 or Old Happy Jack Road (Highway 210) in the Medicine Bow National Forest. The area is known for spectacular granite rock formations and forested "high lonesome" vistas nearly 8,000 feet high. Rock climbers revere the area, and local visitors sometimes take lawn chairs and picnic lunches to watch them scramble up Veedauwoo's southern exposures. Famous western outlaw and "range detective" Tom Horn once patrolled near here and was later hanged in Cheyenne for his excellent marksmanship. Day campsites and picnic areas are available. Contact the Medicine Bow National Forest at (307) 745-2300. (2 hours)

✳ **Terry Bison Ranch**—Located south of Cheyenne, this working bison ranch also has a collection of tourist-related attractions, including wagon tours through the bison (or buffalo) herds, chuckwagon dinners, private fishing, a petting zoo, horseback riding, and authentic collections of turn-of-the-century ranch buildings. Details: 51 I-25 Service Road East; (307) 634-4171. Costs for tickets vary with activity. (1 hour)

✳ **Wyoming Hereford Ranch**—Established in 1883, the Wyoming Hereford Ranch is the oldest continuous registered livestock operation in the United States. The ranch is a well-preserved example of what a major ranch operation used to look like as well as a monument to whiteface Hereford cattle. Details: 114 Hereford Ranch Road; (307) 638-3243. Tours are not always available, so call ahead. (30 minutes)

Curt Gowdy State Park—Named after the native son broadcaster and sportsman, the park is located just before the Veedauwoo area and has camping, boating, hiking, and fishing. Details: (307) 632-7946. Daily entrance permits, $2; overnight permits, $4. (2 hours)

Wyoming Transportation Museum—Located in the historic Union Pacific Depot that stares down the Wyoming State Capitol on the other end of Capitol Avenue, the Wyoming Transportation Museum opened in summer of 1997. As renovations continue, displays will include historic trails, railroads, highways, and air transportation. Details: 115 West 15th Street; (307) 637-3376; open Tuesday through Friday 9 a.m. to 2 p.m., Saturday and Sunday noon to 6 p.m.

Wyoming State Museum—The museum is now closed for building renovations, with the grand reopening slated for the fall of 1998.

Small exhibits from this museum are temporarily displayed at the
Wyoming Arts Council Gallery. Details: 2320 Capitol Avenue; (307)
777-7022; open Monday through Friday 8 a.m. to 5 p.m. Free.
(30 minutes)

CHEYENNE FRONTIER DAYS

For over 100 years, Cheyenne Frontier Days has taken place the last
full week in July. It's the largest outdoor rodeo and Western festival
in the world, attracting upwards of 350,000 people. "The Daddy of
'Em All" offers free pancake breakfasts on Monday, Wednesday, and
Friday mornings, parades, a carnival, and the fastest moving rodeo
you'll ever see, at 1:15 p.m. each day, followed by top-name country
entertainment. It takes 2,000 volunteers to make Frontier Days
happen. For more information, write Cheyenne Frontier Days at
P.O. Box 2477, Cheyenne, WY 82003, or call (800) 227-6336 or
(307) 778-7222.

FITNESS AND RECREATION

You can experience Cheyenne's Victorian cattle-baron era and get
some exercise at the same time by taking the **Cheyenne Historic
Downtown Walking Tour**. The entire loop, filled with some 40
noteworthy buildings and sites spans 24 blocks. A walking tour
brochure and map can be obtained from the Cheyenne Downtown
Development Authority, 2101 O'Neil Avenue, Room 207, (307) 637-
6281.

More vigorous hiking (even rock climbing, if you're so inclined)
can be found at both the **Veedauwoo Recreation Area**, Old Happy
Jack Road (Highway 210), in the Medicine Bow National Forest,
(307) 745-2300; and **Curt Gowdy State Park**, (307) 632-7946, both
located west of Cheyenne. The new and attractive **Cheyenne
Greenway** is almost complete throughout the city. You can catch it
anywhere for walks or bike rides.

To work out while immersing yourself in a little local color, go
to the **Cheyenne YMCA**, 1426 East Lincolnway, (307) 634-9622, for
swimming, weightlifting, and a full-sized gym (if you go over
lunchtime, you'll find *me*). Open Monday through Saturday 6 a.m.
to 9 p.m., Sunday noon to 8 p.m. Admission is free to out-of-town
YMCA members, $5 for nonmembers.

FOOD

The downtown **Medicine Bow Brewery**, 115 East 17th Street, (307) 778-BREW, offers good hand-crafted beers and inexpensive, well-prepared food. Try the buffalo chili or the mufaletta with a pint of Lazy Boy Bitter. Kids will like the atmosphere, the portions, and the homemade root beer. Winning the title of "best steakhouse" in a town known for rodeos and cattle ranches is no small feat, but the **Little Bear Inn**, 1700 Little Bear Road, (307) 634-3684, has recently reclaimed the honor it has held for 30 years. This is a classic American steakhouse with good fresh seafood as well. If you're feeling decadent and wealthy, order a steak and the French-fried lobster tail. The **Owl Inn**, 3919 Central Avenue, (307) 638-8578, is a Cheyenne tradition with hearty, simple food and sassy waitresses. It's one of those places where the local business crowd meets to gossip over coffee every morning. The **Cheyenne Cattle Company**, inside the Best Western Hitching Post Inn, 1700 West Lincolnway, (307) 638-3301, can give Little Bear steaks a run for their money on its best nights.

I followed the owners from their previous incarnation at the Luxury Diner to **Lexie's Café**, 216 East 17th Street, (307) 638-8712, and I would follow them just about anywhere. They have wonderful, big homemade breakfasts and the best burgers in Cheyenne. **La Costa**, 317 East Lincolnway, (307) 638-7372, offers excellent authentic Mexican food with a coastal flair, featuring especially tasty (and unique) seafood recipes. **Los Amigos**, 620 Central Avenue, (307) 638-8591, is more "traditional" Tex-Mex—always a fine value with good service. **Parkway Pizza**, 3751 East Lincolnway, (307) 778-2949, despite its chain-like name, is an independent pizzeria serving the best New Jersey–style pizzas and sandwiches in Wyoming. The white pizza and the home-baked sandwich breads are excellent. And they deliver.

If the walls could talk, you would surely know just about all the dirt there is to know in Cheyenne if you ate at **The Albany**, 1506 Capitol, (307) 638-3507, a historic restaurant and bar across from the Union Pacific Depot. **Poor Richard's**, 2233 East Lincolnway, (307) 635-5114, offers a nice atmosphere in which blackened steaks and seafood are specialties. **Twin Dragon**, 1809 Carey Avenue, (307) 637-6622, one of many surprisingly good Chinese restaurants in southern Wyoming, is a real local favorite. **Senator's Steak House**,

CHEYENNE

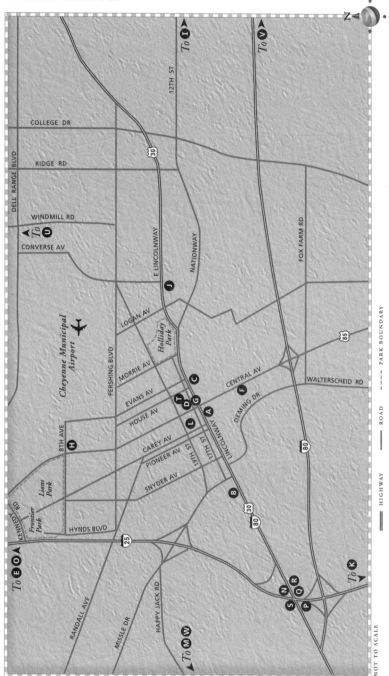

Food

- **A** The Albany
- **B** Cheyenne Cattle Company
- **C** La Costa
- **D** Lexie's Café
- **E** Little Bear Inn
- **F** Los Amigos
- **G** Medicine Bow Brewery
- **H** Owl Inn
- **I** Parkway Pizza
- **J** Poor Richards
- **K** Senator's Steak House
- **L** Twin Dragon

Lodging

- **M** A. Drummond's Ranch Bed and Breakfast
- **B** Best Western Hitching Post Inn

Lodging (continued)

- **N** Comfort Inn
- **O** Diamond Guest Ranch
- **P** Fairfield Inn
- **Q** Holiday Inn
- **R** La Quinta
- **S** Little America Hotel and Resort
- **T** Rainsford Inn Bed and Breakfast
- **U** Storyteller Pueblo Bed and Breakfast

Camping

- **V** AB Camping
- **W** Curt Gowdy State Park
- **K** Terry Bison Ranch

Note: Items with the same letter are located in the same town or area.

at the Terry Bison Ranch, 51 I-25 Service Road East, (307) 634-4995, serves lunch and dinner daily in the summer but only on weekends in the winter. The specialty: bison. A piano player keeps things hopping for the kids.

LODGING

The unofficial capitol of Cheyenne is undoubtedly the **Best Western Hitching Post Inn**, a sprawling 175-room hotel located at 1700 West Lincolnway; (307) 638-3301. Nearly all of Wyoming's legislators stay here during the legislative session (January to March, if that long). It also hosts a throng of cowboys and entertainers during Frontier Days.

Winter rates average $55 to $70 per night; $73 to $94 in the summer. Its AAA four-diamond competitor is the **Little America Hotel and Resort**, with 188 rooms on 80 acres. Rooms are spacious, the restaurants are decent, and there are a nine-hole golf course and lots of trees (unique in Cheyenne). Rates are comparable to the Hitching Post's.

Being at the crossroads of I-25 and I-80, Cheyenne hosts a number of chain hotels, including the **Holiday Inn**, 204 W. Fox Farm Road, (307) 638-4466; **La Quinta**, 2410 W. Lincolnway, (307) 632-7117; **Comfort Inn**, 2245 Etchepare Drive, (307) 638-7207; and the **Fairfield Inn**, 1415 Stillwater, (307) 637-4070.

The **Rainsford Inn Bed and Breakfast**, 219 East 18th Street, (307) 638-2337, is a registered historic home in downtown Cheyenne with large rooms and private baths. An excellent value with interesting hosts, its rates are $60 to $95 depending on the room. The **Storyteller Pueblo Bed and Breakfast**, 5201 Ogden Road, (307) 634-7036, has a Southwestern Native American theme and rates of $45 to $80.

Outside of Cheyenne, you'll find "ranch B&Bs" such as **A. Drummond's Ranch Bed and Breakfast**, 399 Happy Jack Road, (307) 634-6042; as well as more traditional dude ranches like the **Diamond Guest Ranch**, P.O. Box 236, Chugwater, WY 82210, (307) 422-3564 or (800) 932-4222. Rates range from $50 to $70; campsites are $18 per night.

(Note: Disregard all of the above rates during Cheyenne Frontier Days, when rooms generally cost at least twice as much.)

CAMPING

Terry Bison Ranch, (307) 634-4171, offers the most private sites (89 with full RV hookups and literally hundreds of "dry camps" for tents) just 7 miles south of Cheyenne on I-25, with amenities (restaurant, wagon rides, bison herds, petting zoo), for $10 to $19.50. **AB Camping**, 1503 West College Drive, (307) 634-7035, has 100 RV sites and 20 tent sites on 5 acres with a playground and rec room for $12.50 to $17.50. **Curt Gowdy State Park**, 25 miles west of Cheyenne on Highway 210, 1351 Hynds Lodge Road, (307) 632-7946, is open all year and offers 280 sites with $4 fees (plus $2 to $3 vehicle fees) but no hookups and few amenities.

6

SARATOGA/THE PLATTE VALLEY

Definitely off the beaten path, the lush North Platte River Valley is rimmed on three sides by the Snowy Range and Sierra Madre Mountains. Those familiar with the North Platte River in eastern Wyoming or Nebraska won't recognize it here. As the river enters Wyoming and courses through the valley it becomes a 65-mile blue-ribbon trout fishery that includes major technical white water—some of the best in the state of Wyoming. (Saratoga's motto is "Where the Trout Leap in Main Street.")

The valley is home to beautifully appointed old cattle ranches, two small but engaging communities (Saratoga, population 2,000, and Encampment, population 700), hot springs, thousands of wilderness and forest acres, two excellent golf courses, several exclusive private resorts, art galleries, and the third largest airport in the state (private aircraft only). Despite all of these amenities, the area is, strangely enough, not well-known even within the state.

Though it had always been an Indian gathering place because of the river, hot springs, and game-rich mountains and valley, a huge copper find in 1897 near Encampment transformed the valley for a brief time. However, by 1908, the area was virtually abandoned. Downriver, Saratoga was becoming a supply center for the mine, the vast cattle ranches, and the Union Pacific Railroad. A small mining boom (this time, coal) in the 1970s briefly swelled. Today the area feels more "settled in" and comfortable with itself, with tourism, recreation, timber, and agriculture as the mainstays of the local economy. ◪

SARATOGA/PLATTE VALLEY REGION

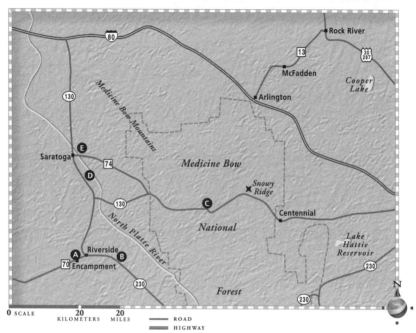

Sights

A Grand Encampment Museum

B Indian Bathtubs

C Kennaday Peak Lookout

D North Platte River

E Saratoga Hot Pool

E Saratoga Museum

E Saratoga National Fish Hatchery

A PERFECT DAY IN SARATOGA/THE PLATTE VALLEY

After catching and releasing a few midsize trout caught literally in the middle of town, have a big ranch breakfast at the Saratoga Inn. Then proceed down Highway 130/230 to Encampment and the glories of the Grand Encampment Museum, stopping for a moment to puzzle over the two-story outhouse. Take a half-day scenic float trip on the lovely North Platte River and try, for once, to keep your fishing rod in its case. Have dinner with your sweetheart in the historic Wolf Hotel, then end the evening in the Saratoga Hot Pool, relaxing in the steaming water while the river flows deep and cold just a few feet away.

SIGHTSEEING HIGHLIGHTS

★★★ **North Platte River**—For nearly 65 miles, from the Colorado state line to I-80, the North Platte River has been designated as a blue-ribbon trout stream. As the North Platte flows from south to north through the valley, it changes from a wild, muscular, technical white-water river to a perfectly swift trout stream to a wide and almost lazy waterway that's terrific for floating and relaxing. Along the way, the river flows through rugged mountains with bald eagles and bighorn sheep to high country plains filled with deer, antelope, coyotes, and waterfowl. The river produces a large natural trout population, and there are specially designated fishing limits and regulations. River access is limited through mostly private ranchlands, so the best way to experience it is by boat or raft. Details: Saratoga-Platte Valley Chamber of Commerce, Saratoga, (307) 326-8855. (3 hours)

★★★ **Grand Encampment Museum**—One of the best museums of its kind in the tri-state area, the Grand Encampment Museum is a 14-building complex housing artifacts and memorabilia. It recalls Encampment's great copper-mining period, the settlement of the Platte River Valley by the American Indians who camped in the area (thus the name of the town), and the exploits of fur trappers, tie cutters, cattle barons, hunters, copper miners, loggers, and ranchers. Encampment itself was once the site of the world's largest (at the time) tram, which carried copper ore down from the mountains to the smelter at the valley floor. The tour of a two-story outhouse is worth the trip alone—it will set you to thinking. (OK, the two-story outhouse was built because the mountain snow got so deep that users would eventually need to climb up to the second story as snow buried the first.) Details: Encampment; (307) 327-5308; open Memorial Day through Labor Day Monday through Saturday 10 a.m. to 5 p.m., Sunday 1 p.m. to 5 p.m., Labor Day through October daily 1 p.m. to 5 p.m., and by appointment the rest of the year. Free. (2 hours)

★★ **Saratoga Hot Pool**—For as long as humans have inhabited the valley, they've taken advantage of the large hot water flows that pulse through the ground near the banks of the North Platte River. American Indians used the waters for bathing and relaxing, and a white entrepreneur later constructed a house and tubs for travelers. The water is hot—117 to 128 degrees. Don't be goofy and dive in it without slowly getting used to the heat. Saratoga acquired the pool in 1982, with the provision that it must always be free to the public and open 24 hours a day. Renovated in 1995, it has changing rooms, restrooms, and showers. Details: East Walnut Street. Open 24 hours a day. Free. (1 hour, or as long as you can take it)

★ **Indian Bathtubs**—The "bathtubs" are deep holes in a granite outcropping east of the Encampment River that naturally gather melting snow and rainwater. The valley was a nineteenth-century gathering place for Ute, Arapaho, and Cheyenne Indians, who used these "bathtubs" for bathing and relaxing. The tubs are accessible via a ¾-mile trail off WYO 230 near Riverside. Details: Saratoga-Platte Valley Chamber of Commerce, Saratoga; (307) 326-8855. (1 hour)

★ **Kennaday Peak Lookout**—Built at 10,810 feet in 1964 in order for lookouts to keep an eye on fire danger in the huge Brush Creek District of the Medicine Bow National Forest, the station affords spectacular mountain and river valley views. The lookout on duty lives in a 470-square-foot facility. A display room in the bottom portion of the lookout station features photos of previous forest service lookouts and former rangers, plus a firefighting display. Details: North Brush Creek Road No. 100; (307) 326-5258; open July through Labor Day. Free. (1 hour)

★ **Saratoga Museum**—Located in a 1917 Union Pacific Railroad depot, this museum has historical and archeological artifacts depicting the settlement and growth of the Platte Valley. Displays and exhibits include the Kathryn Bakeless Nason archeological exhibit of prehistoric settlers, a regional railroad depot, a pioneer home, and a general store. Details: SR 130, Saratoga; (307) 326-5511; open daily Memorial Day through Labor Day 1 p.m. to 5 p.m. and by appointment the rest of the year. Free. (1 hour)

★ **Saratoga National Fish Hatchery**—One of the oldest of its kind in the Rockies, this hatchery was built in 1915 and continues to produce prized strains of rainbow, brook, Snake River cutthroat, and Colorado River cutthroat trout for the rest of the state of Wyoming. Endangered Greenback cutthroat, brown, and lake trout are also kept for breeding. Details: SR 130, Saratoga; (307) 326-5662; open daily 8 a.m. to 4 p.m. Free. (1 hour)

FITNESS AND RECREATION

As mentioned, the North Platte River is unique in its combination of highly technical and exciting white-water rapids upstream, extremely productive trout waters midstream, and relaxing floating downstream. **Great Rocky Mountain Outfitters**, 216 East Walnut Street, Saratoga, (307) 326-8750, has offered all three kinds of trips for more than a decade. Canoe, boat, and raft rentals are available from **Hack's Tackle & Outfitters**, 407 North First, (307) 326-9823, although I would strongly recommend taking your first few trips on the river with either Great Rocky Mountain or Hack's before renting a boat and doing it on your own.

Hikers can enjoy hundreds of scenic miles in the Medicine Bow National Forest and feel virtually alone while doing so. The **Encampment River Trail**, with its trailhead at the Encampment River Campground, offers a challenging 14-mile trek along the river on which you can easily stumble over elk, bighorn sheep, deer, bald eagles, and possibly black bears. For trail maps and information about hiking, biking, and horseback riding, contact the National Forest Service at (307) 324-4841.

Golfers will enjoy the par-36, nine-hole **Saratoga Inn Golf Course**, (307) 326-5261. The course is both gorgeous and difficult, as it crosses and recrosses the wide river.

Winter brings more than 340 miles of groomed snowmobile trails and 181 miles of ungroomed trails at the Brush Creek and Laramie Districts of the Medicine Bow National Forest. Maps are available by calling (307) 777-7550. A big January event in the valley is the **Saratoga Ice Fishing Derby**, which occurs on frozen Saratoga Lake the weekend between the NFL playoffs and the Super Bowl. The Derby attracts ice

SARATOGA/PLATTE VALLEY REGION

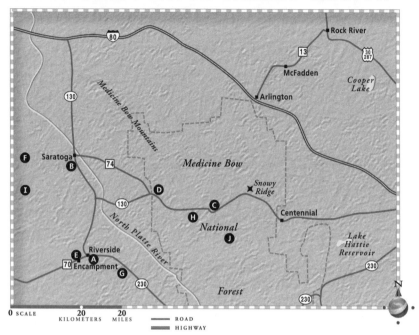

Food

- **A** Bear Trap Café
- **B** Bubba's Bar-B-Que Restaurant
- **B** Lazy River Cantina
- **B** River Street Deli
- **B** Saratoga Inn
- **B** Wolf Hotel

Lodging

- **C** Brush Creek Guest Ranch
- **B** Cary's Sage & Sand Motel
- **B** Far Out West
  Bed and Breakfast
- **B** Hacienda Motel
- **B** Hood House
  Bed and Breakfast

Lodging *(continued)*

- **D** Medicine Bow Guest Ranch &
  Lodge
- **B** Riviera Lodge
- **E** Rustic Mountain Lodge
  Bed and Breakfast
- **B** Saratoga Inn
- **B** Wolf Hotel

Camping

- **F** Corral Creek and
  Bennett Peak
- **G** Lazy Acres Campground
- **H** Ryan Park, Jack Creek,
  and South Brush Creek
- **I** Jack Creek
- **J** South Brush Creek

Note: Items with the same letter are located in the same town or area.

anglers from around the region, offering cash prizes for first fish, biggest fish, and most fish. (Why mention an ice-fishing derby? Simple . . . when I lived here in the early 1980s, I started it.) For details, contact the Saratoga-Platte Valley Chamber of Commerce, Saratoga, (307) 326-8855.

FOOD

Considering its tiny size, Saratoga is a good place to eat. As with other small, out-of-the-way mountain towns, there are a couple of good reasons for that. The first is that although tourism is certainly important, it is not the primary reason for the town's—or the valley's—existence. In order for a restaurant to survive, it must consistently please the locals or it will go the way of the passenger pigeon. A fourth-generation cattle rancher, for example, will not tolerate a substandard steak in his own hometown. Saratoga resorts also host some well-heeled guests who like to eat well.

The **Wolf Hotel**, 101 East Bridge Street, Saratoga, (307) 326-5525, is one of my favorite places to eat and drink in the state. Featuring excellent steaks and sandwiches, a good salad bar, and a fully Victorian atmosphere, it's listed on the National Register of Historic Places and anchors the tiny downtown. The two best things about the Wolf are its authenticity and the hospitality of owners Doug and Cathy Campbell.

The **Saratoga Inn**, 601 East Pick Pike Road, (307) 326-5261, has recently been remodeled and saved from disrepair, but its food has always been substantial and good. The **Lazy River Cantina**, 110 East Bridge Street, Saratoga, (307) 326-8472, is fairly new to town, offering Mexican cuisine in a lively atmosphere made even more lively by excellent margaritas. The **River Street Deli**, 106 North River Street, Saratoga, (307) 326-8683, is a good place to pick up pastrami sandwiches before heading out on the river. **Bubba's Bar-B-Que Restaurant**, 119 North River Street, Saratoga, (307) 326-5427, features spare ribs, chicken, pork, beef, baby back ribs, and combination platters of good barbecue. The **Bear Trap Café**, 120 East Riverside, Riverside, (307) 327-5277, occupies an old log building, and sports a comfortable hunting-camp atmosphere, and features hearty food in quantity.

LODGING

The largest property in town is the **Saratoga Inn**, 601 East Pick Pike Road, (307) 326-5261, recently remodeled to better capture the spa/resort atmosphere it was built for. The rooms are fairly small, but it's a short walk to the pool, the golf course, the driving range, and the river. Rates are $125 to $160. The **Wolf Hotel**, 101 East Bridge Street, Saratoga, (307) 326-5525, offers a couple of restored rooms and one very exclusive suite. This is a dandy place for $26 to $79 per night.

The **Hacienda Motel**, SR 130, Saratoga, (307) 326-5751, offers the most modern motel accommodations in Saratoga, with 32 rooms, suites and family units, and $33 to $56 rates. **Cary's Sage & Sand Motel**, 311 South First Street, Saratoga, (307) 326-8339, is a comfortable favorite of fishermen and hunters that has rates of $30 to $40.

The **Riviera Lodge**, 303 North First Street, Saratoga, (307) 326-5651, is a tiny place that has a few excellent rooms with river views and a nice lawn to relax on. Rates are $33 to $85 per night. The **Rustic Mountain Lodge Bed and Breakfast**, Star Route 49, Encampment, (307) 327-5539, provides four rooms in a mountain lodge at one of the valley's original ranches. Rates are $45 to $65. **Far Out West Bed and Breakfast**, 304 North Second Street, Saratoga, (307) 326-9864, has six rooms in a historic home with a hot tub. Rates range from $45 to $65. **Hood House Bed and Breakfast**, 214 North Third Street, Saratoga, (307) 326-8901, with four rooms, is one of Wyoming's first and best bed and breakfasts. Rates are $50 to $60.

The **Brush Creek Guest Ranch**, Star Route Box 10, Saratoga, (307) 327-5241, is a working cattle ranch on the banks of the North Platte, which offers nightly and weekly packages and stays. Rates are $850 to $1,050 per week per person from May through October. Call for other rates. The **Medicine Bow Guest Ranch & Lodge**, Star Route 8A, Highway 130, Saratoga, (307) 326-5439, has remodeled cabins, good food, and good horses in a wooded mountain location. Rates are $55 to $65 per person, all meals included. Children from ages 4 to 10 are half-price.

CAMPING

Lazy Acres Campground, Star Route 230, Riverside, (307) 327-5968, provides 39 sites in a pleasant, shady, off-the-beaten-path location with hookups and $10 rates. The BLM maintains a decent 24-site campground at **Corral Creek** and **Bennett Peak**, 12 miles east on French Creek Road, (307) 324-4841, with $3 rates. **Ryan Park, Jack Creek,** and **South Brush Creek**, near Saratoga, are supervised by the National Forest Service for $5 per night. Call (307) 326-5258 for information on Ryan Park and South Brush Creek, and (307) 327-5481 for information on Jack Creek.

7

WIND RIVER COUNTRY— RIVERTON/LANDER/DUBOIS

Probably no other place in Wyoming is bigger, more diverse, more interesting, or harder to get a handle on than Wind River Country, which includes the communities of Riverton (population 9,200), Lander (population 7,300), and Dubois (population 900). All three towns, as well as the towering Wind River Mountain Range and the huge Wind River Indian Reservation, are located in 5.8-million-acre Fremont County, Wyoming's melting pot. The region is a study in the different cultures, philosophies, factions, and politics that define the "new" mountain West. This bubbling stew includes Shoshone and Arapaho Indians, cattle ranchers, environmental groups, conservative political factions, go-go developers, fourth-generation families, newcomers, mountain-man throwbacks, granola-head slackers, laconic cowhands, climbers, hikers, fishers, and hunters.

The Wind River Range consists of rugged and spectacularly beautiful mountains that include Gannett Peak, Wyoming's highest at 13,804 feet, as well as dozens of other "thirteeners." Crossing this range duly intimidated early settlers, until explorer Jim Bridger discovered South Pass. Hundreds of thousands of emigrants later used the route on what became known as the Oregon Trail. Much of the range now belongs to the Wind River Indian Reservation and its stewards, the Shoshone and Arapaho Indians. Despite all it has to offer, Wind River Country is not as heavily visited as other locations that share its attributes. That alone is a good enough reason to go there. ◼

WIND RIVER COUNTRY

Map Legend

- Thermopolis
- Shoshoni
- Owl Creek Mountains
- Boysen Reservoir
- Muddy Creek
- Riverton
- St. Stephens
- Sand Draw
- Sweetwater Station
- Pavillion
- Ocean Lake
- Wind River
- Hudson
- Lander
- Atlantic City
- Sweetwater River
- **C** **G**
- **J**
- **A**
- **D**
- **I**
- **E**
- **G** **F**
- Ft. Washakie
- **G**
- **K**
- Shoshone National Forest
- Wind River Indian Reservation
- Bull Lake
- Crowheart
- Continental Divide
- **H**
- Dinwoody Lake
- **B** Dubois
- Wind River Canyon
- Gannett Peak
- Bridger-Teton National Forest
- Cora
- Daniel
- Marbleton

Highways: 20/26, 136, 135, 287, 220, 789, 134, 26, 133, 28, 191, 189, 352, 351

0 SCALE 22 KILOMETERS 22 MILES

ROAD — HIGHWAY — PLACE OF INTEREST ✈ FOREST/RESERVATION BOUNDARY - - - -

N

Sights

- **A** Fremont County Pioneer Museum
- **B** National Bighorn Sheep Interpretive Center
- **C** Riverton Museum
- **D** Sinks Canyon State Park
- **E** South Pass City State Historic Park
- **F** Washakie Cemetery
- **G** Wind River Indian Reservation Cultural Centers
- **H** Wind River Mountain Range

Food

- **I** Atlantic City Mercantile
- **C** Broker Restaurant
- **J** Club El Toro
- **A** Gannett Grill
- **A** Hitching Rack
- **J** Hudson Market and Grill
- **A** Magpie
- **B** Old Yellowstone Garage
- **B** The Ramshorn
- **B** Rustic Pine Steakhouse
- **A** Sweetwater Grille/Popo Agie Brewing Co.

Lodging

- **A** Best Western Inn at Lander
- **B** Bitterroot Ranch
- **A** Black Mountain Ranch
- **B** Brooks Lake Lodge
- **A** Bunk House
- **A** Pronghorn Lodge
- **C** Riverton Holiday Inn
- **A** Three Quarter Circle Ranch
- **C** Tomahawk Motor Lodge
- **B** Twin Pines Lodge & Cabins
- **A** Whispering Winds Bed & Breakfast

Camping

- **B** Brooks Lake, Double Cabin, Falls, Horse Creek, and Pinnacle Campground
- **B** Circle Up Camper Court
- **B** Dickinson Park, Fiddlers Lake, Lewis Lake, and Worthen Meadows Reservoir
- **A** K-Bar RV Park
- **C** Owl Creek Campground
- **C** Riverton RV Park
- **K** Shoshone National Forest
- **D** Sinks Canyon State Park

Note: Items with the same letter are located in the same town or area.

A PERFECT DAY IN WIND RIVER COUNTRY

After coffee and rolls at the Magpie in Lander, drive up Sinks Canyon to
see the Popo Agie River vanish into the mountain ("the Sinks") to re-
emerge a quarter-mile later ("the Rise") in a trout-filled pool. Tour some
of the sites on the Wind River Indian Reservation, including St. Stephens
Mission, Sacajawea's grave, and Crowheart Butte en route to the
mountain town of Dubois. After a walk along the main street of Dubois,
continue to Riverton, a bustling city and home of Central Wyoming
College. For dinner, choose one of the two restaurants in Hudson for
perhaps the biggest steaks and side dishes known to humankind.

PRONUNCIATION TIPS

Perhaps no other section of Wyoming has as many place names that
are as easily mispronounced as does Fremont County. The locals love
to correct you when you screw up a name—and you are instantly
branded a tourist. Here are a few of the basics.

The Popo Agie River (and there are lots of other Popo Agie
locations, including creeks, roads, etc.) is pronounced "puh-POE-jha."
The town of Dubois is easily mispronounced, especially if you know
French. What should be "due-BWA" is actually pronounced "DUE-
boise," just like it looks. You can just hear the French Minister of
Culture gasping at that one. The Shoshone Indians aren't
pronounced "show-SHONE," as you might guess, but "shuh-
SHOW-nee." The town of Shoshoni near Riverton is simply
misspelled—I have no idea why. The great Shoshone Chief Washakie
is pronounced "WASH-uh-key." The town of Ethete on the Wind
River Indian Reservation is pronounced "EE-thuh-tee." The
Absaroka Mountain Range is pronounced "ab-SORE-uh-kuh."

THE WIND RIVER INDIAN RESERVATION

To get an idea how big the Wind River Reservation is, consider that
this 2.2-million-acre reservation is almost exactly the same size as
Yellowstone National Park. Within its borders are some of Wyoming's
most scenic mountain and foothill vistas, including 1,100 miles of
streams and more than 260 lakes. It is populated by 2,500 Shoshone
and 5,167 Arapaho Indians.

The Shoshone tribe is unique in that its people were allowed to choose where they wanted to live because of cooperation between Shoshone Chief Washakie and the United States government. They were the only tribe offered that option. The Shoshones chose this area in 1868 because it was their traditional hunting and wintering lands. In what was supposed to be a temporary arrangement, the Arapahos, traditionally Shoshone enemies, were relocated to the Wind River Reservation in 1878. The "temporary arrangement" became permanent, and now both tribes jointly own and control the lands.

SIGHTSEEING HIGHLIGHTS

★★★ **Wind River Indian Reservation Cultural Centers**—There are three cultural centers on the Wind River Reservation. The **Shoshone Tribal Cultural Center** at Fort Washakie contains displays of Shoshone artifacts and art, historical and modern photographs, and histories of Chief Washakie and Sacajawea. A small gift shop features Shoshone beadwork and crafts. The **Arapaho Cultural Center Museum** at Ethete is on the grounds of historic St. Michael's Episcopal Mission. Museum exhibits include Arapaho artifacts and clothing, photographs of Arapaho chiefs, and contemporary photos. The **Heritage Center** at the St. Stephens Mission displays clothing, crafts, and beadwork. The church is painted with indigenous geometric designs. Details: Shoshone Tribal Cultural Center, P.O. Box 1008, Fort Washakie, WY 82514, (307) 332-9106; St. Stephens Indian Mission, P.O. Box 278, St. Stephens, WY 82524, (307) 856-7806; Shoshone and Arapaho Tribes, 15 North Fork Road, Fort Washakie, WY 82514, (307) 332-3040. Centers open weekdays 9 a.m. to 5 p.m., closed weekends; please call ahead to confirm hours and directions. Free, but donations are appreciated. (2 hours)

★★★ **Wind River Mountain Range**—The vast and rugged Wind River Mountain Range divides the north-central part of Wyoming from the northwest section. On one side of the range are Pinedale, Big Piney, and Jackson Hole, and on the other are Lander, Riverton, and Dubois. To get from one area to the other by car, visitors must either drive north or south to eventually cross over. No direct route exists because the Wind Rivers are huge and almost impassable. Much of the eastern side of the range belongs to the Wind River Indian Reservation and is accessible only with permission from the Shoshone and Arapaho tribes.

Because of this remoteness, the "Winds" contain thousands of acres of pristine mountain terrain, from the highest peak in the state (Gannett,

13,804 feet) to Fremont Peak (13,745 feet), Wind River Peak (13,200 feet), and dozens of other mountains. Although some wonderful drives are listed below, the best way to see and experience the Winds is by foot, horseback, or with specialty outfitters using llamas or goats. Some of the most spectacular country in the Winds is part of the reservation, and visitors must be guided by licensed Indian outfitters. Contact the **Tribal Fish and Game Office**, P.O. Box 217, Fort Washakie, WY 82514; (307) 332-7207. Many people first experience the Wind River Mountains via classes offered by the nationally renown **National Outdoor Leadership School** (NOLS), 288 Main Street, Lander, (307) 332-6973.

There are several very good drives into the Winds, starting in either Lander or Dubois. The Pinnacles route is located near Dubois. It's a 3-mile trip from the highway on Brooks Lake Road showcasing the red **Pinnacle Buttes** that jut skyward from the forest. They were formed by thick layers of volcanic ash and rocks deposited more than 40 million years ago. The **Horse Creek-Double Cabin Road** is a 28-mile route starting in the center of Dubois and following Horse Creek into the Absaroka Range. The **Union Pass** road, also out of Dubois, follows an old trail first blazed by fur trappers and mountain men over the Continental Divide. For more information, contact the Dubois Chamber of Commerce, P.O. Box 632, Dubois, WY 82513; (307) 455-2556.

The **Lander-Loop Road** is a very popular 30-mile drive accessed via Sinks Canyon State Park through the Shoshone National Forest to the historic South Pass area along the Popo Agie River. Sites along the way include Red Canyon Rim, Atlantic City, South Pass City, Grannier Meadows, and Louis, Fiddlers, and Frye Lakes. Details: Wind River Visitors Council, P.O. Box 1449, Riverton, WY 82501, (800) 645-6233; Lander Area Chamber of Commerce, 160 North First Street, Lander, WY 82520, (307) 332-3892. (2 hours)

★★ **Sinks Canyon State Park**—Located 7 miles from Lander on Highway 131, the park offers camping, picnic opportunities, a visitor's center, and its showpiece attraction: the unique "sinks" formation. The water from the middle fork of the Popo Agie River rushes down the mountain canyon and plunges into the ground itself, only to re-emerge a quarter-mile later in a large, still pool (called the "Rise") filled with large trout. Despite studies, scientists are still not sure where the water goes underground, although they do know that more water comes out at the "Rise" than goes into the "Sink" and that the water at the "Rise" is warmer than at the "Sink." A deck and walkway allow visitors to look down into the pool and watch native trout feed from the springs. Fishing is not allowed. Details: Highway 131; (307) 332-6333; open daylight hours throughout the year. Admission: free to view the sinks, $4 for overnight camping. (1 hour)

★★ **South Pass City State Historic Park**—Located 37 miles south of Lander off Highway 287, this restored ghost town on the Oregon Trail once boasted 2,000 inhabitants because of a significant gold discovery that played out in less than ten years. The small collection of buildings that have remained are currently undergoing restoration, including a saloon, hotel, jail, livery stable, and butcher shop. A visitor's center details local history and interprets the site where 300,000 emigrants once crossed the continent from east to west. Call ahead to see if living history programs are planned. Details: SR 28, South Pass City; (307) 332-3684; open daily May 15 through September 9 a.m. to 5:30 p.m. Admission: $1 adults, under 18 free. (2 hours)

★★ **Washakie Cemetery**—Near Roberts Mission on the Wind River Indian Reservation, this small, solemn graveyard features a headstone for the famous Shoshone guide Sacajawea, who aided Lewis and Clark and the Corps of Discovery from 1804 to 1806. Chief Washakie and many of his family members are also buried here. Although historians argue about whether she really is buried here or if the body actually belonged to another woman, there is some historical data that suggests it could be Sacajawea. Of equal interest is the haunting graveyard itself. Instead of headstones, the dead were literally buried in their beds, and the brass and iron headboards and footboards stick out of the ground. This site is not well-marked, with no gates, interpretive signs, or hours. It is not a "tourist" site, although respectful visitors are welcome. (1 hour)

★ **National Bighorn Sheep Interpretive Center**—Because of the large free-roaming bighorn sheep herd in the local mountains, Dubois has become known as a place to view and hunt these animals. This new center is devoted almost entirely to the species from a scientific and biological perspective and includes a 20-foot "sheep mountain," dioramas, interactive videotape displays, and hands-on exhibits. Details: 907 West Ramshorn, Dubois; (307) 455-3429; open daily Memorial Day weekend to Labor Day 9 a.m. to 8 p.m., September 9 a.m. to 5 p.m. Call for days and hours for the rest of the year. Admission: $2 adults, 75 cents children under 13, $5 families. (1 hour)

★ **Fremont County Pioneer Museum**—Early settlers to Fremont County thought ahead and, as early as 1886, formed the Pioneer Association and began to collect their personal effects and artifacts. In 1915 they built a log structure that became the Pioneer Museum, and the building still stands. Exhibits are drawn from area history, including the Pony Express, the first oil well in Wyoming, ranching and farming, the coal and uranium industries, forestry, women's suffrage, and American Indian displays. It's an impressive local collection. Details: 630 Lincoln, Lander; (307) 332-4137; open year-round Monday through Friday 9 a.m. to 5 p.m., Saturday noon to 5 p.m., closed on Sunday. Free, but donations appreciated. (1 hour)

★ **Riverton Museum**—A better than usual local museum dedicated primarily to local settlement and events. Displays include re-creations of rooms including a general store, beauty salon, church, post office, schoolroom, and church. Other exhibits depict local Shoshone and Arapaho artifacts and history. Details: 700 East Park Avenue; (307) 856-2665; open Tuesday through Saturday 10 a.m. to 4 p.m. Free. (1 hour)

Oregon Trail ruts

Wyoming Tourism

FITNESS AND RECREATION

Within **Sinks Canyon State Park**, Highway 131, (307) 332-6333, are trailheads for short, easy walks and rigorous hikes. An easy one is the **Popo Agie Nature Trail**, located near the northern border of the park. Much more challenging is the 16-mile **Middle Fork Trail**, which leads to the heart of the **Popo Agie Wilderness Area**, including Shoshone Lake, Three Forks Park, Sweetwater Gap, and Popo Agie Falls. The 6½-mile **Volksmarch Trail** begins at the visitor's center and borders the Popo Agie River and the highway through the park.

The number of hiking, biking, and horseback trails in the Wind River Mountains is too vast to list here. Obtain information, permits, and advice by contacting the **Shoshone National Forest**, Lander, (307) 332-5460. For guided trips with expert outfitters who can offer excursions of varying lengths, variety, and prices, I recommend the following folks: **Allen Brothers Wilderness Ranch & Outfitting**, Box 243, Lander, WY 82520, (307) 332-2995, or **Rocky Mountain Horseback Vacations**, 7696 Highway 287, Lander, (307) 332-9149, for horsepack trips and wilderness survival skills; **Lander Llama Company**, 2024 Mortimore Lane, Lander, (307) 332-5624 or (800) 582-5262, for llama treks; and **Wind River Pack Goats**, 6668 Highway 26, Dubois, (307) 455-2410—yes, you read that correctly . . . *pack goats.*

FOOD

Locals will say—and I tend to agree—that Fremont County has the best restaurants in the state. Given the population, distances, and relatively low tourist traffic, it's amazing what Wind River Country offers both the patently hungry as well as the discriminating.

The tiny town of Hudson, between Riverton and Lander, consists primarily of two restaurants and a bar. The restaurants appear to stare at each other across the street, and they offer virtually identical menus, atmosphere, and prices. If this sounds strange, you're right. But once you see the size of the steaks and the volume of side dishes served at either **Hudson Market and Grill**, Highway 789, (307) 332-9853, or **Club El Toro**, 132 South Main, Hudson, (307) 332-4627, you'll understand why people travel sometimes hundreds of miles just for dinner. The steaks are delicious and absolutely massive, and a vegetable platter, *sarma*, and ravioli come with dinner (and dinner is all these places serve). These are arguably Wyoming's best steaks.

In Lander, fine dining is available at the **Hitching Rack**, Highway 287 South, (307) 332-4322, specializing in steaks, fresh pasta, a huge salad bar, and microbrews. **Sweetwater Grille/Popo Agie Brewing Co.**, 148 Main Street, (307) 332-7388, is Lander's only microbrewery. Live music (jazz, blues, C&W) can be heard on weekends. The **Gannett Grill**, 126 Main Street, (307) 332-8228, adjacent to the cool Lander Bar, offers terrific burgers and sandwiches, including a "Cluck Boob"—the worst name ever for a good chicken breast sandwich. At **Magpie**, 159 North Second Street, (307) 332-5989, you'll see cowboy hats at one table, Nike caps at the next, and long hair filled with pine needles at the next. Good coffees and breakfasts.

In Riverton, the **Broker Restaurant**, 203 East Main Street, (307) 856-0555, is the restaurant of choice for business deals and the place to impress out-of-town relatives in a historic hotel atmosphere. In Dubois, both **The Ramshorn**, 202 East Ramshorn, U.S. Highway 287, (307) 455-2400, and the **Rustic Pine Steakhouse**, 119 East Ramshorn, (307) 455-2400, are classic old steak-and-potatoes venues populated by locals down from the mountains for the day. Also in Dubois, **Old Yellowstone Garage**, 112 East Ramshorn, (307) 455-3666, features very good Italian food and a menu that changes daily. Closed in April and November.

The **Atlantic City Mercantile**, 100 East Main Street, Atlantic City, (307) 332-5143, would be worth the trip to the South Pass area for the rustic, authentic cowboy-miner atmosphere and "above-the-timberline views" alone. The "Merc" is open all week but serves large steaks grilled over aspen wood Thursday through Sunday and a seven-course Basque feast on Wednesday.

LODGING

Wind River Country offers an eclectic blend of lodging, from the expected to the very offbeat. Riverton offers the most rooms by far at the most consistent prices. Travelers can find some real bargains in the area. The **Riverton Holiday Inn**, 900 East Sunset, Riverton (307) 856-8100, is the area's only large convention-style property, with 121 rooms, pool, restaurant, atrium, and airport transportation at $45 to $56 per night. The **Tomahawk Motor Lodge**, 208 East Main Street, Riverton, (307) 856-9205, is well-maintained and located in the heart of downtown, with $28 to $40 rooms.

In Lander, the **Pronghorn Lodge**, 150 East Main Street, (307) 332-3940, is a local favorite that's very easy to find because of its beautiful bronze sculptures along the highway. Rates are modest, ranging from $28 to $44. Lander's newest is the **Best Western Inn at Lander**, 260 Grand View Drive, (307) 332-2847, with 46 rooms, many amenities, and competitive rates. The **Bunk House**, 2024 Mortimore Lane, (307) 332-5624, is a rustic lodgepole home owned by the Lander Llama Company that sleeps up to six people for $65 a night. **Black Mountain Ranch**, 548 North Fork Road, (307) 332-6442, offers the entire beautifully restored rustic ranch house to guests for $350 per week. **Whispering Winds Bed & Breakfast**, 695 Canyon Road and Seventh Avenue South, (307) 332-9735, features well-appointed rooms in a midtown location for $45 to $55 per night.

Dubois offers a variety of lodgings, which, to be honest, primarily exist to accommodate travelers for one night on their way to Yellowstone. **Twin Pines Lodge & Cabins**, 218 Ramshorn, (307) 455-2600, is a unique, historic group of restored rooms and new cabins in an attractive setting, with $30 to $50 rates. The Dubois area also hosts more than ten established guest and dude ranches, offering nightly, minimum stay, and weekly programs and rates. Contact the **Bitterroot Ranch**, 10 Stallmaker, (800) 545-0019, if your primary interest is horseback riding, or **Brooks Lake Lodge**, 458 Brooks Lake Road, (307) 455-2121, for a resort-type ranch. Those wanting to live and work on a real cattle ranch should check out the **Three Quarter Circle Ranch**, U.S. Highway 287, Lander, (307) 332-2995, for riding, roping, fence-fixing, and other cowpoke activities.

CAMPING

As with so many places described in this book, campgrounds abound in and around local communities. Including the **Shoshone National Forest**, there are more than 30 campgrounds within 40 miles of the area, including the **Circle Up Camper Court**, 225 West Welty Street, Dubois, (307) 455-2238, with 100 private sites, some tipis, hookups, and pull-throughs for $12 per night. The National Forest Service maintains numerous sites around Dubois, including **Brooks Lake, Double Cabin, Falls, Horse Creek**, and **Pinnacle Campground**, for $6 to $8 per night. Call (307) 455-4266 for maps, regulations, and permits.

In and around Lander, the **K-Bar RV Park**, U.S. 87 and Route 789, (307) 332-5460, offers 87 sites on 50 acres near a reconstructed frontier town for $8 to $12 per night. **Sinks Canyon State Park**, Highway 131, (307) 332-6333, provides 30 sites in an excellent location for $9 to $12 per night. The National Forest Service maintains sites at **Dickinson Park**, **Fiddlers Lake**, **Lewis Lake**, and **Worthen Meadows Reservoir**. Call (307) 332-5460 for maps, regulations, and permits. The Riverton area has two private campgrounds: **Owl Creek Campground**, U.S. 26, Riverton, (307) 856-2869, with 40 pull-through sites for $15 per night; and **Riverton RV Park**, 1618 East Park Avenue, (307) 856-3913, with 60 sites, hookups, tipi tent sites, and $17.50 to $19.50 rates.

Scenic Route: Wind River Canyon

Named after the Indian tribe, **Shoshoni** is the gateway to **Boysen State Park** and **Wind River Canyon**. In 1911 the Chicago, Burlington, and Quincy Railroad tunneled through the canyon only after fur trader William Ashley had journeyed through a century before. Take U.S. Highway 20/Wyoming Route 789 along the Wind River. **Boysen Dam** has tamed the once completely wild **Wind River** into a river with many slow and lazy sections, but some impressive technical white water and excellent fishing still remain. (But anglers should note that much of the river is within the Wind River Indian Reservation, which requires a special fishing license. Same with rafters and hikers.)

Signs along the canyon provide information about specific geological formations. Amateur and professional geologists can drive through various rock and sedimentary periods of the earth as they descend the canyon, including the Jurassic and Pre-Cambrian "dinosaur" periods. As the 2,000-foot canyon walls rise on either side and the road winds through several tunnels, a strange optical illusion occurs: Because of the grade of the road, the river appears to be

WIND RIVER CANYON

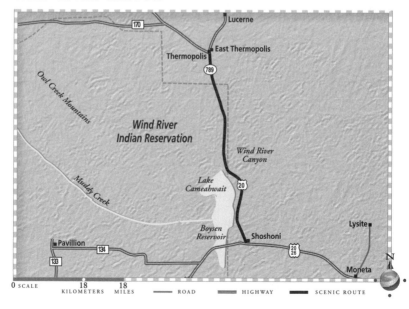

flowing uphill instead of downhill. This illusion has caused many visitors to pull to the side of the road and rub their eyes.

The canyon finally opens 10 miles before you reach **Thermopolis** (population 3,200), considered one of Wyoming's secret places. It is certainly worth visiting, hosting the world's largest hot springs (2.8 million gallons flow out of the ground every day). Three notable pool areas within **Hot Springs State Park** include a free soaking pool and two indoor/outdoor recreation pools with soaking and swimming areas, plus waterslides. The best of the three is the **Star Plunge**—it's more conventional than its predecessor, the rickety wooden "Screaming Mimi," but it's still a kick. Short walks within Hot Springs State Park lead to **Bighorn Hot Spring**, **Black Sulphur Springs**, **White Sulphur Springs**, and **Ponce de Leon**. A new attraction is the **Wyoming Dinosaur Center**, 110 Carter Ranch Road, which was founded by two German paleontologists who bought a local ranch because the terrain looked as if it contained significant fossil beds . . . and they were right. Visitors can view fossils being prepared within the Preparation Lab, the archeological site where the bones are recovered, and see interpretive displays on the massive finds occurring right now. Call (307) 864-2997 for hours. Admission is $5. For more details on Thermopolis, contact the Thermopolis–Hot Springs Chamber of Commerce, P.O. Box 768, Thermopolis, WY 82443; (307) 864-3194. ◼

8

JACKSON HOLE

As a friend of mine once said between beers, "Dude, everybody's got to do the 'Stone and the Hole once in their lives." He was referring, of course, to Yellowstone and Jackson Hole. Since Yellowstone was the first destination chapter in this book, we can say we've done it. Now it's time for Jackson Hole. Hold on to your hats.

Originally called "Jackson's Hole" after nondescript trapper Davey Jackson, Jackson Hole proper encompasses the entire valley 60 miles from the town of Jackson to the south entrance of Yellowstone Park. All of Grand Teton National Park is within "Jackson Hole." Prior to the nineteenth century, there was little human activity in the valley. American Indians—Blackfoot, Gros Ventre (pronounced "grow vahnt"), Shoshone, and Crow—passed through but didn't stay long. Mountain men followed in search of beaver. A few hardy ranchers were next. Then came hunters, hikers, tourists, and merchants. Skiers arrived in the late 1960s, when Paul McCollister opened the Jackson Hole Ski Area. The rich and famous (Harrison Ford, President Clinton and family) soon followed.

As my friend said, you are going to end up doing the Hole. If you do it right, you'll enjoy the heck out of it. ◼

JACKSON HOLE

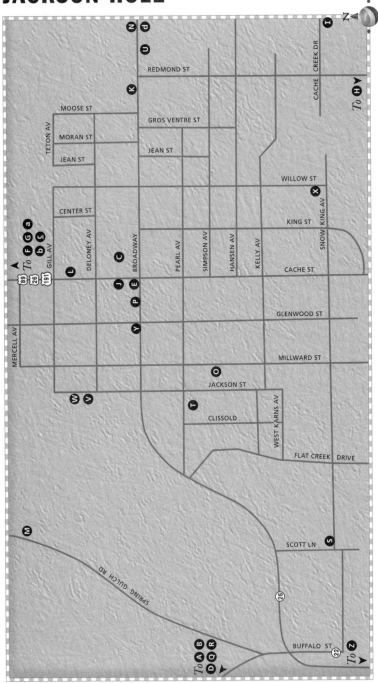

NOT TO SCALE

ROAD

Sights

- **Ⓐ** Grand Targhee Ski and Summer Resort
- **Ⓑ** Grand Teton Music Festival
- **Ⓒ** Jackson Town Square
- **Ⓓ** Jackson Hole Ski Area
- **Ⓔ** Million Dollar Cowboy Bar
- **Ⓕ** National Elk Refuge
- **Ⓖ** National Museum of Wildlife Art
- **Ⓗ** Snow King Mountain

Food

- **Ⓘ** Bar-T-Five Chuckwagon Cookout & Wild West Show
- **Ⓙ** Billy's Giant Hamburgers
- **Ⓚ** Bubba's Barbeque
- **Ⓛ** The Bunnery
- **Ⓙ** Cadillac Grille
- **Ⓜ** The Granary
- **Ⓝ** Gun Barrel Steakhouse
- **Ⓞ** Jackson Hole Pub & Brewery
- **Ⓟ** Jedediah's House of Sourdough
- **Ⓠ** Stieglers

Lodging

- **Ⓑ** Alpenhof Lodge
- **Ⓡ** The Antler
- **Ⓑ** Best Western Inn at Jackson Hole
- **Ⓢ** Best Western Lodge at Jackson Hole
- **Ⓣ** Forty-Niner Inn and Suites
- **Ⓠ** Jackson Hole Racquet Club Resort
- **Ⓤ** Nowlin Creek Inn
- **Ⓥ** The Parkway
- **Ⓦ** Rusty Parrot Lodge
- **Ⓑ** Sojourner Inn
- **Ⓡ** Spring Creek Resort
- **Ⓡ** Teton Pines Resort
- **Ⓧ** Twin Trees Bed and Breakfast
- **Ⓨ** Wort Hotel

Camping

- **Ⓩ** Astoria Hot Springs
- **ⓐ** Curtis Canyon
- **ⓑ** Grand Teton Park KOA
- **ⓒ** Snake River Park KOA
- **ⓓ** Virginian Lodge RV Park

Note: Items with the same letter are located in the same town or area.

A PERFECT DAY IN JACKSON HOLE

Start the day with fresh-baked bread and a large egg dish at The Bunnery, just off the square. If you're visiting in the summer, be sure to finish your coffee in time to meet your white-water float trip company. Experienced guides will steer you through Kahuna and Lunch Counter rapids, and *you will get wet*. In the afternoon visit the National Museum of Wildlife Art or stroll down the wooden sidewalks of downtown Jackson. If you're with children, take a short covered-wagon trip with Bar-T-Five into the foothills above Jackson for a chuckwagon cookout, songs, and entertainment.

On a winter day, be the first to make some tracks in the powder. Jackson has recently added two new gondolas and hundreds more acres of terrain. The lack of lift lines and the challenging terrain of Jackson Hole can wear you out—take the afternoon off from skiing. Instead, take a sleigh ride on the National Elk Refuge under a thick blanket and find yourself in the midst of 10,000 or so elk on their winter feed grounds. For après ski, do the Mangy Moose in Teton Village or the intimate Beaver Dick's, followed by a great big sloppy cheeseburger and beer at Billy's Giant Burgers. Next door, there's a cowboy band at the Million Dollar Cowboy Bar.

THE THREE JACKSON HOLES

There are several different Jackson Holes. The first is the most obvious—the tourist town with wooden sidewalks, Ralph Lauren, Benetton, and J. Crew factory outlets on the square and staged shootouts on the street. The second Jackson is populated by a wealthy elite who have recently chosen Jackson to build second or third million-dollar houses tucked away in the aspen and pine groves. Locally, these houses are referred to as "starter castles" (they aren't hard to recognize).

The third Jackson, the one I recommend, is the middle tier made up of working men and women (many who were either born in the region or might as well have been), who do the work of running the hotels, pumping the gas, guiding hunters or hikers, and selling the lift tickets; these people choose to live here because they love the area. They're sure to know what flies are working on the river or which ski runs are good given current snow conditions. Don't be afraid to approach them and ask.

SIGHTSEEING HIGHLIGHTS

★★★ **Jackson Hole Ski Area**—Located at Teton Village, the Jackson Hole Ski Area has the longest continuous vertical rise of any United States ski resort—4,139 feet from the valley floor to the top of Rendezvous Mountain, with a 63-passenger aerial tram that transports skiers to the top in 12 minutes. Jackson Hole is unique for its challenging skiing and expert slopes. Many skiers will swear that in Jackson Hole a green run (easiest) is a blue run (moderately difficult) at most other ski areas, and that a blue run is a double blue, a black diamond is a double-black diamond, and so on. In other words, you learn soon enough why skiers from all over the world come to "ski the big one." A Jackson Hole average I like is that there are only 1,750 skiers on 2,500 acres of ski terrain, offering one of the lowest skier densities of any area in the country. This means that fewer people see you crash and burn. In summer, the **Jackson Hole Aerial Tram** whisks visitors from the heart of Teton Village to the top of 10,450-foot Rendezvous Mountain. Details: WYO 390, Teton Village; (800) 443-6931 or (307) 733-2292; open 9 a.m. to 5 p.m. but call ahead for conditions. Tickets are $15. (1 hour)

★★★ **Jackson Town Square**—Everything in Jackson revolves around the square, which is exactly that—a small wooded park in the center of town that can be entered by passing under massive **Elk Antler Arches**. The arches were originally built from shed antlers found on the National Elk Refuge in the '50s and '60s. Surrounding the square are wooden sidewalks fronted by shops and galleries. Jackson *is* a tourist town, evidenced by shops that include Benetton, The Gap, J. Crew, and Polo. But some jewels can also be found, like **Jack Dennis Sports** and the **Valley Bookstore** (located in Gaslight Alley), the best local book store in Wyoming. Details: For a *Guide to Shopping in Jackson Hole*, write ahead or stop by the Jackson Hole Chamber of Commerce and Visitor Center, P.O. Box E, Jackson, WY 83001, (307) 733-3316; for an art gallery guide, call (307) 739-8911. (2 hours)

★★★ **National Elk Refuge**—Established in 1912 to protect elk from being killed in the winter, when they are most visible, the National Elk Refuge is now home to upwards of 10,000 elk in the winter months. Although the feeding program and the constantly increasing herd is the subject of growing controversy, the opportunity to see elk in an intimate winter setting is impressive. Operated by the U.S. Fish and Wildlife

Service, sleigh rides into the herds are available in the winter. Details: Elk Refuge Road, Jackson; (307) 733-9212; open mid-December through March. Admission: $8 adults, $4 children ages 6 to 12; tickets available at National Museum of Wildlife Art. (1 hour)

★★★ **National Museum of Wildlife Art**—This 51,000-square-foot facility, opened in 1994, is considered to be the nation's premier public collection of fine art devoted to North American animals. It's a spectacular collection in a spectacular location, featuring 2,000 paintings by more than 100 artists, including Carl Rungius, George Catlin, Albert Biestadt, John Clymer, John J. and John W. Audubon, and Charlie Russell. It's best visited in the winter with its epic view of the National Elk Refuge. Details: Rungius Road; (307) 733-5771; open daily (except Christmas) 10 a.m. to 5 p.m. Admission: $5 adults, $4 children, $12 families. (2 hours)

★★ **Grand Targhee Ski and Summer Resort**—"Over the hill" from Jackson via Teton Pass, Grand Targhee sits high in the Tetons between Mount Moran and The Grand on the Idaho side. Grand Targhee is legendary for its powder, which averages over 500 inches a year. The area's vertical rise is 2,200 feet, with base elevation at 8,000 feet. Its 1,500 acres are served by lifts, with an additional 1,500 available by snowcat. The terrain is 10 percent beginner, 70 percent intermediate, and 20 percent advanced. Details: Ski Hill Road, Alta; (307) 353-2300 or (800) TARGHEE; lift tickets cost $39 for a daily value card. (3 hours)

★★ **Grand Teton Music Festival**—Every summer for 35 years, world-renowned musicians have participated in this unique classical music phenomenon. Conductors and composers such as Zubin Mehta, Robert Shaw, and Stanislaw Skrowaczewski have visited, along with the New York Philharmonic in its first-ever summer residency. Details: Teton Village; (307) 733-3050; Tuesday through Saturday 8 p.m. to 10 p.m. Admission: from $5 for open rehearsal to $30 for festival orchestra.(2 hours)

★ **Million Dollar Cowboy Bar**—Even though it's kitschy and corny and you sometimes wonder where your waitress went, it *does* have the original cowboy barstools made of real saddles and the rotating western dioramas on the chandeliers. And it's got that great buckaroo marquee sign out front. An institution. Details: 25 North Cache (on the square);

(307) 733-2207; open Monday through Saturday 9 a.m. to 2 a.m., Sunday noon to midnight. Cover charge for live bands. (2 hours)

★ **Snow King Mountain**—Wyoming's first ski area was the Snow King, which opened in 1939 and is considered the "town hill" because of its location within Jackson city limits. Don't let the "town hill" moniker lull you, though. The area has a vertical rise of 1,571 feet, with 400 acres of skiable terrain—15 percent beginner, 25 percent intermediate, and 60 percent advanced. Details: 400 East Snow King Avenue; (307) 733-5200 or (800) 522-KING; lift tickets are $28. (2 hours)

FITNESS AND RECREATION

Like other mountain resort towns, it sometimes seems as if just about everybody in and around Jackson Hole is into fitness and recreation—and talks about it, sometimes ad nauseam. If you gain weight while visiting Jackson, it is *your fault*, because even though there are great places to eat, there are equally great places to work off the meals.

Grand Teton National Park

Hikers, bikers, trekkers, joggers, runners, and walkers have literally hundreds of trail miles at their disposal within the length of the Jackson Hole valley. For outdoor trail and recreational information, contact **Grand Teton National Park**, Drawer 170, Moose, WY 83012, (307) 739-3600; and Bridger Teton National Forest, P.O. Box 1888, Jackson, WY 83001, (307) 739-5500.

According to your mood, available time, and sense of adventure, there are scenic, white-water, combo scenic/white-water, and fishing river trips available on the **Snake River**. I recommend the white-water trips because they are short (four to five hours including ground transportation), high-quality (some darned good rapids), lots of fun (U-paddle boats and skilled guides), and a good value. Choose from the following: **Barker Ewing Whitewater River Trips**, (307) 733-1000, adults $26 and up; **Charles Sands' Wild Water River Trips**, (307) 733-4410, adults $30 and up; and **Lewis & Clark Expeditions**, (307) 733-4022, adults $30 and up.

FOOD

Jackson Hole hosts plenty of dining options. The trick is to avoid what I call "resort food," food that looks good on your menu and pretty on your plate (e.g., "Savory Vegan Risotto" or "Ziti tossed with Provencal Herbs, Sundried Tomatoes, and Chevre"—actual menu items) but leaves you unsatisfied, poor, and feeling slightly . . . *false*. So, for your dining pleasure, we will include no resort food on this list or in this book.

For breakfast, do **The Bunnery**, 130 North Cache Street, (307) 733-5474, for excellent omelettes, fresh-baked pastries, and strong coffee; or **Jedediah's House of Sourdough**, 135 East Broadway, (307) 733-5671, for sourdough pancakes and wheat cakes. Both are local favorites and very affordable.

For lunch or dinner, try the **Cadillac Grille**, 55 North Cache, (307) 733-3279, which sometimes dances with my resort food definition but generally serves wildly creative, well-prepared game, steak, seafood, and pasta dishes in a comfortable art deco atmosphere. Just inside the Cadillac's front door is **Billy's Giant Hamburgers**, 55 North Cache, (307) 733-3279, where you grab a stool at the counter, yell out your order, and watch the cooks prepare your big burger with cheese, lettuce, tomato, and attitude. **Bubba's Barbecue**, 515 West Broadway, (307) 733-2288, features down-home smoked meats and sauces. The **Jackson Hole Pub & Brewery**, 265 Millward, (307) 739-2337, serves up simple and good pizza and sausages with Snake River Lager, Pale Ale, and Zonker Stout. The **Gun Barrel Steakhouse**, 862 West Broadway, (307) 733-3287, features mesquite-grilled steaks and baked sweet potatoes, plus an excellent selection of single-malt Scotch and bourbons.

For more elegant dining, visit **The Granary** at Spring Creek Ranch, Spring Gulch Road, (307) 733-8833. It has a wonderful elevated view of the Teton Range and a romantic ambiance. **Stieglers**, Jackson Hole Racquet Club, (307) 733-1071, features Austrian continental dishes like paprika schnitzel and apple strudel.

Sure, some of the jokes are a little corny, but my family loves the **Bar-T-Five Chuckwagon Cookout & Wild West Show**, Cache Creek Road, (307) 733-5386. Joyce makes good beans.

LODGING

In Jackson Hole there are three primary lodging areas: the town itself; Teton Village, 12 miles from Jackson; and points in between. In town, the historic and refurbished **Wort Hotel**, at Glenwood and Broadway, (307) 733-2190, is a half-block off of the square. Rates run from $115 to $169. Good, solid, locally owned properties include the **Best Western Lodge at Jackson Hole**, 80 Scott Lane, (307) 739-9703; **The Antler**, 43 West Pearl, (307) 733-2535; the **Forty-Niner Inn and Suites**, 330 West Pearl Street, (307) 733-7550; **The Parkway**, 125 North Jackson Avenue, (307) 733-3143; and the **Rusty Parrot Lodge**, 175 North Jackson, (307) 733-2000. Rates are from $98 to $450.

In Teton Village (in summer or winter), try the **Best Western Inn at Jackson Hole**, SR 390, (307) 733-2311; the **Alpenhof Lodge**, SR 390, (307) 733-3242; or the **Sojourner Inn**, SR 390, (307) 733-3657. **Spring Creek Resort**, on Spring Gulch Road, (307) 733-8833, sits between Jackson and Teton Village. **Teton Pines Resort**, 3450 North Clubhouse Drive, (307) 733-1005, is located on the road to Teton Village with rates from $75 to $250.

Quality bed and breakfasts in the valley include the **Nowlin Creek Inn**, 660 East Broadway, (307) 733-0882; and the **Twin Trees Bed and Breakfast**, 575 South Willow, with rates from $90 to $120.

CAMPING

The **Snake River Park KOA** (April 15 to October 5), 11 miles from Jackson on Highway 89, has 100 sites with hookups, (307) 733-7078.

Astoria Hot Springs (May 15 to September 5) is 3 miles south of Hoback Junction on Highway 89, with 102 sites with hookups and a mineral hot pool, (307) 733-2659. The **Virginian Lodge RV Park** (summer only), 750 West Broadway, (307) 733-2792, offers 110 large spaces with RV hookups in the middle of town. **Curtis Canyon,** (307) 733-7455, is a National Forest Service public campground with 12 sites and an excellent Teton view. The **Grand Teton Park KOA** (April through September), (307) 733-1980, 6 miles east of Moran Junction on U.S. 287, has 200 immaculate sites with hookups.

NIGHTLIFE

You can sit on a saddle instead of a barstool at the **Cowboy Bar**, 25 North Cache (on the square), (307) 733-2207, and listen to solid live country music. The **Mangy Moose** in Teton Village, SR 390, (307) 733-4913, has a stuffed moose suspended from the ceiling and good (sometimes excellent) live blues, jazz, rock, and reggae bands. **J.J.'s Silver Dollar Bar** in the Wort Hotel, Glenwood and Broadway, (307) 733-2190, is generally more quiet and contemplative, with a Lone Ranger singer on occasion. **Dornan's Bar**, Moose Junction, (307) 733-2522, offers one of the best Teton views and the best wine list in Jackson Hole. Try to get there before dark to watch the sunset.

9

GRAND TETON NATIONAL PARK

W e've all seen the Teton Mountains so many times that they're burned into our collective brains even if we've never been to the park. The Tetons are unique and spectacular, a mountain range that seems to be thrusting 7,000 feet out of the flats into the air like sabers. They have provided the background for countless movies, commercials, advertisements, and presidential proclamations. The mountains are so young, they're still growing. They're so blue and jagged, the air is so clear and sharp, it almost hurts your eyes to look at them. Even the best nature artist couldn't do justice to the sight of the Snake River doing a lazy "S" curve beneath the looming blade-like summit of the Grand Teton.

Grand Teton is almost 500 square miles, about 24 by 38 miles in a north-to-south rectangle, boasting more than 200 miles of hikeable trails. The Teton Range comprises the western border of the park; Jackson and Jenny Lakes (along with dozens of other lakes and flats) and the Snake River occupy the valley floor. Even though Grand Teton is directly south of Yellowstone, the park doesn't share its thermal features or varied landscapes and wildlife. Grand Teton does, however, play host to more moose in its willow-filled wetlands, and it's a thoroughfare for southbound elk exiting Yellowstone in the late fall. ◨

GRAND TETON NATIONAL PARK

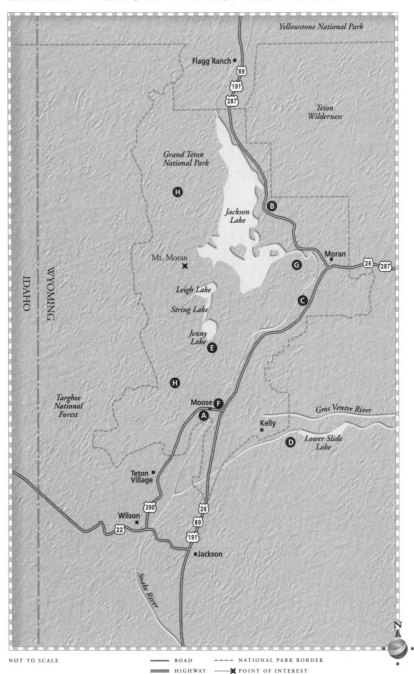

Yellowstone National Park

Flagg Ranch ■

89
191
287

Teton
Wilderness

Grand Teton
National Park

H

Jackson
Lake

B

Mt. Moran ✕

G

Moran ■

26 287

Leigh Lake

C

String Lake

Jenny
Lake

E

H

Targhee
National
Forest

Moose F

A

Gros Ventre River

Kelly ■

D   Lower Slide
Lake

Teton ■
Village

390

26

Wilson ■

89

22

191

■ Jackson

Snake River

IDAHO   WYOMING

N

NOT TO SCALE

———— ROAD   ----- NATIONAL PARK BORDER

═══════ HIGHWAY   ✕ POINT OF INTEREST

Sights

Ⓐ Chapel of the Transfiguration

Ⓑ Colter Bay Indian Arts Museum

Ⓒ Cunningham Cabin

Ⓓ Gros Ventre Slide

Ⓔ Hidden Falls and Inspiration Point Trails

Ⓕ Menor's Ferry

Ⓖ Signal Mountain

Ⓗ The Tetons

A PERFECT DAY IN GRAND TETON NATIONAL PARK

Start the morning with a breakfast trail ride and fill up on Dutch-oven biscuits, eggs and ham, and hot coffee followed by apple cobbler baked in that same Dutch oven. Walk off breakfast by exploring some of the many hiking trails around Moose, the park's headquarters, and make sure to visit the beautifully simple Chapel of the Transfiguration, which frames the Teton Range in its window. A scenic boat cruise on the Snake River allows increasingly magnificent views of the mountains as well as the occasional moose and bald eagle. Relax before dinner with a beverage in the Mural Room at Jackson Lake Lodge, watching the late afternoon sun play on the mountains through the 100-foot picture windows. Have your steak broiled to order at the outside Pool Grill and BBQ while you enjoy the brisk mountain air.

GRAND TETON 101

As stunning as the Tetons are, only a French trapper far away from home could look at them and call them "Les Trois Tetons" (The Three Breasts). Compared to its bigger northern neighbor, Yellowstone, Grand Teton National Park is a pup. The present park border and its actual designation as "Grand Teton National Park" didn't occur until 1950, even though there was a move afoot since the 1920s to create the park. Even today there are still small pockets of private land and "grandfathered" concessions within the park. It is also the only United States national park that contains an airport, the Jackson Hole Airport.

Grand Teton offers an ambiance of elegance that is missing from much of Yellowstone as well as from most other national parks. This elegance is probably attributable to the man who built and designed such signature accommodations as Jackson Lake Lodge and Jenny Lake Lodge, John D. Rockefeller. Rockefeller also donated the majority of the land to the National Park Service, a move that wasn't popular with everyone in the state of Wyoming, who saw the "donation" as confiscatory. You can still stir up a hornet's nest with some old-timers if you choose to broach the topic. So don't. Instead, enjoy the view—you'll never see mountains like this anywhere else.

Park admission was raised to $20 per car in 1997, up from $10 the previous year. If you've already paid and entered in Yellowstone there is no additional charge, and vice-versa. This "two parks for one fee" might just be the best vacation deal in the world.

SIGHTSEEING HIGHLIGHTS

Except where otherwise noted, for information on all sites and activities within Grand Teton Park, contact Superintendent, Grand Teton National Park, P.O. Drawer 170, Moose, WY 83012, (307) 739-3300.

★★★ **Chapel of the Transfiguration**—This small chapel, located by the Moose headquarters, is a log structure patterned after a similar chapel built on the Wind River Indian Reservation near Ethete, Wyoming. Built in 1925, the chapel's picture window within the chapel frames the Teton Range so beautifully that it looks like a Moran painting. Episcopal services are held during the summer, and schedules are posted outside. (30 minutes)

★★★ **Signal Mountain**—A steep narrow road located 2 miles south of Jackson Lake Junction on Teton Park Road delivers an epic panorama of Grand Teton Park and beyond. From the top of this mountain, you can see views to the east, north, and south, including the valley, Jackson Lake, southern Yellowstone, the Gros Ventre and

Hoback Mountains, and, of course, the Tetons. The best views occur at sunset. (30 minutes)

★★★ **The Tetons**—All of Grand Teton National Park is, in essence, a 500-mile plot of land offering views of the Teton Range from different angles and altitudes. Arguments erupt over where the best view is, but really there is no "best" view. Mount Moran through the picture window at Jackson Lake Lodge is no more breathtaking than Mount Moran looming over Oxbow Bend near Moran Junction. The Grand can take your breath away, not only from the Snake River Overlook on U.S. Highway 89, but also from any number of pullouts along the road. The whole range is spectacular when viewed from a boat on the Snake (although your neck aches from looking up all the time) and from Valley Trail.

Impress the other tourists by pointing out each of the mountains in the Teton Range as follows, descending from the tallest: Grand Teton, 13,770 feet; Mount Owen, 12,928 feet; Middle Teton, 12,804 feet; Mount Moran, 12,605 feet; South Teton, 12,804 feet; Mount Teewinot, 12,325 feet; Thor Peak, 12,028 feet; Buck Mountain, 11,938 feet; Nez Percé Peak, 11,901 feet; Mount Wister, 11,490 feet; and Mount St. John, 11,430 feet. (2 hours)

★★ **Menor's Ferry**—Down a trail from the chapel is Menor's Ferry, named after the bachelor brothers Bill and Holiday Menor, who were among the first white settlers in the valley. Legend has it they didn't really like each other; they apparently lived on opposite sides of the river and didn't speak for years, though they were virtually alone in the wilderness. The Park Service has reconstructed a replica of the watercraft that was used to ferry passengers across the Snake River; the Menors' original cabin still exists and can be toured daily in the summer. (30 minutes)

★ **Cunningham Cabin**—Located 6 miles south of Moran Junction, this homesteader's cabin became the base for a ranch. This is a good spot to ponder how rough and rugged it really was for Teton settlers before jet airplanes, electricity, and delivered pizza. (30 minutes)

★ **Gros Ventre Slide**—Ten miles west of Moose is the unique geological site of the Gros Ventre Slide (pronounced "grow vahnt," a French trapper's term for local American Indians who had "big

bellies"). On June 23, 1925, a large section of the mountain
dislodged and slid down the hill into the Gros Ventre River,
damming it and obliterating the small town of Kelly, Wyoming. A
self-guided tour prepared by the Bridger-Teton National Forest
provides further details. (1 hour)

★ **Hidden Falls and Inspiration Point Trails**—Not really "hidden"
anymore, thanks to tourism, Hidden Falls and Inspiration Point
Trails at the southern shore of Jenny Lake can be accessed in the
summer via boat ride. Hidden Falls itself is an icy, foamy, furious
little falls worth the hike to see. Ranger-guided tours are available
daily during summer. (2–3 hours)

Colter Bay Indian Arts Museum—American Indians didn't spend a
lot of time in the mountainous and rugged Jackson Hole/Grand Teton
area. Understandably, they preferred country that was lower in
elevation, more temperate, and easier for traveling and hunting.
Nevertheless, some natives did occupy the area, struggling in a near-
primitive state. Well-preserved artifacts from these and other regional
tribes are displayed at the small museum. Details: John D. Rockefeller
Memorial Parkway, Colter Bay Village; (307) 739-3594; open mid-May
through September 8 a.m. to 8 p.m., to 5 p.m. before Memorial Day
and after Labor Day. (30 minutes)

FITNESS AND RECREATION

Activities available within Grand Teton National Park run the gamut
from the sublime (sitting back and enjoying a relaxing Snake River raft
ride) to the adventurous (climbing the 13,000-foot Grand Teton
Mountain). We'll start at the top, so to speak.

The climbing season in Grand Teton runs from mid-June through
mid-September, and although fit and experienced climbers can obtain
maps and do it alone, most of the locals, including the National Park
Service, recommend a guided trip. **Jackson Hole Mountain Guides**,
(307) 733-4979, as well as other authorized services, provide
professional climbing instruction. Multiday trips are also available.
Ascents of peaks like the Grand, Mount Moran, and Mount Owen are
not easy jaunts, taking at least two days. Lesser peaks can be scaled in
one to two days. Climbers and/or climbers-to-be should contact the
Park Service at (307) 739-3300.

Guided horseback riding as well as breakfast and dinner rides are available from both **Jackson Lake Lodge** and **Colter Bay Village**. Trail rides are offered for one hour ($19), two hours ($29), three hours ($39), or four hours ($46). A breakfast ride on horseback is $32 and $18 by wagon, $14 for children. A dinner trail ride is $36 for adults, $25 for children, or $24 and $18 by wagon. Make your reservations with the **Grand Teton Lodge Company**, the park concessionnaire, at (307) 543-3100.

The **Glacial Lakes** of the Tetons include Leigh, String, Jenny, Taggart, Bradley, and Phelps—all accessible to the hardy by foot. For detailed maps, permits, and trail conditions, contact the National Park Service at the **Moose Visitor's Center**, (307) 739-3300. Like many of the trails and lakes in Yellowstone, few Grand Teton visitors ever leave the road, and, even in the height of the season, you can find stunning views and solitude.

Jackson Lake boat cruises lasting 1½ hours from Colter Bay take several trips a day ($11 adults, $6 children). There are also breakfast ($20 adults, $12 children) and dinner cruises ($35 adults, $23 children). For a detailed schedule and exact rates, contact the **Grand Teton Lodge Company**, (307) 543-3100.

A number of companies offer scenic float trips on the Snake River through Grand Teton Park (not to be confused with white-water trips on the same Snake River south of the town of Jackson). Trips vary with the outfitter from 1½-hour, 5-mile floats on **Osprey Snake River Float Trips**, (307) 733-5500, for $15 to $20 for adults, to three-hour, 10-mile trips with dinner from **Grand Teton Lodge Company Float Trips**, (307) 543-2855, at $36 to $41 per adult. **Barker-Ewing Scenic Float Trips**, (307) 733-1800, and **Triangle X Ranch Float Trips**, (307) 733-5500, also offer a variety of quality trips and rates.

FOOD

Even if the food were sub-par (which it isn't), the view of the Tetons through 100-foot windows in the **Mural Room at Jackson Lake Lodge**, (307) 543-2811, ext. 1911, would make a meal here worthwhile. All three meals are served, and diners enjoy well-prepared beef, fish, and pasta dishes. Reservations are recommended in general and are essential during July and August. Open May 23 through October 3. The **Pool Grill and BBQ at Jackson Lake**

GRAND TETON NATIONAL PARK

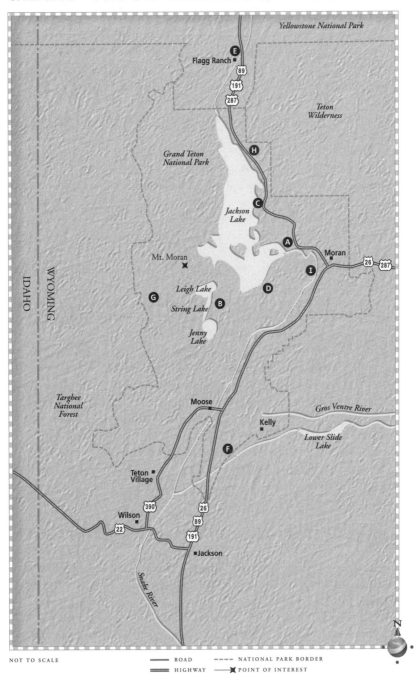

Yellowstone National Park

Flagg Ranch ■ E

89
191
287

Teton
Wilderness

Grand Teton
National Park

H

Jackson
Lake

C

A

Moran ■
26
287

Mt. Moran ✖

I

Leigh Lake

G

D

String Lake

B

Jenny
Lake

IDAHO

WYOMING

Moose ■

Gros Ventre River

Kelly ■

Lower Slide
Lake

Targhee
National
Forest

F

Teton ■
Village

390

26

Wilson ■

22

89

191

■ Jackson

Snake River

N

NOT TO SCALE

ROAD   ---- NATIONAL PARK BORDER
HIGHWAY   ✖ POINT OF INTEREST

Food

Ⓐ Jackson Lake Lodge (Mural Room and Pool Grill and BBQ)

Ⓑ Jenny Lake Lodge Dining Room

Ⓒ John Colter Grill

Ⓐ Pioneer Grill at Jackson Lake

Ⓓ Signal Mountain Lodge

Lodging

Ⓒ Colter Bay Village and Cabins

Ⓔ Flagg Ranch

Ⓐ Jackson Lake Lodge

Ⓑ Jenny Lake Lodge

Ⓓ Signal Mountain Lodge

Camping

Ⓒ Colter Bay RV and Trailer Park

Ⓒ Colter Bay Tent Village

Ⓔ Flagg Ranch Campground

Ⓖ Grand Teton Park KOA

Ⓕ Gros Ventre Campground

Ⓖ Jenny Lake Camp

Ⓗ Lizard Creek Campground

Ⓘ Signal Mountain Campground

Note: Items with the same letter are located in the same town or area.

Lodge (same phone) is a personal favorite, although anything outdoors in the mountains of Wyoming can be a bit of a gamble. Open during July and August for outside dining, sandwiches, pizza, and burgers are served from 11:30 a.m. to 3:30 p.m., followed by an all-you-can-eat Western barbecue of steaks, chicken, and ribs from 6 to 8 p.m.

The **Jenny Lake Lodge Dining Room**, (307) 733-4647, is well-known for excellent food in a rustic atmosphere. Starting in June, reservations are required for dinner and breakfast. The **John Colter Grill at Colter Bay Village**, (307) 543-2811, is better than the above dining experiences if you have small children or are on a budget. Open from 6 a.m. to 10 p.m. daily, the grill features basic breakfasts, burgers, and sandwiches. Reservations aren't required. The **Pioneer Grill at Jackson Lake**, (307) 543-2811, offers the same kind of menu and hours. **Signal Mountain Lodge** in the Signal Mountain complex,

(307) 543-2831, offers good American food at midrange prices with a lovely view of Jackson Lake; make reservations based on when you can get a window table.

LODGING

Please keep in mind that, like Yellowstone, there are no in-room televisions and few telephones. If you or your family need the average hotel or motel amenities, consider staying outside the park in Jackson, Wyoming, and day-tripping into the park during your stay.

There are four lodging complexes within Grand Teton Park. **Jackson Lake Lodge**, 5 miles northwest of Moran Junction, (307) 543-3100, is a full-service resort hotel overlooking Willow Flats and Mount Moran. The view from the Mural Room is reason enough for staying (or at least visiting) this lodge. There are 385 rooms, not all of which have the Teton view everybody wants. Jackson Lake Lodge has a "corporate" feel to it, unusual for National Park properties, primarily because of the many conventions and meetings it hosts. Prices range from $99 for main lodge rooms to $175 for "view" rooms. Suites run $315 to $450. Open mid-May through mid-October.

Jenny Lake Lodge, 3 miles off of Interpark Road, (307) 733-4647, is much more rustic (although elegantly so with a Mobil four-star rating and AAA four-diamond rating) than Jackson Lake Lodge and has a tendency to make people fall passionately in love with it. Thirty-seven cabins surround a main lodge and the property has a relaxed guest-ranch feel to it; lots of log cabins, quilts, and stunning Teton views from the porch. Stunning prices as well, with cabins starting at $335 per night for two. Breakfast, dinner, and horseback riding are included in the room rate. The property is open from June through September.

Signal Mountain Lodge, (307) 543-2831, is an attractive hideaway on Jackson Lake with a 79-room main lodge and 34 cabins. Signal Mountain is not as well-known or expensive as the former Rockefeller properties (Jackson Lake Lodge and Jenny Lake Lodge) but has a charm of its own, with many water-based family activities, including a beach, fishing, rental canoes and boats, and water-skiing. Rooms and cabins range from $69 to $155. Open May 12 to October 16.

Colter Bay Village and Cabins, (307) 543-3100, is the budget and family place to stay within Grand Teton Park, with cabins, tent cabins, an RV park, and camping. The 208 cabins vary according to size, layout, and facilities. Rates per day for one or two persons are $30 for a semiprivate room, $60 to $85 for a room with bath, and $87 to $109 for two rooms with connecting bath. The village also offers Colter Bay Tent Cabins, cool little canvas tents with woodburning stoves, outdoor grills, bunk beds, and picnic tables for $26 per day. Your kids will like them. Open May 31 to September 7.

Just outside the park, **Flagg Ranch**, (307) 543-2861, sits on the John D. Rockefeller Memorial Parkway between Grand Teton Park and Yellowstone. Talk about location! Flagg Ranch is a sprawling complex that has just undergone some extensive construction and remodeling. The main lodging facility has 110 rooms, and new cabins are within walking distance of the lodge and restaurant. Flagg Ranch is closed from March 15 through May 15 and October 15 to December 14. It's a prime location for winter activities, partly because it's the "end of the road" and staging area for snowmobile and snowcoach activity. Summer rates range from $91 to $117, with winter rates dropping to $70 to $80.

CAMPING

Nearly 1,460 designated campsites exist within Grand Teton Park, and they're a mixture of public (National Park Service) and private (Grand Teton Lodge Company). Like Yellowstone, the private campgrounds encourage reservations and deposits are required, while the public campgrounds won't accept reservations except for large groups, in writing. **Colter Bay RV and Trailer Park**, 10 miles northwest of Moran Junction, has 112 sites with hookups, (307) 543-3100. Rates are $25 from June 9 to September 5, $19 from May 12 to June 8 and September 6 to October 6. **Colter Bay Tent Village**, within the Colter Bay complex, is described above under Lodging. The season runs from June 2 to September 10. **Flagg Ranch Campground**, May 20 to September 20, is located 2 miles south of the Yellowstone entrance, 171 sites with hookups, reservations and deposit required, (307) 543-2861. **Grand Teton Park KOA**, April 1 to October 1, located 6 miles east of Moran Junction on U.S. 287, 200 sites with hookups, immaculate appearance, $16 to $24 depending on season, (307) 733-1980.

Campsites maintained by the National Park Service all cost $10 per night and include **Gros Ventre Campground**, May 3 to October

15, 360 sites, 6 miles north of Jackson on U.S. 89; **Jenny Lake Camp**, May 23 to September 30, 49 sites, 7 miles north of Moose on Teton Park Road; **Lizard Creek Campground**, 62 sites, June 13 to September 30, 18 miles north of Moran Junction on U.S. Highway 89; and **Signal Mountain Campground**, 86 sites, May 10 to October 10, 18 miles north of Moose on Teton Park Road.

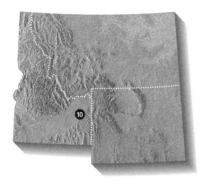

10
IDAHO FALLS

I daho Falls grew up around the rapids of the Snake River, known as the "Mad River" by early explorers. The town's namesake is scenic falls in the river that serves as the centerpiece of the community. Like many other Western towns, Idaho Falls began as a crossroads to elsewhere. In the 1860s freighters and prospectors traveling north from Salt Lake City to gold mines in northern Idaho and western Montana crossed the Snake River in this vicinity. In 1865 the settlement (then called "Eagle Rock") began. When the mines had been exhausted and the economy bottomed out, the remaining residents decided to stick around and try something new. They dug channels from the river to irrigate the land, and today the area has more than a million acres of farmland. This community of 50,000 residents is now Idaho's third largest city.

Idaho Falls is a likable, pleasant small city and still a hub, with spokes to Yellowstone to the northwest, Jackson Hole and Grand Teton National Park to the east, West Yellowstone to the north, Craters of the Moon National Monument to the west, and Salt Lake City to the south. ◣

IDAHO FALLS

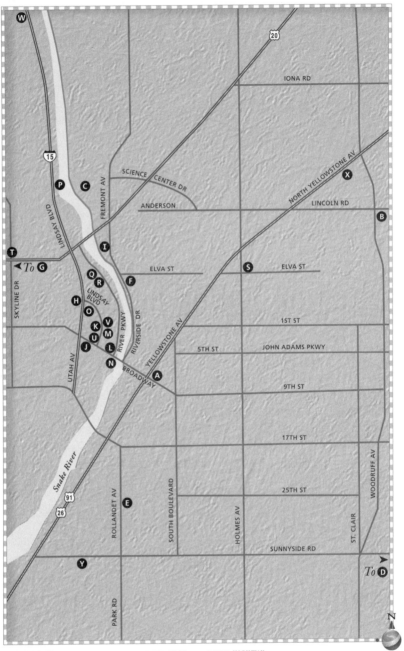

NOT TO SCALE ——— ROAD ━━━ HIGHWAY

Sights

A Bonneville Historical Museum

Idaho Falls Parks:

    B Lincoln Park

    C Russell A. Freeman Park

    D Sandy Downs

    E Tautphaus Park/Idaho Falls Zoo

F Idaho Falls Temple Visitor Center

G Idaho National Engineering Laboratories

H Ridge Avenue Historic District

I Snake River Greenbelt Park

Food

J Jake's Steak and Fish House

K O'Callahan's

L Rutabaga's Espresso Bar

M The Sandpiper

N The Snake Bite, Inc.

Lodging

O Ameritel Inn

P Best Western Cottontree

Q Best Western Driftwood

R Holiday Inn Westbank

S Littletree Inn

T Motel West

U Quality Inn

V Shilo Inn

Camping

W Idaho Falls KOA

X Shady Rest Campground

Y Sunnyside Acres

A PERFECT DAY IN IDAHO FALLS

Start out with a brisk walk around the Snake River Greenbelt (be sure to take along popcorn to feed the friendly ducks and geese). Stroll downtown to one of the bread stores for a slice of hot homemade bread or a muffin and a cup of espresso. Golf a round at one of Idaho Falls' three excellent municipal golf courses. When you're done, drive down West Broadway to Reeds Dairy for a scoop of homemade potato ice cream. In the evening sit in the bleachers of McDermott Field, soak up the hometown atmosphere, munch on a couple of hot dogs, and watch the Pioneer League Idaho Falls Braves play ball.

SIGHTSEEING HIGHLIGHTS

★★★ **Snake River Greenbelt Park**—The pleasant 14-mile greenbelt loops around the falls and the Snake River in a track enjoyed by pedestrians, joggers, and bicyclists. The falls itself is long and fairly calm, not a thundering splashdown of water. Canada geese and ducks hang out along the walkway, and it isn't unusual to see an occasional trumpeter swan, loon, or brown pelican. (1 hour)

★★ **Bonneville Historical Museum**—This museum does a much better-than-average job of presenting county history. Maybe it's because the county is such an interesting place—from the first explorers and settlers at "Eagle Rock USA," to mining, the birth of agriculture, and the atomic age. The building itself is on the National Register of Historic Places. Details: Eastern and Elm Avenues, Idaho Falls; (208) 522-1400; open weekdays 10 a.m. to 5 p.m., Saturday 1 p.m. to 5 p.m. Admission: $1 adults, 25 cents children. (1 hour)

★★ **Idaho Falls Parks**—This small city is big on parks. There are 39 within city limits. **Tautphaus Park**, located off Boulevard, provides 80 acres of grass and activity fields, including softball diamonds, tennis courts, picnic shelters, and an artificial ice hockey rink. The **Idaho Falls Zoo**, (208) 529-1470, is also housed within this park. **Russell A. Freeman Park**, on Science Center Drive, sits on the bank of the Snake River and, in addition to ballfields and picnic shelters, contains the unique Idaho Vietnam Memorial. **Sandy Downs**, a 200-acre park southeast of town, (208) 529-8722, contains the rodeo grounds and parimutuel horse racing. **Lincoln Park**, on Lincoln Road, has shelters, playground equipment, and tennis courts. Details: Idaho Falls Parks and Recreation Department, (208) 529-1480. (2 hours)

★ **Idaho Falls Temple Visitor Center**—Southern Idaho has a large Mormon (LDS) population. Its temple is closed to the public, but its visitor's center offers exhibits, artwork, films, and displays on Mormon history and culture. Details: 1000 Memorial Drive; (208) 523-4502; open daily 9 a.m. to 9 p.m. Free. (1 hour)

★ **Idaho National Engineering Laboratories**—A great deal of government-sponsored nuclear research and experimentation has occurred in and around Idaho Falls. The 890-square-mile Idaho National Engineering Laboratories (INEL) employs many locals here. Tours of some of the facilities are available with advance permission; contact the public affairs office. Details: 1955 Fremont Avenue; (208) 526-0050. Free. (1–4 hours)

★ **Ridge Avenue Historic District**—This 67-site, self-guided walking tour is a well-put-together, well-documented look at historic Idaho Falls. Most of the homes on tour were built from 1890 to 1920 and exhibit distinct architectural styles. Details: Greater Idaho Falls Chamber of Commerce, 505 Lindsay Boulevard; (208) 523-1010. (2 hours)

FITNESS AND RECREATION

Walking, jogging, biking, or blading—the **Snake River Greenbelt** is the place of choice when the weather is nice. Idaho Falls also offers four good golf courses, including **Sandy Creek Golf Course**, 5230 Hackman Road, (208) 529-1115; **Pinecrest Golf Course**, 701 Elva, (208) 529-1485; **Heise Hills**, 5136 East Heise, (208) 538-7327; and the **Idaho Falls Country Club**, 11611 South Country Club Drive, (208) 523-5757. Indoor workout facilities, including aerobics, super circuit, free weights, etc., are available at the **Downtown Athletic Club**, 1769 West Broadway, Idaho Falls, (208) 529-8600.

FOOD

Idaho Falls is not known for a wealth of exclusive or specialty restaurants, and the fare is generally fairly traditional. However, many of the better restaurants sit along the banks of the Snake, affording excellent river views. **Jake's Steak and Fish House**, 851 Lindsay Boulevard, (208) 524-5240, receives high marks for fine steaks and a quality Idaho wine list. **The Sandpiper**, 750 Lindsay Boulevard, (208) 524-3344, features steak and seafood in a nice atmosphere with a river view. **Rutabaga's Espresso Bar**, 415 River Parkway, (208) 529-3990, has good sandwiches and salads. The **Snake Bite, Inc.**, 425 River Parkway, (208) 525-2522, has tasty burgers and lunch. **O'Callahan's**, part of the Shilo Inn, 780 Lindsay Boulevard, (208) 523-1818, features a good prime rib, salmon buffet, and patio seating.

LODGING

Because of its crossroads location and vibrant economy, Idaho Falls hosts a wealth of quality lodging properties at competitive rates. Most are located in the vicinity of the Snake River Greenbelt, and many offer river views. It's pleasant and convenient to stroll from your hotel along the river to a nice meal (see Food, above). Check out the **Holiday Inn Westbank**, 475 River Parkway, (208) 523-8000, offering 142 singles or doubles for $85 a night. The shiny new **Ameritel Inn**, 645 Lindsay Boulevard, (208) 523-1400 or (800) 600-6001, has 126 oversized rooms for $69 to $89, wheelchair accessible. The **Shilo Inn**, 780 Lindsay Boulevard, (208) 528-0088, offers 161 rooms, including mini-suites, for $89 to $119. The **Best Western Cottontree**, 900 Lindsay Boulevard, (208) 523-6000, has 94 rooms from $65 to $70. The **Quality Inn**, 850 Lindsay Boulevard, (208) 523-6260, offers 127 rooms at $44 to $50. The **Best Western Driftwood**, 575 River Parkway, (208) 523-2242, has 74 rooms from $43 to $75. Downtown lodging includes **Motel West**, 1540 West Broadway, (208) 522-1112 or (800) 582-1063, $32 to $46; and the **Littletree Inn**, 888 North Holmes Avenue, Idaho Falls, (208) 523-5993, $55 to $69.

CAMPING

Because Idaho Falls is surrounded by public lands and forests with many campsites, the town itself offers limited choices. They include the **Idaho Falls KOA**, 1440 Lindsay Boulevard, (208) 523-3362, with 175 sites and hookups at a well-maintained facility. Open all year, rates are $15 to $17.50 per night. Others include the **Shady Rest Campgrounds**, 2200 North Yellowstone, (208) 538-7944; and **Sunnyside Acres**, at 905 West Sunnyside Road, (208) 523-8403.

NIGHTLIFE

Live music is generally on tap at the **Holiday Inn Westbank Lounge**, 475 River Parkway, (208) 523-8000. If you prefer country music in a country atmosphere, choose **Dusters**, at the Best Western Stardust, 700 Lindsay Boulevard, (208) 529-8361. To catch the game, try the **Pressbox Sports Bar**, 1551 West Broadway, (208) 253-8413.

Scenic Route: Teton Scenic Byway

One thing to remember as you take Idaho Highway 26 East to **West Yellowstone** is that Idahoans get a little testy if you refer to the magnificent horizon as "the back of the Tetons." I was once reprimanded by a waitress in Victor, Idaho, who reminded me, correctly, that there was no "back" to the Tetons, and that the citizens of Jackson Hole over the top of the mountain had no right to refer to their view of the Tetons as the "front."

This route includes Idaho Falls east to **Swan Valley**, then to **Victor** on Idaho Highway 31, Victor to **Tetonia** on Idaho Highway 33, Tetonia to **Ashton** on Idaho Highway 32, and U.S. 20 to West Yellowstone, Montana. It's not as complicated as it sounds, and the route is extremely well-marked. The "Road to Yellowstone" is a two-lane roadway with no passing lanes, some 35 mph curves, and, frequently, snow in the winter.

Drivers enjoy beautiful views of the **Snake River Valley**, the western slope of the Tetons, and **Falls River**, as well as the **Targhee National Forest**. The stunning **Teton Range** looms through the

TETON SCENIC BYWAY

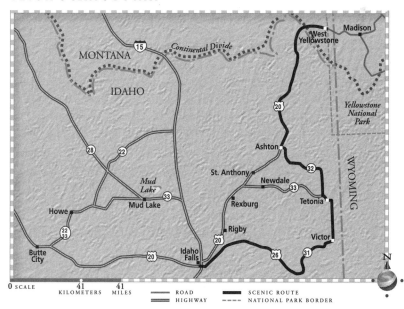

passenger window as you continue northward. The famous **Henry's Fork of the Snake River**, known worldwide to fly fishers, parallels the highway north of Ashton. ◼

11

SUN VALLEY/KETCHUM

Sun Valley offers winter and summer activities that rival or surpass those at any other Rocky Mountain resort, including indoor and outdoor skating rinks with professional ice shows and stars, sleigh rides, snowmobiling, and heliskiing. *Ski* magazine readers recently named Sun Valley the "Best Ski Resort in the Nation." The area boasts 18 lifts, 78 runs, 2,067 skiable acres, and 3,400 vertical feet. Bald Mountain is widely considered the single-best ski mountain in the country, some say the world. Because Sun Valley's base sits at 6,000 feet, much lower than most ski areas, the weather is temperate and generally more pleasant than at other Rocky Mountain resorts. In summer, which surprisingly attracts more visitors than winter, the valley offers golf, tennis, swimming, white-water rafting, camping, horseback riding, shooting, mountaineering, kayaking, and fishing. More than 20 art galleries accompany scores of unique shops.

After a lull, the Hollywood celebrities have returned to the area. Clint Eastwood has a home in Sun Valley, and Bruce Willis and Demi Moore own most of the town of Hailey as well as the Soldier Mountain Ski Area in Fairfield. More than 30 Olympians live nearby as well, including native Picabo Street ('94 Olympic silver medalist), Gretchen Fraser, and Dick Fosbury (creator of the "Fosbury Flop"). ◨

SUN VALLEY/KETCHUM

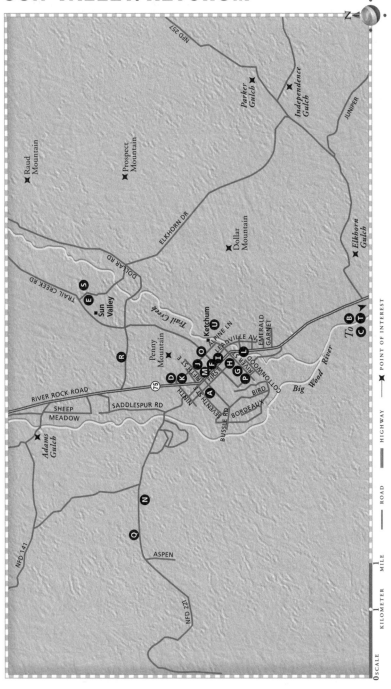

Sights

- Ⓐ Art Gallery Tours
- Ⓑ Craters of the Moon National Monument
- Ⓒ Hailey
- Ⓓ Hemingway Memorial
- Ⓔ Sun Valley Ice Shows
- Ⓔ Sun Valley Ski Area

Food

- Ⓕ Buffalo Café
- Ⓖ Evergreen Bistro
- Ⓗ The Kitchen
- Ⓘ The Kneadery
- Ⓙ Michel's Christiania and Olympic Bar
- Ⓒ The Mint
- Ⓚ Pioneer Saloon
- Ⓛ Sawtooth Club
- Ⓜ Sun Valley Brewery
- Ⓝ Warm Springs Ranch Restaurant

Lodging

- Ⓞ Best Western Christiana Motor Lodge
- Ⓟ Best Western Tyrolean Lodge
- Ⓠ Clarion Inn of Sun Valley
- Ⓔ Elkhorn Resort and Golf Club
- Ⓠ Heidelberg Inn
- Ⓡ Idaho Country Inn
- Ⓓ Knob Hill Inn
- Ⓒ Povey Pensione
- Ⓔ Sun Valley Inn
- Ⓔ Sun Valley Lodge

Camping

- Ⓢ Ketchum Ranger District
- Ⓣ The Meadows
- Ⓤ Sun Valley RV Resort

Note: Items with the same letter are located in the same town or area.

A PERFECT DAY IN SUN VALLEY/KETCHUM

In the summer, start with a 6 a.m. hike up Dollar Mountain to be one of the first to view the magnificent sunrise over the Sawtooths. Return to Ketchum and pound some pancakes at The Kneadery, and then strap on your day pack and head for the Trail Creek Area. Corral Creek Trail is a challenging 7-mile trek through mountain aspen and pine. Return in the afternoon, relax, and soak up some sun beside the pool at Sun Valley Lodge. That evening, enjoy watching a famous skater at the Ice Shows, followed by a lively dinner and show at The Mint (owned by Bruce Willis) in Hailey.

On a winter day, take a couple of quick runs on Dollar Mountain to get your legs ready, hop on the KART bus, and transfer to Bald Mountain. With seven high-speed detachable quads, four triples, two double lifts, and cruiser runs as long 3 miles, you'll see why Baldy is considered such hot stuff. *Skiing* magazine has called Baldy "the best cruising mountain on the planet." Do the après ski thing at Grumpy's or Baldy Base Camp, followed by an elegant dinner with someone special at Michel's Christiania.

SUN VALLEY 101

In 1935 Union Pacific Railroad magnate, former New York governor, diplomat, and entrepreneur Averell Harriman dispatched Austrian Count Felix Shaffgotsch west to find the best place for a great ski resort that would be served, obviously, by the Union Pacific. Shaffgotsch toured the Rocky Mountains and Pacific Northwest, passing up mountains that would later become Aspen, Mount Hood, and Jackson Hole, and settling on a small Sawtooth Mountain mining community in central Idaho's Wood River Valley called Ketchum. Upon recommendation, Harriman quickly bought the 4,300-acre Brass Ranch, dubbed the place "Sun Valley," and began construction of both a magnificent lodge and the first motor-driven chair lift.

America's first destination ski resort attracted lots of attention, not the least of which came from such Hollywood stars as Clark Gable and Gary Cooper. The movie *Sun Valley Serenade* was filmed at the resort, adding another layer of glamour. Novelist Ernest Hemingway fell in love with Ketchum and lived there until his death. The Union Pacific eventually sold the resort in order to focus on running the railroad; it is currently owned by Earl Holding.

SIGHTSEEING HIGHLIGHTS

★★★ **Sun Valley Ski Area**—Sun Valley is comprised of two mountains, Dollar and Bald Mountain. Dollar is primarily a beginner's area, with 13 runs, 70 percent of which are easy. Bald Mountain features 13 lifts and 64 runs (38 percent easy, 45 percent intermediate, 17 percent most difficult). The ski area is open from Thanksgiving Day through May 1, and though massive snowmaking facilities have been installed, they're rarely used. The world's first alpine skiing chair lift was (and still is) located in Sun Valley. Built by Union Pacific Railroad engineers, it was designed after a banana-boat loading device. The 1936 fee: 25 cents per ride. Sun Valley sponsors lots of theme weeks and events throughout the winter as well as specific "kids ski free" periods. Hot spots for après ski include **Baldy Base Club**, Warm Springs Lift, (208) 726-3838; **Apples Bar & Grill**, 215 Lloyd Drive, (208) 726-7067, for local color; and **Grumpy's**, 860 Warm Springs Road, Ketchum (no phone), for locals. Details: Sun Valley/Ketchum Chamber of Commerce, P.O. Box 2420, Sun Valley, ID 83353; (800) 634-3347 or (208) 726-3423. (4–8 hours)

★★ **Art Gallery Tours**—The walking tour features 20 galleries located within easy access of each other throughout Ketchum. Details: Sun Valley/Ketchum Chamber of Commerce, P.O. Box 2420, Sun Valley, Idaho, 83353; (800) 634-3347 or (208) 726-3423; guided tours Thursday at 10 a.m. during summer. Free. (2 hours)

★★ **Craters of the Moon National Monument**—Located 1½ to two hours from Sun Valley on U.S. 93, this 83-square-mile area contains more basaltic volcanic features than any other comparable area in the continental United States. Its moonscape-like surface starkly contrasts with the green hills and towering mountains of Ketchum and Sun Valley. Craters of the Moon National Monument contains nearly 40 separate lava flows, some formed as recently as 250 years ago. The otherworldly area was used as a training ground for early astronauts. See it in June, when a lavish display of wildflowers adds to the surreal quality of the landscape. Details: U.S. 20/26 and U.S. 93; (208) 527-3257; 7-mile loop drive open mid-April to early November; visitor's center open daily mid-June through Labor Day 8 a.m. to 6 p.m., 8 a.m. to 4:30 p.m. the rest of the year. Admission: $4 per vehicle. (2 hours)

★★ **Hailey**—Charming Hailey had a long history well before the arrival of Bruce Willis and Demi Moore. Laid out in spring of 1881 by John Hailey, the town was the bustling center of a rich mining district and the first town in Idaho to have electric lights. While you're there, check out the **Blaine County Historical Museum**, North Main Street, (208) 788-4185, which features an interesting collection of American political campaign memorabilia as well as a replica of a mine tunnel. Details: Hailey Chamber of Commerce, 14 West Bullion; (208) 788-2700. (1 hour)

★★ **Hemingway Memorial**—When Pulitzer and Nobel Prize–winner Ernest Hemingway moved permanently from Cuba to his beloved Ketchum in 1960, he was already in bad shape. Hemingway had known Sun Valley as far back as 1939 and had continued to hunt, fish, ski, and drink in Idaho throughout his career, until he finally decided to make it his home. He killed himself in July 1961, but not before making his mark. Details: Ketchum Cemetery on State Highway 75; a simple memorial to Hemingway sits in the trees along Trail Creek. (1 hour)

★ **Sun Valley Ice Shows**—Featuring such performers as Nancy Kerrigan, Oksana Baiul, Kristi Yamaguchi, Katarina Witt, Victor Petrenko, Scott Hamilton, and Brian Boitano, with scenic Bald Mountain in the background, the Sun Valley Ice Shows have been popular for decades. Shows begin with an optional buffet and run Saturdays at dusk, from mid-June through mid-September. Details: Sun Valley; (208) 622-4111; call for schedules. Admission: show, $24 adults, $20 children; show and buffet, $63 adults, $44 children. (2 hours)

FITNESS AND RECREATION

In both summer and winter, the number of quality outdoor activities in the Sun Valley/Ketchum area can be daunting. The thing to do in winter is fairly obvious: ski. For more information, see the Sun Valley Ski Area listing, above. As for summer activities, here are some suggestions: Hiking ranges from easy 1- and 2-mile loops near town to challenging treks in the Sawtooths. National Forest Service trail maps for hikes leading out of Sun Valley are available at the Sun Valley/Ketchum Chamber of Commerce or from the National Forest Service. **Sawtooth National Recreation Area** headquarters and visitor's center is located 8 miles north of Ketchum, near Galena Summit. Trail maps, advice, and information can be obtained there before setting out, or call (208) 726-8291.

Horseback riding in the Sawtooths area is an impressive experience, and many experienced outfitters can accompany you. For a listing, contact the chamber of commerce. One outfitter is the **Galena Stage Stop Corrals and Trail Rides**, (208) 726-1735, leading trips daily from May 31 through Labor Day. One- or two-hour excursions cost $24; half-day, $48; and all-day, $75.

River rafting, boating, and kayaking are also offered from local outfitters in single-day, half-day, or multiday intervals. Kayak school is conducted by **Cascade Recreation**, (208) 462-3292. Scores of outfitters provide single-day river trips, but **Cascade Recreation, Far and Away Adventures**, (208) 726-8888, and **Middle Fork River Tours**, (208) 788-6545, are most notable.

The Elkhorn, (208) ELKHORN, and **Sun Valley Golf**, (208) 622-2251, boast 18-hole courses designed by Robert Trent Jones Jr. The nine-hole **Bigwood Golf Course**, (208) 726-4024, is a good value.

Some of the most challenging and rewarding fly fishing in the Rockies can be had on Silver Creek and the Big Wood and Little Wood Rivers. Silver Creek is particularly awesome and tough, yielding big trout that you must promptly release. **Silver Creek Outfitters**, (208) 726-5282, **Venture Outdoors**, (208) 788-5049, and **Sun Valley Outfitters**, (208) 622-3400, are quite knowledgeable.

Mountain biking, ice skating, llama treks, horsepack trips, inline skating, rock climbing, tennis, trap and skeet shooting, and more are available in Sun Valley. For a complete inventory, contact the Sun Valley/Ketchum Chamber of Commerce at (208) 726-3423 or (800) 634-3347.

FOOD

It's been said that there are no bad places to eat in Ketchum. That's a bit of a stretch. (For my definition of "resort food," see the Food section in the Jackson Hole chapter.) However, local restaurant patrons in Sun Valley do seem more discriminating than most and weed out the real losers in a hurry. What's left is a fine collection of restaurants.

For breakfast, do omelettes at **The Kitchen**, Second and Main Streets, (208) 726-3856, or homemade muffins at local favorite **The Kneadery**, 260 Leadville, (208) 726-9462. Both are also good for lunch, and so is the **Sun Valley Brewery**, 202 North Main, (208) 788-5777, boasting excellent sandwiches, pub food, and hand-crafted beer. The **Buffalo Café**, 320 East Avenue, Ketchum, (208) 726-9795, serves a fine lunch, and its Buffalo Chips are said to cure hangovers.

A wealth of worthy dinner choices includes the solid **Pioneer Saloon**, North Main Street, (208) 726-3139, for steaks and prime rib; and the **Sawtooth Club**, South Main, (208) 726-5233, serving seafood, steak, pasta, and sandwiches. The whole family will love **Warm Springs Ranch Restaurant**, Warm Springs Road, (208) 726-2609, for its beef, chicken, and children's specials.

The **Evergreen Bistro**, First Avenue and River Street, (208) 726-3888, is high-end with a great wine list and wonderful jazzy food. **The Mint**, 116 South Main Street, Hailey, (208) 788-MINT, owned by Bruce Willis, features fine dining and headline shows upstairs. **Michel's Christiania and Olympic Bar**, Walnut Avenue, (208) 726-3388, delivers discreet, classy service and old-fashioned great food. I recommend the lamb shank.

LODGING

Five areas within the Big Wood River Valley offer lodging: The best known, of course, is Sun Valley itself; the Elkhorn area is just over the hill from Sun Valley and the closest to Dollar Mountain; Warm Springs Lodge and River Run Plaza are base areas for lifts to the top of Bald Mountain; finally, there's the town of Ketchum.

If you want to stay at a resort, Sun Valley Resort offers the elegant **Sun Valley Lodge** and the comfortable (but somewhat dorm-like) **Sun Valley Inn**, (800) 786-8259. The Lodge's standard rooms start at $134 in the summer and, in winter, go up and up from there. A standard room in the Inn is $99 in winter and $109 and up in summer. Condos start at $115, and cottages range from $550 to $1,000. Prices drop in the spring and fall. The **Elkhorn Resort and Golf Club**, Sun Valley, (800) 355-4676 or (208) 622-4511, is a roomy, more modern hotel offering 184 rooms for $89 to $285 in the winter, $95 to $295 in the summer. Condos are also available.

If you'd rather stay at a hotel or motel, the **Heidelberg Inn**, Warm Springs Road, Warm Springs, (800) 284-4863 or (208) 726-5361, is a very pleasant property and a fine value. Rooms start at $65. Another good deal is the **Best Western Tyrolean Lodge**, 260 Cottonwood, Ketchum (River Run), (800) 333-7912 or (208) 726-5336, offering quality rooms from $70 up. The **Best Western Christiana Motor Lodge**, 651 Sun Valley Road, Ketchum, (208) 726-3351, has rooms from $65 to $85. The **Clarion Inn of Sun Valley**, 600 North Main, Ketchum, (800) 262-4833, bills itself as "The Best Little Hotel in Idaho." Rooms go for $90 to $175.

If you're in the mood for a bed and breakfast, try one of the following: The **Povey Pensione**, 128 West Bullion, Hailey, (208) 788-4682, offers a good alternative for travelers on a budget—rates are $45 for singles and $55 for doubles. The **Idaho Country Inn**, 134 Latigo Lane, Ketchum, (208) 726-1019, is a beautiful, upscale place. Its 11 rooms range from $125 to $185 per night. Even more upscale is the European-style **Knob Hill Inn**, 960 North Main Street, Ketchum, (208) 726-8010. Rooms run from $160 to $300.

An excellent way to access a wide range of accommodations throughout the valley is by contacting **Premier Resorts**, 500 South Main, (800) 635-4444 or (208) 727-4000. Premier offers everything from condos to houses, in just about any price range.

CAMPING

Although it's surrounded by hundreds of miles of ruggedly beautiful mountains and forests (and hundreds of U.S. Forest Service campsites—call (800) 280-CAMP), Sun Valley itself is not exactly renowned for its camping, if you get my drift. However, you'll find a few good campsites around town. The **Sun Valley RV Resort** in Ketchum, (208) 726-3429, is right on the river and fills up quickly. It has 80 spaces with hookups, at rates of $17.50 to $31 per day. **The Meadows** in Ketchum, (208) 726-5445, offers 45 spots at $18 per day. The **Ketchum Ranger District** in Ketchum and Sun Valley, (208) 622-5371, provides 22 free spaces without hookups.

NIGHTLIFE

According to age and taste, there are plenty of things to do and see at night in Ketchum, Hailey, and Sun Valley. For the very young there are the ice rink, movies, and bowling alley at the **Sun Valley Lodge**. For the young of drinking age, do **Grumpy's**, 860 Warm Springs Road, Ketchum (no phone), for $2.75 schooners and the "Sorry—We're Open" sign; or **The Beach**, Main Street and Sun Valley Road, (208) 726-0051. And, of course, check out **The Mint**, 116 South Main

Street, Hailey, (208) 788-MINT, if there's a show. "Hemingway Haunts" (which means serious watering holes) include **The Casino** and the **Pioneer Saloon**, North Main Street, (208) 726-3139. For the seasoned, there's the **Duchin Room** at the Sun Valley Lodge, a.k.a. the "Wrinkle Room" or the "Doo-Dah Room."

12

RIVER OF NO RETURN COUNTRY— SALMON/CHALLIS/STANLEY

When you hear "Idaho," you think of potatoes, right? Well . . . OK, *right*. But you should also think of white water. Idaho has 3,100 white-water river miles, far more than any other state in the country. And the Salmon/Challis/Stanley area in central Idaho is absolutely prime white-water country, as good as anything in the United States. The Wild and Scenic Rivers Act helped preserve a number of rivers, and the Salmon River System is the longest undammed system in any state. The area still looks much like it did when the first white explorers found it. Lewis and Clark dubbed the Salmon the "River of No Return." Mountain men Jim Bridger and Kit Carson used to winter here. Surrounding the river is the Frank Church River of No Return Wilderness, the largest forested wilderness in the lower 48. We're talking real wild country here, nearly all of it public land.

The small communities here are authentic and historic, a real step back in time. Each is, in its way, a staging area for adventures. Salmon is the favored starting point for pack trips into the wilderness and float trips into the wildest part of the river. Stanley is the center of the Sawtooth National Recreation Area, Sawtooth Valley, and the Sawtooth Basin, with most Middle Fork float trips outfitted there. The area north of Challis on Highway 93 is considered the "White Water Capital of the World." ◾

RIVER OF NO RETURN COUNTRY

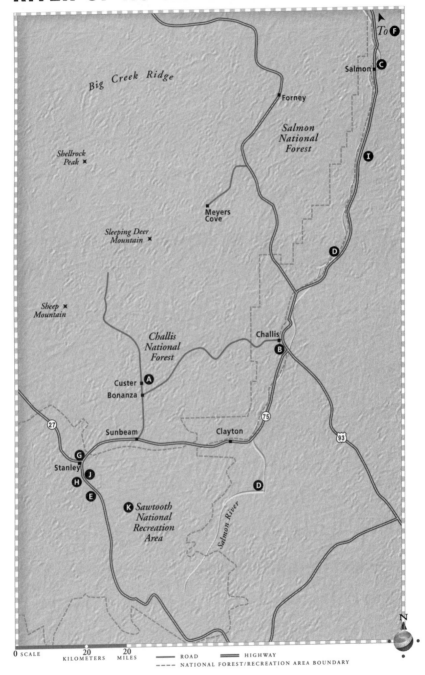

To **F**

Salmon **C**

Big Creek Ridge

Forney

Salmon
National
Forest

Shellrock
Peak ✕

I

Meyers
Cove

D

Sleeping Deer
Mountain ✕

Sheep ✕
Mountain

Challis
National
Forest

Challis

B

Custer **A**
Bonanza

27

75

Sunbeam

Clayton

93

G
Stanley
J
H
E

D

K Sawtooth
National
Recreation
Area

Salmon River

N

0 SCALE 20 20
KILOMETERS MILES

—— ROAD —— HIGHWAY

- - - NATIONAL FOREST/RECREATION AREA BOUNDARY

Sights

A Custer

B Land of the Yankee Fork Historical Area

C Lemhi County Historical Museum

D Salmon River

E Sawtooth Fish Hatchery

Food

F Broken Arrow Family Restaurant

C Salmon River Coffee Shop

C Salmon River Inn

G Sawtooth Hotel

C Shady Nook

Lodging

G Jerry's Country Store and Motel

H Redfish Lake Lodge

C Stagecoach Inn

C Suncrest Motel

C Syringa Lodge Bed and Breakfast

I Twin Peaks Ranch

Camping

J Elk Mountain RV Resort

K Sawtooth National Recreation Area

Note: Items with the same letter are located in the same town or area.

A PERFECT DAY IN RIVER OF NO RETURN COUNTRY

The rubber raft is being packed with dry bags, and the outfitter is doing last-minute checks of the equipment, extra oars, and life jackets. The sun is brilliant, and the morning is warm. You've already had your safety talk and know what to do if you get washed out of the boat. You and your friends get into the boat, and the guide noses it out into the water—the Middle Fork of the Salmon River. Someone jokes nervously about the name, the "River of No Return." You grip your paddle. You hear a rumble ahead that turns into a roar . . . .

TIPS FOR WHITE-WATER SAFETY

White-water trips on the Salmon are available, as the guides put it, from "mild to wild." The trick is to challenge yourself enough to have fun but not overdo it. Here are some tips that have stood the test of time:

- Always know the section of the river you intend to run, its hazards, put-ins, take-outs, and rapids.
- Check weather conditions. Make sure you have proper clothing and insulation against water temperature and the elements.
- Insure that rafting and kayaking equipment is in good condition and properly suited to the river sections you intend to negotiate.
- Make sure your skill level—and that of your companions—is up to the challenges of the river.
- Carry safety equipment for self-rescue and know how to use it.
- If you find yourself swimming in a rapid, know the hazards. Float on your back and use your feet to fend off rocks and obstacles. If not fending off obstacles, don't try to collect your gear, just swim quickly to shore.
- Have a plan to communicate with your group in case a bad situation arises. Choose a leader and think ahead.
- If you're not absolutely sure you can accomplish any of the preceding seven tips, take a commercially guided raft trip.

SIGHTSEEING HIGHLIGHTS

★★★ **Land of the Yankee Fork Historical Area**—This is an informative interpretive center detailing historic central Idaho mines and the role mining played in state and local development. An 18-minute slide presentation features area ghost towns, mining history, and Challis-area settlers. The center also leads to several real ghost mining towns, including Custer and Bonanza, both part of a 91-mile scenic loop on a narrow gravel road. The loop hosts a gold dredge open for tours June through September. Details: junction of Idaho Highways 75 and 93, Challis; (208) 879-5244; open daily May through September 8 a.m. to 6 p.m., rest of the year 8 a.m. to 5 p.m. Admission: free, but gold dredging tour is $2.50 adults, $1.50 children. (1 hour for interpretive center, 3 hours for scenic loop)

★★★ **Salmon River**—The Salmon River is one of the few remaining undammed waterways in America. Surrounding the river are heavily forested mountains with pine meadows and deer, elk, black bear, and mountain goats. The best way to experience the river is with a licensed and bonded outfitter and guide on a raft trip of one to six days. There are three sections of the river, the Main Salmon or "River of No Return," the Middle Fork, and the Lower Salmon. Two of the three sections, the Main and the Middle Fork, are located in this area. Both sections offer Class III–IV rapids. In a nutshell, the Main Salmon offers anything from gentle floats to long challenging rapids, while the Middle Fork is ranked one of the top ten white-water rivers in the world. (1–7 days)

★★ **Custer**—A gold-mining ghost town on the Yankee Fork of the Salmon River, Custer was a thriving community during the late 1870s. Today the old Custer schoolhouse is used as a museum. Visitors can walk though the venerable Empire Saloon, take a self-guided tour of the town, and see a slide show about Custer history in the old opera house. Details: 10 miles north of Sunbeam on Highway 75; (208) 879-5244; open Memorial Day through Labor Day 8 a.m. to 5 p.m. Free. (1 hour)

★ **Lemhi County Historical Museum**—An eclectic mix of Asian antiques from China, Japan, and Tibet, as well as local historical items and American Indian artifacts. Details: 210 Main Street, Salmon; (208) 756-3342; open July and August Monday through Saturday 10 a.m. to

© Jean Higgins/Unicorn Stock Photos

Rancher in Central Idaho

5 p.m.; April, June, and September 1 p.m. to 5 p.m. Free, but donations are appreciated. (1 hour)

★ **Sawtooth Fish Hatchery**—The hatchery produces steelhead and Chinook salmon eggs by trapping and holding both species. We're talking big fish. Details: 5 miles south on State Road 75, Stanley; (208) 774-3684; open Memorial Day weekend through Labor Day 8 a.m. to 5 p.m; guided tours at 10:30 a.m., 1:30 p.m., and 3 p.m. Free. (1 hour)

FITNESS AND RECREATION

Recreation is the primary reason for visiting River of No Return Country, specifically its river trips. Trips run for one to six days and vary greatly in diversity depending on the particular stretch of river you choose. Outfitters I can recommend include **Barker-Ewing River Trips**, who provide six-day excursions on the main channel of the Salmon. Prices range from $900 to $1,300 per person. For details, contact them at Box 3032-A, Jackson, WY 83001; (307) 733-1000. **ROW (River Odysseys West)** offers Main Salmon trips plus other Idaho River excursions, including float/horseback trips and raft and ranch holidays. Contact P.O. Box 579, Coeur d'Alene, ID 83816; (800) 451-6034. For a list of bonded and licensed river outfitters as well as descriptions of their trips, contact the **Idaho Outfitters & Guides Association** (the model for what an association like this should be), P.O. Box 95, Boise, ID 83701; (208) 342-1919.

Of course, you aren't limited only to river trips. Horseback rides from 1½ hours to all day and longer are available from **Redfish Lake Corrals and Trail Rides**, (208) 774-3591. Open Memorial Day through Labor Day, with fees starting at $30 for short rides.

For magnificent hiking and trekking, sample the 4.3 million acres (think you'll have enough *room*?) of the **Salmon and Challis National Forests**. The forest contains over 2,800 miles of trail—I'm not making this up. *Twenty-eight hundred miles.* For details and trail maps, contact the Salmon and Challis National Forest headquarters, at RR 2M Box 600, Salmon, ID 83467; (208) 756-5100.

FOOD

Expect your food to be basic and big, with an ever-so-slight nod toward the health-conscious. The **Salmon River Coffee Shop**, 606 Main Street,

Salmon, (208) 756-3521, serves decent steaks and chicken. It gets more rustic at the **Broken Arrow Family Restaurant**, HC 10, Box 1108, Gibbonsville, (208) 865-2241, a good place for the kids to blow off steam and maybe even catch a fish in the trout pond. The **Sawtooth Hotel**, Main Street, Stanley, (208) 774-9947, offers some decent local fare. The **Salmon River Inn**, Main and Andrews Streets, Salmon, (208) 756-3643, is a popular watering hole and eatery usually featuring live bands. The **Shady Nook**, U.S. 93, Salmon, (208) 756-4182, open 5 p.m. to 10 p.m., serves basic steak and seafood in a relaxed atmosphere. Abundant trophies on the walls.

LODGING

In Salmon, the **Stagecoach Inn**, 201 Highway 93H, (208) 756-2231, has 24 rooms and decent amenities (microwaves, refrigerators) for $47 to $63 per single. Many rooms overlook the Salmon River. The **Suncrest Motel**, 705 Callis Street, (208) 756-2294, is another good choice with some nice extras—like a horseshoe pit—for $32 per single. The **Syringa Lodge Bed and Breakfast**, 2000 Syringa Drive, (208) 756-4424, is a beautifully refurbished old homestead with six porches for $40 per single, $60 per double. One of the better dude/guest ranches in the region is **Twin Peaks Ranch**, 20 miles south of Salmon on U.S. 93, (208) 894-2290. $1,195 to $1,395 per person per week (about $170 to $199 per night) buys you a spectacular location with activities, room, horses, shooting, and everything else included.

In Stanley, **Redfish Lake Lodge**, Sawtooth Valley, (208) 774-3536, is an Idaho tradition. Some folks swear by its stunning views and rambling, old-fashioned lodge-like personality the same way they swear by places like the Old Faithful Inn. Rooms go from $40 up, and cabins range from $85 to $200. A nice basic motel without pretension is **Jerry's Country Store and Motel**, HC 67M (208) 774-3566, charging $45 to $53 for a single.

CAMPING

Finding a camping space in River of No Return Country is a little like finding a trail in the Salmon and Challis National Forests (see above). Or like trying to locate a coffee shop in Seattle. There are 29 campgrounds in the **Sawtooth National Recreation Area** alone, seven of which take advance reservations (Easley, 13 miles north of

Ketchum; Boulder View, 14 miles north of Ketchum; Glacier View and Point Campground, at Redfish Lake; Elk Creek Campground, 10 miles west of Stanley; Sheep Trail Campground, 9 miles west of Stanley; and Trap Creek Campground, 15 miles west of Stanley). All cost $8 per night plus a $6 reservation fee. Reservations can be had by calling (800) 280-CAMP or (800) 280-2267. The remaining 22 campgrounds charge $4 per night to $8 per night. For detailed maps and information, contact the SNRA at (208) 726-7672. Local private campgrounds include the 27-site **Elk Mountain RV Resort**, SR 21, Stanley, (208) 774-2202, at $16.50 per night. It's open May 1 through October 15.

NIGHTLIFE

At night on the shore of the Salmon River, after a long day of exhilarating rapids, read in your tent by the light of a flashlight until the six-pack or the batteries wear out.

Scenic Route: Salmon River Scenic Byway

North of Stanley on U.S. Highway 93, the Salmon River Scenic Byway parallels the Salmon River, nicknamed the "River of No Return" by the first white explorers to see it, Captains Meriwether Lewis and William Clark, between 1804 and 1806. It's easy to imagine the name's origins judging by the wild and rolling river and roaring white-water rapids. The Salmon is now considered to be one of the best and most challenging white-water rivers in North America, and dozens of experienced river outfitters take visitors on the ride and experience of a lifetime.

Along Highway 93 north of **Challis** is where the river is considered the "White Water Capital of the World." Rafts can be seen negotiating the rapids, and it's worth stopping at one of the many scenic pullouts to watch experienced oarsmen guide the boats through. The road along the river is two lanes with very few passing opportunities and some winding, 35-mph curves. The hardest thing about the drive is keeping your eyes on the road and not on the undammed, completely wild river. (Although this scenic route is created

SALMON RIVER SCENIC BYWAY

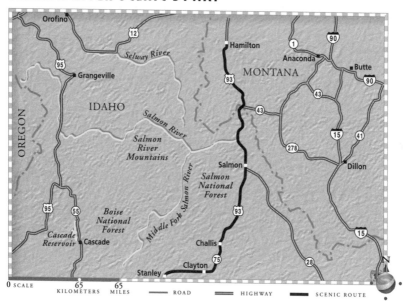

for driving, be sure to see the same route from the river itself. For a list of bonded and licensed river outfitters and details of their trips, contact the **Idaho Outfitters & Guides**, P.O. Box 95, Boise, ID 83701; 208-342-1919.)

The highway also courses through narrow rocky canyons all the way to the Montana border and cuts through Idaho's **Salmon National Forest** and Montana's **Bitterroot National Forest**. The route includes **Clayton, Challis, Ellis, Salmon, North Fork,** and **Jacksonville,** Idaho, and **Darby,** Montana—all very small towns with limited travelers' services. This is the heart of the **Sawtooth National Recreation Area,** widely considered one of the most primitive but picturesque areas in the United States. Depending on the time of year, there is the possibility of seeing salmon-spawning beds at **Indian Riffles** as well as **Land of the Yankee Fork Interpretive Center,** at the junction of Idaho Highways 75 and 93.

The drive will take you past views of **Tower Rock, White Cloud, Lemhi,** and the **Bitterroot Mountains,** and the **Lost River;** and provide access to the **Lewis and Clark National Historic Trail** and **Challis** and **Salmon National Forests.** Look for elk, deer, bald eagles, coyotes, wolves, and bears. For the best weather, travel from April to November, although I also recommend September and October for the stunning fall colors. ◼

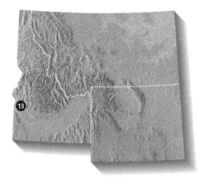

13
BOISE

French-Canadian explorers named the heavily wooded area with the river running through it "Les Bois" (the trees), and the name, like so many others in the mountain West, became corrupted and stuck. Agriculture and mining helped the town grow, and it became territorial capital, then the state capital. Today Boise is the largest city (population 130,000) in Idaho, bigger than any other city in Wyoming or Montana. It's also the largest metropolitan area for 300 miles in any direction (Salt Lake City is the closest large city). Because it's a rather remote destination, Boise has always been somewhat self-contained and self-reliant.

It's also much more sophisticated than people might imagine—certainly hipper and more metropolitan than any other city with a similar population I know. Boise boasts a university, symphony orchestra, summer-long Shakespeare festival, opera and ballet companies, outstanding museums, a 25-mile river greenbelt, and corporate headquarters for such Fortune 500 companies as Boise Cascade, Albertson's, Ore-Ida (H.J. Heinz), Hewlett-Packard, Micron Technology, Morrison-Knudsen, and T.J. International. One of the fastest-growing cities in the West, its temperate climate, friendliness, and vibrant economy continues to attract newcomers, primarily from California.

BOISE

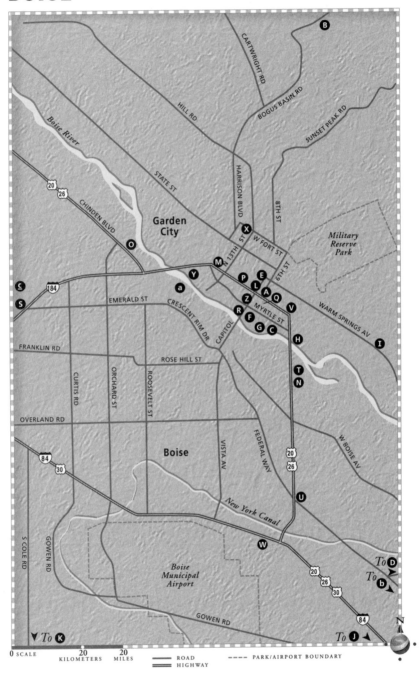

Boise River

20 26

HILL RD

CARTWRIGHT RD

BOGUS BASIN RD

SUNSET PEAK RD

B

STATE ST

HARRISON BLVD

8TH ST

CHINDEN BLVD

Garden City

Military Reserve Park

O

X

W FORT ST

N 15TH ST

9TH ST

M

Y

a

P E

L A Q

Z

R F

G C

V

Warm Springs Av

184

C

S

EMERALD ST

CRESCENT RIM DR

CAPITOL

MYRTLE ST

H

I

FRANKLIN RD

ROSE HILL ST

T

N

CURTIS RD

ORCHARD ST

ROOSEVELT ST

OVERLAND RD

Boise

VISTA AV

FEDERAL WAY

W BOISE AV

20 26

U

New York Canal

S COLE RD

GOWEN RD

Boise Municipal Airport

W

To D

To b

20 26 30 84

▼ To K

GOWEN RD

To J ◄

N

0 SCALE		
20 KILOMETERS	20 MILES	

——— ROAD   - - - - PARK/AIRPORT BOUNDARY

——— HIGHWAY

Sights

- **A** Basque Museum and Cultural Center
- **B** Bogus Basin
- **C** Discovery Center of Idaho
- **D** Idaho City
- **E** Idaho State Capitol
- **F** Idaho State Historical Museum
- **G** Julia Davis Park Boise Tour Train
- **H** Morrison-Knudsen Nature Center
- **I** Old Idaho State Penitentiary
- **J** Snake River Birds of Prey National Conservation Area
- **K** World Center for Birds of Prey
- **G** Zoo Boise

Food

- **L** Bittercreek Alehouse
- **M** Brick Oven Beanery
- **L** Millford's Fish House and Oyster Bar
- **N** Murphy's Seafood Chophouse
- **O** Oñati–The Basque Restaurant
- **P** Peter Schott's Restaurant and Lounge
- **Q** Renaissance Ristorante Italiano
- **R** Tablerock Brewpub & Grill

Lodging

- **A** Ameritel Inn
- **T** Boise River Inn
- **U** Courtyard by Marriott
- **S** Doubletree Club Hotel at Park Center
- **V** Heritage Inn Bed and Breakfast
- **P** Idanha Hotel
- **W** Inn America
- **X** J.J. Shaw House Bed and Breakfast Inn
- **M** Owyhee Plaza Hotel
- **Y** Red Lion Hotel Riverside
- **H** Shilo Inn Riverside
- **Z** West Coast Hotel

Camping

- **a** Americana Kampground
- **b** Boise KOA
- **c** Fiesta RV Park
- **w** Mountain View RV Park

Note: Items with the same letter are located in the same town or area.

A PERFECT DAY IN BOISE

Start the morning with a brisk walk or jog along the 25-mile greenbelt on the banks of the Boise River. Afterwards, take your appetite to the historic downtown for breakfast at Fletcher's Café & Bakery or the Buckin' Bagel. Then find out why Boise is known as "the City of Trees" and "the City of Museums" by visiting the Discovery Center of Idaho, the World Center for Birds of Prey, the Basque Museum, and the Idaho State Historical Museum. Start the evening at Tablerock Brewpub and finish it at one of the funky restaurants at the Eighth Street Marketplace.

SIGHTSEEING HIGHLIGHTS

★★★ **Old Idaho State Penitentiary**—The names Harry Orchard, Lady Bluebeard, and Diamondfield Jack still echo through the halls of the Old Idaho Penitentiary, a fascinating Boise tourist attraction that offers one of the most informative prison tours in the West. The cornerstone of the "Old Pen" was set in 1870, and the last prisoners were moved out in 1973. Built of sandstone quarried by those sentenced to hard labor, the Pen allows visitors to walk through the courtyards, cells, gallows, and "coolers," where prisoners were sentenced to solitary confinement. Visitors can also see the **Museum of Electricity** and the **Idaho Transportation Museum** within the walls. The **Idaho Botanical Garden** is located nearby. Details: 2445 Old Penitentiary Road; (208) 368-6080 or (208) 334-2844; open daily Memorial Day through Labor Day 10 a.m. to 5 p.m., rest of the year noon to 5 p.m. Admission: $4 adults, $3 seniors and children ages 6 to 12. (2 hours)

★★★ **World Center for Birds of Prey**—Established in 1971, this 7,200-square-foot facility is the headquarters of the Peregrine Fund, a nonprofit organization dedicated to raptor conservation. The interpretive center features multimedia exhibits and interactive displays. Visitors can see live bird presentations and learn how the Peregrine Fund breeds endangered birds in captivity and reintroduces them into the wild. A recent addition to the complex is the Tropical Birds of Prey building. Details: 5666 West Flying Hawk Lane; (208) 362-3716; open Tuesday through Sunday 9 a.m. to 5 p.m., November to February 10 a.m. to 4 p.m. Admission: $4 adults, $3 seniors, $2 children. (1 hour)

★★ **Bogus Basin**—Just 16 miles north of town, Bogus Basin is Boise's "town hill" for skiing. With a vertical drop of 1,800 feet, Bogus has one quad, six doubles, one rope tow, one paddle tow, and 48 runs on 2,000 acres. Bogus Basin is a "sleeper," with good, long, black diamond runs, spine-tickling bumps, tree and bowl getaways, and a broad variety of intermediate cruiser runs. Earlier this year, a ground-breaking ceremony signaled the start of the resort's master development plan.

Recent additions: a $3-million quad lift at Deer Point, extended Nordic ski trails, and a flattened, double-chair, beginner enclave. Planned for the near future: a new quad to Shaffer Butte, new lodge and mountainside skier service facilities, and increased Nordic development. Bogus Basin is one of the "big three" of nonprofit community areas, a trio that includes Winter Park, Colorado, and Bridger Bowl, Montana. Details: 2405 Bogus Basin Road; (208) 332-5115 or (800) 367-4397 (out of state only). Ticket prices: $29 adults, $24 students (age 13 to college), $22 seniors (65+), $20 children under age 13, preschoolers free. (3 hours)

★★ **Discovery Center of Idaho**—Offering more than 150 interactive science exhibits, this hands-on science museum is excellent for families. Visitors are encouraged to see, touch, feel, smell, and hear displays. Details: 131 Myrtle Street; (208) 343-9895; open Tuesday through Saturday 10 a.m. to 5 p.m., Sunday noon to 5 p.m. Admission: $4 adults, $3 seniors, $2.50 children. (2 hours)

★★ **Morrison-Knudsen Nature Center**—This 4½-acre facility features living displays via underwater windows on kokanee salmon, steelhead, cutthroat trout, and other fish, from spawning through old age. Other exhibits include aquatic ecology, stream hydraulics, various habitats, and riparian ecology. Details: 300 South Walnut; (208) 334-2225; open daily sunrise to sunset. Free. (1 hour)

★★ **Snake River Birds of Prey National Conservation Area**—Encompassing 483,000 acres of public land along 80 miles of the Snake River 15 miles south of Boise, this area is managed by the Bureau of Land Management (BLM) to provide habitat for nesting birds of prey. Such birds include golden eagles and multiple species of hawks, falcons, vultures, and owls. The area is accessed via a driving loop tour starting in the town of Kuna. An excellent brochure produced by the BLM, Idaho Travel Council, and Kuna Futures narrates each mile.

Details: brochures available at the Boise Convention and Visitors Bureau, 168 North Eighth, Suite 200, (208) 344-7777; or at the Idaho Department of Commerce, 700 West State Street, (208) 334-2470; open sunrise to sunset, weather permitting. Free. (4 hours)

★ **Basque Museum and Cultural Center**—Boise is home to the largest community of Basque people outside of Europe. This historic boardinghouse housed Basque immigrants from 1910 through the 1970s. The museum and center explore Basque history, culture, and cuisine. Details: 607 Grove Street; (208) 343-2671; open Tuesday through Friday 10 a.m. to 3 p.m., Saturday 11 a.m. to 2 p.m. Free, but donations appreciated. (1 hour)

★ **Idaho City**—Located in the Boise Basin, 38 miles north of Boise, Idaho City was once the largest town in the Pacific Northwest. Placerville and Centerville were Idaho City's neighbors and between them formed a rip-roaring gold mining area rivaling anything the California '49ers created. Today Placerville and Centerville are relatively quiet areas. Idaho City has been rebuilt, with some original buildings still in use. Visitors can browse the local museum and arts and crafts center and see hand-carved woodwork, pottery, and quilts made by the Boise Basin Quilters. A tourist information center is located on Highway 21 at the town entrance. Idaho City has several annual celebrations to relive its history. Details: Idaho City Hotel, Idaho City; (208) 392-4290. (3 hours)

★ **Idaho State Capitol**—Located in the heart of downtown and built with local sandstone and marble from Alaska, Georgia, Italy, and Vermont, the state capitol is topped by a large bronze eagle. The self-guided tour begins at the visitor's center in the lower level. Guided tours can be arranged by calling ahead. Details: Jefferson, West State, Sixth, and Eighth Streets; (208) 334-2470; open Monday through Friday 8 a.m. to 5 p.m. Free. (1 hour)

★ **Idaho State Historical Museum**—Objects tell Idaho's story from prehistoric times through the present. Exhibits cover American Indian, Basque, and Chinese populations. Guided tours are available with advance notice. Details: 610 North Julia Davis Drive; (208) 334-2120; open Monday through Saturday 9 a.m. to 5 p.m.; Sunday 1 p.m. to 5 p.m. Free, but donations appreciated. (1 hour)

★ **Julia Davis Park Boise Tour Train**—A good introduction to Boise. This open passenger car is pulled by a replica of an 1890 puff-belly engine through the shopping, historic, and modern districts. Reservations are a good idea. Details: departure from Julia Davis off Capitol Boulevard; (208) 342-4796 or (800) 999-5993; open June through Labor Day, Monday through Saturday tours at 10 a.m., 11:15 a.m., 12:30 p.m., 1:45 p.m., and 3 p.m.; Sunday at noon, 1:15 p.m., 2:30 p.m., and 3:45 p.m.; also open in May, September, and October—call for departure times. Fares: $6.50 adults, $3.50 children ages 4 to 12, $6 seniors. (1 hour)

★ **Zoo Boise**—The collection includes birds and animals native to Idaho and the Pacific Northwest as well as monkeys, camels, tigers, zebras, and other exotic species. Tours are self-guided. Run by the Boise Parks Department. Details: Julia Davis Park, off Capital Drive and Battery Street; (208) 384-4260; open daily 10 a.m. to 5 p.m. Admission: $4 adults, $2 seniors, $1.75 children. (1 hour)

FITNESS AND RECREATION

The **Boise River Greenbelt**, (208) 384-4240, is one of the best river walks I've ever come across, stretching a total of 25 miles on both sides of the Boise River, through the heart of town and many local attractions. The path accesses additional recreation facilities, such as the **Willow Lane Athletic Complex** (soccer fields, playgrounds, fitness course) near Willow Lane, a fishing lake in **Veteran's Memorial State Park**, picnic groves in **Riverside Park**, Wheels-R-Fun skate and bike concession in **Shoreline Park**, the urban wildlife and ¾-mile walking loop at **Kathryn Albertson Park**, the vistas, playgrounds, and reflecting pools of **Ann Morrison Memorial Park**, the zoo and museums of **Julia Davis Park**, the picnic shelters and groves of **Municipal Park**, the **Morrison-Knudsen Nature Center**, the waterpark in **Warm Springs Park**, the 8-acre pond for windsurfing and fishing at **ParkCenter Park**, **Warm Springs Municipal Golf Course**, the Class A Habitat of the **Natural Habitat Area**, and **Barber Park**, where 250,000 summer river tubers start their float.

FOOD

Boise has plenty of good food and lots of variety. From Asian, Basque, and Northern Italian to cowpoke cuisine, Boise's eclectic choices belie its size, population, and reputation. For lunch, try the **Bittercreek Alehouse**, 246 North Eighth Street, (208) 345-1813, for a pub-style menu and selection of Northwest microbrews or the **Brick Oven Beanery**, 801 Main Street, (208) 342-3456, features slow-roasted meats, fresh breads, and beans.

Dinner choices include the **Tablerock Brewpub & Grill**, 705 Fulton Street, (208) 342-0944, for excellent Whitebird Wheat beer and pub grub. **Millford's Fish House and Oyster Bar**, 405 South Eighth Street (Eighth Street Marketplace), (208) 342-8382, reminds us that the Pacific Ocean is actually getting closer, with a fresh oyster bar and seafood flown in daily. **Murphy's Seafood Chophouse**, 1555 Broadway, (208) 344-3691, serves fresh seafood as well as big steaks. **Oñati–The Basque Restaurant**, 3544 Chinden Boulevard, specializes in authentic Basque foods and wines and is known for its lamb dishes as well as its exceptional soups and salads. You can find elegant dining in Boise, at prices that will pleasantly surprise you. The **Renaissance Ristorante Italiano**, 110 South Fifth, (208) 344-6776, features innovative Northern Italian dishes. **Peter Schott's Restaurant and Lounge**, Tenth and Main in the Idanha Hotel, (208) 336-9100, excels in fresh pasta, veal, and lamb.

LODGING

Boise's location of choice for lodging is along the greenbelt. Weekend rates in several of the better hotels are sometimes very good bargains, so shop around. The mother of Boise accommodations is the **Idanha Hotel**, 928 Main Street, (208) 342-3611, a funky, elegant old place that's a little bit creaky (and noisy on the Main Street side on weekends—ask for a room on the other side) but filled with character and history. Rooms go for $45 to $62, and they still pour champagne for breakfast on weekends. Likewise, the **Owyhee Plaza Hotel**, 1109 Main Street, (208) 343-4611, is a little younger than the Idanha (1910 versus 1901) but also has real character and was recently remodeled.

The **J.J. Shaw House Bed and Breakfast Inn**, 1411 West Franklin Street, (208) 344-8899, is a distinctive Queen Anne Victorian 1907 home that's well-run. Rooms range from $75 to $114. The **Heritage Inn Bed and Breakfast**, 109 West Idaho, (208) 342-8066, is a historic bed and breakfast, formerly home to Idaho Governor Chase Clark. Rooms are $60 to $95.

Boise offers a number of quality business hotels that offer excellent values and amenities for travelers. They include the **Shilo**

Inn Riverside, 4111 Broadway Avenue, (208) 343-7662, $58 to $89; the **Red Lion Hotel Riverside**, 2900 Chinden Boulevard, (208) 343-1871, with a great location near the Greenbelt and downtown, $69 to $109; **Doubletree Club Hotel at Park Center**, 475 West Park Center, (208) 345-2002, $53 to $86; **Courtyard by Marriott**, 222 S. Broadway, (208) 331-2700, mountain and greenbelt view, $89 to $109; and **Ameritel Inn**, 7965 West Emerald Street, (208) 378-7000, $75 to $130. The 250-room **West Coast Hotel**, 245 South Capitol Boulevard, is slated to open in January 1998.

A nice, clean, new budget property is the **Inn America**, 2275 Airport Way, (208) 389-9800, $37 to $49. The **Boise River Inn**, 1140 Colorado Avenue, (208) 344-9988, an apartment hotel, runs $45 to $55.

CAMPING

The **Fiesta RV Park**, 11101 Fairview Avenue, (208) 375-8207, is considered the best in Boise, with 100 sites, hookups, and pull-throughs; the location is near shopping and restaurants; rates are $16 per night. The **Mountain View RV Park**, 2040 Airport Way, (208) 345-8207, provides 63 sites near the interstate and rates of $19 per night. The **Americana Kampground**, 3600 Americana Terrace, (208) 344-5733, is a good Sampark containing 111 sites for $19 a night in downtown Boise. The **Boise KOA**, 7300 Federal Way, (208) 345-7673, has 120 sites for $25 to $40 per night.

NIGHTLIFE

For those who are sick of bars and brewpubs, Boise offers both the **Boise Opera Company**, 910 Main Street, (208) 345-3541, and the **Boise Philharmonic**, 205 North Tenth Street, (208) 344-7849. Call for schedules and ticket prices. The **Idaho Shakespeare Festival**, P.O. Box 9365, Boise, ID 83707, (208) 323-9700, schedules open-air performances on weekends (and some weekdays) from mid-June through mid-August. Tickets are $11 for adults, $7 for students. Call for the schedule. Wednesday evenings from May and the end of September come alive in downtown Boise with the **Alive After Five** performances on the Grove, (208) 371-LIVE, featuring local musicians, entertainers, and food.

Parimutuel horse racing at **Les Bois Park**, Fairgrounds on Chinden Boulevard, (208) 376-7223, is less cultural but you can win more money. The **Boise Hawks** minor-league baseball team plays throughout the summer at Memorial Stadium near the Fairgrounds, (208) 322-5000. End the evening gracefully with a cocktail at the **Gamekeeper Lounge** in the Owyhee Plaza Hotel, 1109 Main Street, (208) 343-4611.

14

HELLS CANYON COUNTRY/LEWISTON

When the Nez Percé Indians met the Lewis and Clark expedition, a remarkable thing happened in the violent annals of the West: nothing. The Nez Percé respected and assisted the strange white men, and the Corps of Discovery admired the Indians' wealth, civility, and their famous Appaloosa war-horses. Lewiston shares the site of the meeting with Clarkston, Washington. The discovery of gold expanded Lewiston, which became a mining camp supply point and, briefly, the territorial capital.

Lewiston is the gateway to Hells Canyon, at 7,900 feet the deepest river gorge in North America. In some places the canyon walls plunge more than a mile down to sandy river banks. Officially called the Hells Canyon National Recreation Area, it is accessible by one- to six-day jetboat or float trips. White-water rafters, jetboaters, campers, anglers, hikers, and hunters all enjoy this protected recreation area.

Surprisingly, Lewiston is also a seaport. Ships travel 470 miles from the Pacific Ocean up the Columbia River to gather cargo. The rampaging Clearwater and Snake Rivers meet here and calm down. Because of its elevation (738 feet), Lewiston sports extremely mild and pleasant weather. ◪

HELLS CANYON COUNTRY/LEWISTON

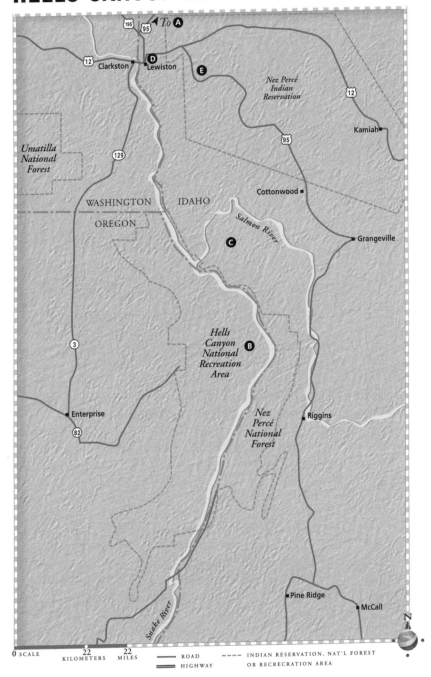

To **A**

195
95

12
Clarkston
Lewiston **D**
E

*Nez Percé
Indian
Reservation*

12

Kamiah■

*Umatilla
National
Forest*

129

95

WASHINGTON   IDAHO

Cottonwood■

OREGON

Salmon River

3

C

Grangeville■

*Hells
Canyon
National
Recreation
Area*

B

*Nez
Percé
National
Forest*

Enterprise■

82

Riggins■

■Pine Ridge

Snake River

■McCall

N

0 SCALE	22	22	ROAD	INDIAN RESERVATION, NAT'L FOREST
	KILOMETERS	MILES	HIGHWAY	OR RECRECRATION AREA

Sights

Ⓐ Appaloosa Horse Club Museum

Ⓑ Hells Canyon Recreation Area

Ⓒ Hells Gate State Park

Ⓓ Luna House Historical Museum

Ⓔ Nez Percé National Historic Park and Museum

Food

Ⓓ Mighty Potato

Ⓓ It Shop

Ⓓ Waffles 'n' More

Ⓓ Zany's

Ⓓ Jonathan's

Ⓓ M.J. Barleyhoppers

Lodging

Ⓓ Carriage House Bed and Breakfast

Ⓓ Inn America

Ⓓ Lewiston Ramada Inn

Ⓓ Pony Soldier Motor Inn

Ⓓ Riverview Inn

Ⓓ Sacajawea Motor Inn

Camping

Ⓒ Hells Gate State Park

Note: Items with the same letter are located in the same town or area.

A PERFECT DAY IN HELLS CANYON COUNTRY/LEWISTON

After a brisk early morning run (or walk) along the scenic Lewiston Levee Parkway, enjoy a big breakfast at Waffles 'n' More. After breakfast, drive west along the river to Beamers Landing to meet your river outfitter and climb into the big jetboat, an aluminum-hulled craft custom-built for the unique river. Soon you're transported upriver on the mighty Snake into Hells Canyon. You see mountain sheep and 3,000-year-old petroglyphs on the walls. You might even have the chance to catch (and release) a 300- to 500-pound sturgeon, one of the most primitive fish that still exists. At your evening camp, enjoy a relaxing soak in a natural hot tub before retiring to the lodge.

SIGHTSEEING HIGHLIGHTS

★★★ **Hells Canyon Recreation Area**—Although a few roads cut through the canyon, including the Rim View Drive, the best way to experience Hells Canyon is via a one-day or overnight jetboat ride into the canyon itself. Experienced jetboat pilots deftly maneuver aluminum-hulled specially built jetboats (some with twin 500-horsepower engines) upstream through rolling rapids and boulders. In addition to pure-sightseeing trips where visitors can see petroglyphs, abandoned mineshafts and communities, and abandoned white and American Indian settlements, other trips include two-day historic mail runs; fishing charters for steelhead, salmon, and sturgeon; dinner cruises; and overnight excursions to excellent lodges. Details: 2535 Riverside Street, Clarkston, WA; (509) 758-0616. Free. (3 hours)

★★★ **Nez Percé National Historic Park and Museum**—For thousands of years the valleys, prairies, and plateaus of north-central Idaho have been home to the Nez Percé Indians. Today the 24 sites in the park bring alive the fascinating past of this successful American Indian nation. Park headquarters are in Spalding. The visitor's center contains the museum and an auditorium with interpretive talks and films on sites such as the **White Bird Battlefield, St. Joseph's Mission**, and the **Heart of the Monster**, the natural basalt monument central to the tribe's mythology. Details: 11 miles east of Lewiston on U.S. 95, Spalding; (208) 843-2001; open daily Memorial Day through Labor Day 8 a.m. to 6 p.m., rest of the year 8 a.m. to 4:30 p.m. Free. (2 hours)

★★ **Appaloosa Horse Club Museum**—Located north of Lewiston in Moscow, the museum traces the lineage of the Appaloosa, an important feature of Nez Percé history. The Indians selectively bred this species to create excellent, sought-after horses noted for their hardiness and spotted markings. Regalia and artifacts used with the Appaloosa are displayed, including Nez Percé items. Appaloosas graze behind the museum during the summer months. You don't have to be a horseman to appreciate these animals and the museum. Details: State Highway 8, Moscow; (208) 882-5578; open June through August Monday through Friday 8 a.m. to 5 p.m., Saturday 9 a.m. to 3 p.m. Free. (1 hour)

★ **Luna House Historical Museum**—Displays at this museum focus on the history of Nez Percé County and the surrounding area. Long-term exhibits include a pioneer kitchen and bedroom. Portraits of noted Nez Percé leader Chief Joseph are permanently displayed. Shows change periodically, so call ahead to see what's being featured. Details: Third and C Streets; (208) 743-2535; open Tuesday through Saturday 9 a.m. to 5 p.m. Free. (30 minutes)

★ **Hells Gate State Park**—The gateway to Hells Canyon Recreation Area and launching point for jetboat tours, the park features an interpretive center that details the history, geology, and culture of the Clearwater, Snake, and Salmon Rivers. The visitor's center has a theater, interpreted photographs, sketches, maps, and artifacts. The historic steamboat *Jean*, a paddlewheeler, is berthed next to the marina. Details: 3620-A Snake River Avenue, Lewiston; (208) 743-2363; open Monday through Friday 8 a.m. to 4:30 p.m. Admission: based on vehicle; contact the park for rates. (1 hour)

FITNESS AND RECREATION

The best reason to visit Lewiston and north-central Idaho is to access the mighty Hells Canyon Recreation Area, and therefore a jetboat tour is a must. Rates vary depending on the length and purpose of the trip, but daylong excursions cost approximately $75 to $85 per person, with overnight trips ranging from $125 up. Recommended outfitters include **Hells Canyon Adventures**, P.O. Box 159, Oxbow, OR 97840, (541) 785-3352, and **Beamers Hells Canyon Tours and Excursions**, P.O. Box 1243, Lewiston, 83501, (800) 522-6966. For a complete listing of outfitters, trips, dates, and rates, contact **Idaho Outfitters & Guides Association**, P.O. Box 95, Boise, ID 83701, (208) 342-1919; or the Lewiston Chamber of Commerce, 2207 East Main Street, Lewiston, (208) 743-3531 or (800) 473-3543.

Before and after the river trip, though, visitors can enjoy walking, running, or biking sections of the 21-mile Lewiston Levee Parkway that hugs the Snake River. The parkway was designated a National Recreation Trail in 1988 and offers two visitor's centers along its length, the Clearwater Landing and the Lewis and Clark Interpretive Center.

Golfers who live in the high-altitude, short-summer Rockies and suffer spring fever while the snow melts on their local courses often venture to low-elevation Lewiston to enjoy the two 18-hole courses: **Bryden Canyon Golf Course**, 445 O'Conner Road, (208) 746-0863, and **Lewiston Golf and Country Club**, 3985 Country Club Drive, (208) 743-3549.

FOOD

Because Lewiston isn't a large community (28,100 residents) and is not yet considered a resort town, restaurants are fairly basic and simple. But thanks to the rich surrounding agricultural lands of the Palouse Valley, fruits and vegetables are fresh and of excellent quality.

The **Mighty Potato**, 826 21st Street, (208) 746-7783, offers good burgers and steaks accompanied by, well, mighty big potatoes. The **It Shop**, 631 Main Street, (208) 746-3054, serves even bigger burgers in an all-American atmosphere. **Waffles 'n' More**, 1407 Main Street, (208) 743-5189, features the big home-cooked breakfasts we love. **Zany's**, 2004 19th Avenue, (208) 746-8131, offers some of the best barbecue in the three-state area. Try **Jonathan's**, 301 D Street, Bollinger Plaza, (208) 746-3438, for well-prepared beef and seafood dishes and fresh, creative pasta and salads. **M.J. Barleyhoppers** brewpub, located in the Lewiston Ramada Inn, 621 21st Street, (208) 799-1000, offers good hand-crafted microbrews and pub food.

LODGING

The big kahuna in Lewiston is the **Lewiston Ramada Inn**, 621 21st Street, (208) 799-1000, a 136-room convention hotel that is comfortable and self-contained, with amenities like hot tubs and Barleyhoppers brewpub. Expect to pay $76 to $96. The **Pony Soldier Motor Inn**, 1716 Main Street, (208) 743-9526, is a local favorite, with 66 rooms and $58 to $66 rates. **Inn America**, 702 21st Street, (208) 746-4600, features oversized rooms at undersized rates of $38 to $47. Worthy accommodations in good locations and at affordable rates are available at the **Riverview Inn**, 1325 Main Street, (208) 746-3311, $38 to $40; and the **Sacajawea Motor Inn**, 1824 Main Street, (208) 746-1393, $40 to $46. The **Carriage House Bed and Breakfast**, 611 Fifth Street, (208) 746-4506, offers four well-appointed rooms for $75 to $85.

CAMPING

Although there are Forest Service sites in the Clearwater National Forest, campsites are scarce in Lewiston. **Hells Gate State Park**, 4 miles south of town on Snake River Avenue, (208) 799-5015, contains 93 basic sites with access to nature trails and the river for $6 to $12 per night.

Scenic Route: The Selway River

The "Wild and Scenic River Corridor" of the Lewis and Clark Trail is U.S. Highway 12 from east of **Kooskia** to **Missoula**, Montana. The **Loschsa River** cascades throughout the narrow valley of the **Crags Mountains**. Within the **Clearwater National Forest**, you'll find small waterfalls and towering cliffs among the pine and fir woods. At **Lolo Pass**, on the Montana border, the route rises to 5,233 feet. Once in Montana, U.S. Highway 12 crosses the **Bitterroot Range**. The roadway parallels mountain streams in the **Lolo National Forest** and passes many interesting geological formations. Information on camping, hiking, and many other recreational opportunities can be found at the Lolo Pass Visitor Center. Note that this is a two-lane roadway with some passing lanes and some 35-mph curves in the Montana portion. ◼

THE SELWAY RIVER

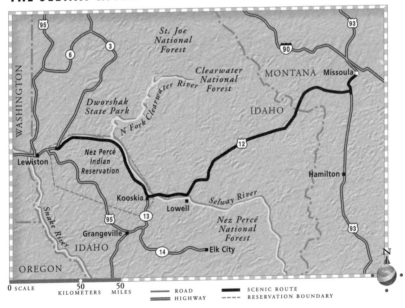

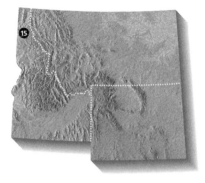

15

COEUR D'ALENE/NORTH IDAHO

T he panhandle of north Idaho is a land of dense forests, mountains, and deep blue glacial lakes. The town of Coeur d'Alene (pronounced "core-duh-LANE") is the hub of north Idaho and its largest community, with a population of 25,000. Coeur d'Alene means "heart of an awl" in French, referring to the sharp, hard bargains the local American Indian tribes drove. The town was once a timber and trading center for the area as well as a playground for the rich silver kings who lived in neighboring Spokane.

Today the community has been reborn as an international resort, a spectacular place to enjoy sailing, water-skiing, golfing, fishing, hiking, biking, and skiing. Lake Coeur d'Alene, 25 miles long by 3 miles wide, has been called one of the most beautiful in the world by *National Geographic*. It is. Where a huge lumbermill once stood on the lakeshore is currently the setting for the elegant and spectacular Coeur d'Alene Resort. One of the most unusual golf courses in North America—complete with a floating green—now occupies the site of a former timber slag heap.

As Coeur d'Alene has changed, so has the surrounding area, as places such as Sandpoint, Wallace, and Post Falls retool their former mining and timbering economies toward tourism. North Idaho's population has grown significantly in recent years as a result of these changes. ◼

COEUR D'ALENE

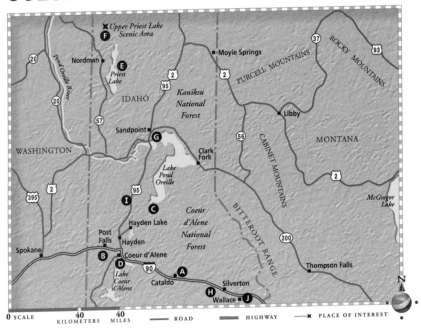

Sights

- **A** Cataldo Mission
- **B** Factory Outlet Stores
- **C** Farragut State Park
- **D** Lake Coeur d'Alene Cruises
- **D** Museum of North Idaho
- **E** Priest Lake
- **F** Roosevelt Grove of Ancient Cedars
- **G** Sandpoint and Pend Oreille Lake
- **H** Silver Mountain Gondola
- **I** Silverwood Theme Park
- **J** Wallace
- **D** Wild Waters

Note: Items with the same letter are located in the same town or area.

A PERFECT DAY IN COEUR D'ALENE

Today let's pretend that money is no object. Start the day with a stroll along the 3,000-foot floating boardwalk through the marina on Lake Coeur d'Alene, followed by breakfast in the Coeur d'Alene Resort at a table overlooking the sailboats. Transfer by motorboat to the resort golf course. Your golfing partners include fellow wealthy industrialists, and you have a wonderful day on the links, despite plunking five golf balls into the water trying to hit the floating 14th green. After lunch, take a scenic drive to the beautiful Catoldo Mission but return to the resort in time to enjoy fresh seafood, wine, and cigars at Beverly's. Leave a big tip.

SIGHTSEEING HIGHLIGHTS

★★★ **Cataldo Mission**—The Coeur d'Alene Indians constructed the mission in 1850 under the direction of Father Ravalli, a Jesuit missionary. The mission walls stand a foot thick, and the structure was built totally without nails, using woven straw, adobe mud, and pegs to secure the walls and ceiling. There are no pews because the Indians preferred to worship in an open room. Living history demonstrations and the visitor's center are must-sees. Details: 20 miles east of Coeur d'Alene via I-90; (208) 682-3814; open daily June through August 8 a.m. to 6 p.m., September through May 9 a.m. to 5 p.m. Admission: $2 per motorized vehicle. (1 hour)

★★★ **Lake Coeur d'Alene Cruises**—Surrounded by mountains and lush forest, Lake Coeur d'Alene is one of the most beautiful glacial lakes in North America. In addition to providing a scenic setting for sailing, powerboating, and fishing, the lake hosts one of the largest populations of osprey nesting sites. During the winter, bald eagles dive into the lake to catch salmon. Lake Coeur d'Alene Cruises explore the bays and inlets of the 100-mile shoreline. Cruise boats depart from the Coeur d'Alene public dock. Details: Coeur d'Alene Resort, 7200 Caller, Coeur d'Alene; (208) 756-4000; cruises depart at 1:30 p.m., 3:30 p.m., and 5:30 p.m.; call ahead for reservations and to confirm times and details. Fares: $11.75 adults, $10.75 seniors, $6.75 children. (2 hours)

★★ **Priest Lake**—The most private of all north Idaho lakes, Priest Lake offers plenty for the camper and fisherperson. World-class

Mackinaw trout and kokanee salmon have been pulled from its waters. The remote beauty of the lake rivals the more developed Lake Tahoe, and the nearby Roosevelt Grove of Ancient Cedars contains trees more than 200 years old. Details: Priest Lake Chamber, Steamboat Bay Road, #21, Coolin, ID 83821; (208) 443-3191. (2 hours)

★★ **Sandpoint and Pend Oreille Lake**—Located at the north end of Pend Oreille Lake via the impressive Long Bridge, Sandpoint is a scenic and growing community of 5,200 residents in a stunning setting. This picturesque small town offers lively visual and performing arts. Pend Oreille rivals Lake Coeur d'Alene for beauty and depth (1,150 feet) and is one of the largest lakes in the Pacific Northwest. Fourteen species of game fish inhabit its waters, including kokanee, largemouth bass, and bluegill. The world's record Kamloops trout and a 32-pound Dolly Varden came from this lake. Guided boat tours and fishing charters are available during the season. Details: Greater Sandpoint Chamber of Commerce, U.S. 95 North, Sandpoint; (208) 263-2161 or (800) 800-2106. (2 hours)

© P. Crist/Idaho Dept. of Commerce

Pend Oreille Lake

★★ **Silver Mountain Gondola**—The world's longest gondola exists at Kellogg, a once-booming silver-mining town. Visitors travel more than 3 miles up in an enclosed tram from the base to the Mountain Haus on Kellogg Peak, a rise of 3,400 feet. From the top, you can view Idaho, Montana, Washington, and even Canada. The Mountain Haus has a restaurant and nature gallery and serves as a jumping-off point for hikers and mountain bikers. The ride takes about 20 minutes one way. Details: 610 Bunker Avenue, Kellogg; (208) 783-1111; open mid-June to mid-September daily 10 a.m. to 5:30 p.m., weekends rest of year. Admission: $9.95 adults, $8 children and seniors. (1½ hours)

★ **Farragut State Park**—During World War II, this unique state park started out as the second largest naval training station in the world, utilizing the incredible depth (1,152 feet) of Pend Oreille Lake. A tour through this 4,000-acre park now includes wildlife (deer, turkeys, mountain goats) viewing and an interpretive center. Located north of Post Falls on State Highway 41. Details: East 13400 Ranger Road, Athol; (208) 683-2425; open year-round, but visitor's center open Memorial Day through mid-September 7:30 a.m. to 9:30 p.m., April 1 through Memorial Day and late September 9 a.m. to 4 p.m. Admission: $2 per motorized vehicle. (2 hours)

★ **Museum of North Idaho**—This regional museum has exhibits exploring Nez Percé, steamboat, logging, and community histories. Details: 115 Northwest Boulevard, Coeur d'Alene; (208) 664-3448; open April through October 11 a.m. to 5 p.m. Admission: $1.50 adults, 50 cents children. (30 minutes)

★ **Roosevelt Grove of Ancient Cedars**—Located 17 miles north of Priest Lake on State Highway 57, this old-growth forest has trees up to 12 feet in diameter and 150 feet tall. Granite Falls is a scenic location with a pretty falls and moss-covered rocks. Details: Idaho Panhandle National Forest, Priest Lake Ranger District; (208) 443-2512. Free. (1 hour)

★ **Wallace**—Until recently, mining was Wallace's lifeblood. The town, established in 1892, served as a supply center for one of the largest silver-producing areas in the world in the late 1800s. Today the entire town is on the National Register of Historic Places. The **Northern Pacific Depot**, an architectural gem, and the **Coeur** d'Alene District Mining Museum serve as interpretive centers for regional history. The **Oasis Bordello Museum** provides a more "colorful" perspective of the town's past, while the **Sierra Silver Mine** gives a good feel for the life of an underground miner. Details: Wallace Chamber of Commerce, 10 River Street, Exit 61, Wallace; (208) 753-7151. (2 hours)

Factory Outlet Stores—Located in Post Falls, the complex includes more than 60 outlet stores including fashion, jewelry, shoes, housewares, and children's shops. Details: 8 miles from Coeur d'Alene on I-90, Post Falls; (208) 773-4555; open April through December Monday through Saturday 9:30 a.m. to 8 p.m., Sunday 11 a.m. to 6 p.m., January through March Monday through Saturday 9:30 a.m. to 6 p.m., Sunday 11 a.m. to 6 p.m. (2 hours)

Silverwood Theme Park—Newly opened and a bit out of place in the lush forest, the Silverwood Theme Park offers a roller coaster, log flume, and other carnival rides with a mining town theme. Details: 15 miles north on U.S. 95, Athol; (208) 683-3400; open Memorial Day weekend through Labor Day 11 a.m. to 8 p.m. Admission: $19.99 adults, $9.99 seniors and children ages 3 to 7. (2 hours)

Wild Waters—This roadside waterpark, always popular with children, features waterslides, spas, and inner-tube rides. Details: Government Way, Coeur d'Alene; (208) 667-6491; open Memorial Day through August 25 11 a.m. to 9 p.m., August 26 to Labor Day 11 a.m. to 7 p.m. Admission: all-day pass $12 adults, $11 children ages 4 to 11. (2 hours)

FITNESS AND RECREATION

As far as outdoor recreation goes, there isn't very much that north Idaho *doesn't* offer. As in the rest of the state, river rafting is readily available, on the Moyie and St. Joe Rivers. Trips can be arranged through outfitters, including **River Odysseys West**, 314 East Garden Street, (800) 451-6034. They run May 1 through September 15 and charge $75 for a one-day trip. Ski boats, pontoons, fishing boats, and canoes for Lake Coeur d'Alene can be rented from **Coeur d'Alene Marine**, (208) 667-9483. Large sailboats can be rented from **Crescendo Charters**, (208) 765-2238. Golfing is a big-time activity in Coeur d'Alene, and courses include the private, $130-a-round **Coeur d'Alene Resort Golf Course**, (208) 667-4653, to the much less expensive (and public) **Avondale-on-Hayden Golf Club**, (208) 772-5963; the **Coeur d'Alene Golf Course**, (208) 667-4653; and the nine-hole **Ponderosa Springs Golf Course**, (208) 664-1101. Mountain bikes can be rented from **Coeur d'Alene Bike Rentals**, (208) 667-2663.

COEUR D'ALENE/NORTH IDAHO IN WINTER

North Idaho boasts two interesting ski areas, Schweitzer Mountain Resort, near Sandpoint, and Silver Mountain Resort, in Kellogg. Both have abundant snow that's plentiful, deep, and not as dry as the powder at other Rocky Mountain ski areas. Both areas harken back to high quality, small resorts of the past and don't glamourize themselves beyond their means or that of their local skier base. They're not well-known in the big winter scheme of things just yet.

    Schweitzer Mountain Resort, (208) 263-9555 or (800) 831-8810, has a vertical drop of 2,400 feet, with one quad, five double chairs, and 55 runs. Ticket prices: $34 adults, $27 after 12:30 p.m.; $15 from 3 p.m. to 9 p.m.; children ages 7 to 12, $20, $16, $10; students and seniors $27, $22, $10; beginner lift $15, $12, $10.

    Silver Mountain Resort, 610 Bunker Avenue, (208) 783-1111, has a vertical drop of 2,200 feet, with one gondola, one quad, two triples, two doubles, one surface tow, and over 50 runs. Ticket prices: $31 adults, $24 students and seniors; $18 children; children under 7 ski free.

FOOD

The consensus in north Idaho is that if you want to impress or romance someone, the place to go is **Beverly's**, at the Coeur d'Alene Resort, 7200 Caller, seventh floor, (208) 765-4000. Not only will you enjoy a magnificent view of the lake, but you'll have food and service (and prices) to match the view. **Cedars Floating Restaurant**, Highway 95 on the Spokane River, (208) 664-2922, is a local favorite popular for its seafood and huge steaks. My favorite is **T.W. Fisher's Brewpub**, 204 North Second, (208) 664-BREW, one of the first in the region. The beer and pizza are both first-rate. **Cricket's Restaurant and Oyster Bar**, 424 Sherman Avenue, (208) 765-1990,

COEUR D'ALENE/NORTH IDAHO

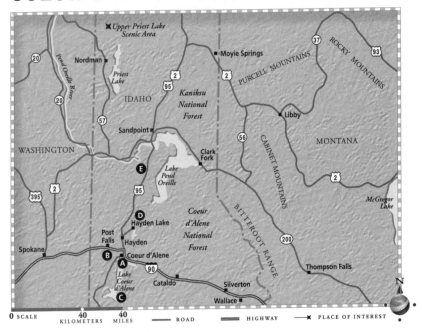

Food

- **A** 3rd Street Cantina
- **A** Beverly's
- **A** Cedars Floating Restaurant
- **A** Cricket's Restaurant and Oyster Bar
- **A** Jimmy D's
- **A** T.W. Fisher's Brewpub

Lodging

- **B** Best Western Templin's Resort Hotel
- **A** Coeur d'Alene Inn and Conference Center

Lodging *(continued)*

- **A** Coeur d'Alene Resort
- **A** Gregory's McFarland House Bed and Breakfast
- **A** Roosevelt Inn Bed and Breakfast
- **A** Shilo Inn

Camping

- **A** Beauty Creek
- **C** Bell Bay Lower Loop
- **D** Coeur d'Alene North KOA
- **E** Silverwood RV Park

Note: Items with the same letter are located in the same town or area.

has a crazed, tons-of-stuff-on-the-walls interior and affordable food with good service. Don't let the name **Jimmy D's**, 320 Sherman, (208) 664-9774, fool you into thinking it's a hamburger-deluxe joint. This place features excellent fresh seafood, a decent wine selection, and a creative menu. The **3rd Street Cantina**, 201 North Third Street, (208) 664-0581, serves some tasty Tex-Mex dishes a heck of a long way from the border.

LODGING

Though the competition might not like it, in Coeur d'Alene there is the **Coeur d'Alene Resort**, 7200 Caller, (208) 765-4000, and then there is every place else. Like it or hate it, this place literally redefined the community and put north Idaho on the "resort" map. The resort offers 338 huge and tastefully appointed rooms with such amenities as two fine restaurants and one excellent restaurant, a floating boardwalk, a world-class golf course, a marina, bowling alley, shops, and a view that by itself is worth the price of at least one night. Go in the off season for surprisingly affordable rates. Singles range from $69 to $299 in the off season to $99 to $355 mid-May through late September. The **Coeur d'Alene Inn and Conference Center**, 414 Appleway, (208) 765-3200, is a sister property, offering access to Resort facilities with rooms from $47 to $77 in the off season, $102 to $132 in summer.

The **Best Western Templin's Resort Hotel**, 414 East First Avenue, Post Falls, (208) 773-1611, is attractively located on the banks of the Spokane River and provides excellent amenities for rates of $59 to $86. The **Shilo Inn**, 702 West Appleway, (208) 664-2300, is a Northwest staple and always a good value, $79 to $149.

Gregory's McFarland House Bed and Breakfast, 601 Foster Avenue, (208) 667-1232, offers five charming rooms in a fin-de-siècle mansion in a quiet neighborhood. Rooms are $85 to $105 per night. The **Roosevelt Inn Bed and Breakfast**, 105 Wallace Avenue, (208) 765-5200, features 16 well-appointed rooms in a renovated turn-of-the-century schoolhouse for $50 to $55.

CAMPING

The **Coeur d'Alene North KOA**, 10 miles north of town at 4850 Garwood Road, (208) 772-4557, contains 65 private sites with hookups and pull-throughs in a quiet, shady location. Rates range from $13 to $15. The **Silverwood RV Park**, 17 miles north on Highway 95, (208) 772-0515, is near the theme park and offers 126 sites at $13 to $16 per night. Public campgrounds include 15-site **Beauty Creek**, 1 mile from Beauty Bay Inlet, (208) 769-3000; and 12-site **Bell Bay Lower Loop**, east side of Lake Coeur d'Alene, (208) 769-3000. Both cost $6 per night and have standard National Forest Service set-ups, meaning clean campsites, pit toilets, good locations, and no amenities.

16

GLACIER NATIONAL PARK

C alled the "Crown of the Continent," Glacier National Park is the
United States portion of the Waterton-Glacier International
Peace Park, which straddles the Montana-Alberta border and is one of
the newest World Heritage sites. The park is a million-acre wilderness
containing more than 200 mountain lakes, nearly 50 living glaciers, 60
species of mammals, 200 species of birds, and over 1,000 species of
flowering plant life. As is true of Grand Teton and Yellowstone, it's
possible to blow through Glacier in less than a day, and hundreds of
thousands of people do exactly that every year. But like those two other
parks, the real beauty of Glacier is in the lingering and in seeing it by
foot, horseback, or boat. Glacier may be the greatest hiking park in the
entire national park system, with more than 700 miles of trails offering
hundreds of stunning vistas, overlooks, and alpine scenery. It also
features the spectacular Going-to-the-Sun Road, a 52-mile narrow and
winding mountain road through the heart of the park over the
Continental Divide, which may be the most scenic drive of its kind
anywhere.

Weather can be a problem in Glacier. I've been in May, June, and
July and have been snowed out of traveling the Going-to-the-Sun
Road for at least a day in each of those months. The best time for
travel is August or mid-September to early October. There may be
some snow flurries, but the fall scenery is awesome, and you'll feel as if
you've got the place to yourself. ∎

GLACIER NATIONAL PARK

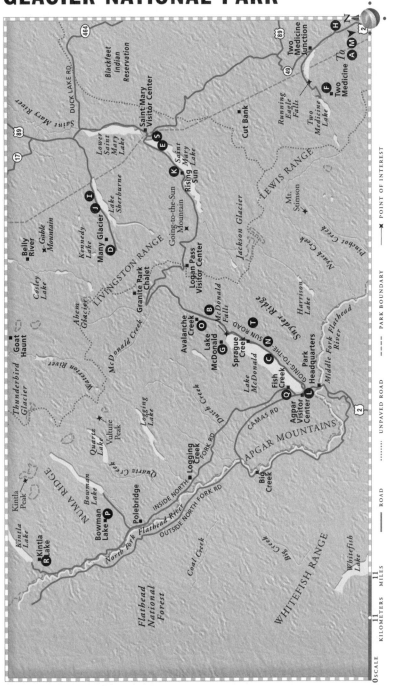

Sights

- **Ⓐ** Goat Lick
- **Ⓑ** Going-to-the-Sun Road
- **Ⓒ** Lake McDonald
- **Ⓓ** Many Glacier
- **Ⓔ** St. Mary Lake
- **Ⓕ** Two Medicine Valley

Food

- **Ⓖ** Cedar Dining Room
- **Ⓗ** Great Northern Steak & Rib House
- **Ⓘ** Ptarmigan Dining Room
- **Ⓙ** Swiftcurrent Italian Gardens Ristorante
- **Ⓚ** Two Dog Flats Mesquite Grill

Lodging

- **Ⓛ** Apgar Village Lodge
- **Ⓗ** Glacier Park Lodge
- **Ⓜ** Izaak Walton Inn
- **Ⓝ** Lake McDonald Lodge
- **Ⓓ** Many Glacier Hotel
- **Ⓚ** Rising Sun Motor Inn
- **Ⓓ** Swiftcurrent Motor Inn

Camping

- **Ⓛ** Apgar
- **Ⓞ** Avalanche
- **Ⓟ** Bowman Lake
- **Ⓠ** Fish Creek
- **Ⓡ** Kintla Lake
- **Ⓓ** Many Glacier
- **Ⓚ** Rising Sun
- **Ⓢ** St. Mary
- **Ⓣ** Sprague Creek
- **Ⓕ** Two Medicine

Note: Items with the same letter are located in the same town or area.

A PERFECT DAY IN GLACIER NATIONAL PARK

Start the morning in West Glacier and leave your car behind. Climb aboard a classic long red "jammer" bus and begin your journey over the spectacular Going-to-the-Sun Road. Pass along the 10-mile shoreline of Lake McDonald as your driver climbs into the sky, past Lake McDonald Lodge to Logan Pass. Despite the altitude, all around you are even higher peaks and U-shaped green glacier valleys. You continue down the other side of the Continental Divide, past Rising Sun, to St. Mary Lake. After some short hikes around the lake, you arrive at the dock, where you're booked on an evening lake cruise to watch the sun set in the spectacular Glacier Park mountains.

GLACIER 101

Once territory of the Salish, Kootenai, Flathead, and Blackfoot Indians, Glacier was a tourist destination 20 years before it was declared a national park in 1910. The Great Northern Railroad was the primary instrument of both visitors and infrastructure, and although modern-day elites may view the promotion of the park as crass and commercial, the brochures and posters that were produced at the time are works of art. The Great Northern built the three primary lodges in the park (Glacier Park Lodge at East Glacier, the Prince of Wales Hotel at Waterton, and the Many Glacier Inn at Many Glacier) as well as smaller accommodations within the boundaries. The Going-to-the-Sun Road was opened in 1933 after 20 years of road construction, and it truly opened up Glacier to the masses. The park became an automobile destination, and the Great Northern faded from the radar screen.

As in other national parks established early in the century, new management proposals addressing park philosophy and the impact of tourism on ecology are extremely controversial, both locally and nationally. Recent proposals to close popular chalets within the park because of sanitation problems have created a firestorm of comment.

For information on lodging and activities within Glacier National Park, contact Glacier Park, Inc., P.O. Box 147, East Glacier Park, MT 59434-0147; (406) 226-9311 or fax (406) 226-9221. During the off season, the Glacier Park staff moves lock, stock, and barrel to Arizona. Reach them there at (602) 207-6000. A seven-day entrance pass to

Glacier is $10 per vehicle, and admission to Waterton Lakes Park, across the Canadian border, is an additional $5. For information on trails and backcountry permits and advice, contact Glacier National Park, National Park Service, West Glacier, MT 59936; (406) 888-5441.

OPENINGS AND CLOSINGS

Like Yellowstone, opening and closing dates can vary depending on weather conditions, but the following generally holds true: The Many Glacier entrance is open May 24 through September 2; St. Mary is open May 24 through October 20; Two Medicine is open May 24 through September 2; and West Glacier is open May 24 through October 20.

SIGHTSEEING HIGHLIGHTS

★★★ **Going-to-the-Sun Road**—Completed in 1933 after 20 years of construction (this road is quite a feat of engineering), Going-to-the-Sun Road is the unabashed highlight of Glacier National Park. Not doing the road is like going to Yellowstone Park and not seeing Old Faithful. It is, without a doubt, one of the most scenic roads in the world. The route includes the **Weeping Wall, Birdwoman Falls, Logan Pass, St. Mary Lake**, and many incomparable mountain vistas. Vehicles and vehicle combinations longer than 21 feet or wider than 8 feet are prohibited from this road. The preferred method of travel is via the historic red jammer buses, which carry 15 to 20 passengers each. In good weather drivers roll back the tops, allowing passengers better opportunity to view the meadows, lakes, and mountains. The road generally opens in mid-June, but the date can vary, so call ahead.

    Avalanche Creek, at the top of Going-to-the-Sun Road, has cut a narrow and deep gorge through brilliant red sandstone. Truly a natural marvel, the creek has formed a series of deep ponds and waterfalls along its length and is accessible by a boardwalk trail. Logan Pass offers a visitor's center as well as naturalist talks at 11 a.m., noon, and 1 p.m. daily June through Labor Day. Details: Logan Pass (elevation 6,680 feet) closes for the season no later than the Monday morning following the third Sunday in October, although weather and snow can close it earlier. Jammer bus fare: $42.75 adults, $22.75 children; one-way trips to Many Glacier are $21.50, $25.50 to East Glacier. (4 hours)

★★★ **Lake McDonald**—The largest lake within Glacier, Lake McDonald is one of those places that looks like it was designed by Disney and painted by Bierstadt or Moran—it is breathtakingly beautiful. Snow-covered mountains rim the lake in all directions, and the lake itself is serene, a massive mirror of mountains and sky. Hiking trails abound, including the wheelchair-accessible **Trail of the Cedars**. Rowboat, canoes, and motorboat rentals are available. Recommended are the scenic boat cruises available from the **Glacier Park Boat Company**. Details: Lake McDonald Lodge; (406) 888-5727; open early June through late September, with departures at 10 a.m., 1:30 p.m., 3:30 p.m., and 7 p.m.; minimum of six adults required. Fares: $6.50 to $8.50 adults, $3.25 to $4.25 children. (1½ hours)

★★ **Many Glacier**—In the northeast part of the park, the Many Glacier region includes Swiftcurrent Lake and multiple scenic glacier valleys. The area is crisscrossed with hiking trails (take your bear bells) to Morning Eagle Falls, Cracker Lake, Ptarmigan Lake, Josephine Lake, Grinnell Glacier, and Iceberg Lake. National park naturalists offer daily field walks and programs. Boat tours are available at 9 a.m. and 11 a.m. and at 2 p.m., 4 p.m., and 7 p.m. Details: Many Glacier dock; (406) 732-4480. Fares: $6.50 to $8.50 adults, $3.25 to $4.25 children. (1½ hours).

★★ **St. Mary Lake**—Peaks of the Lewis Range surrounding St. Mary rise over a mile from the shoreline, and it's one of those places where your neck starts to hurt from looking up at the horizon. You'll see why this is one of the most-photographed lakes in Glacier. In addition to hiking the many trails (Baring Falls, Sun Point, Sunrift Gorge, Siyeh Pass, Preston Park, Gunsight Lake, Red Eagle Trail are the most accessible and notable), you can tour by boat at 2 p.m., 4 p.m., and 7 p.m. Details: St. Mary Lake dock; (406) 732-4480. Fares: $6.50 to $8.50 adults, $3.25 to $4.25 children. (1½ hours)

★★ **Two Medicine Valley**—Just 11 miles from East Glacier, the valley is not as heavily traveled as some of the other sites within the park but is just as scenic, with Two Medicine Lake, Twin Falls, Running Eagle Falls, and hiking trails throughout. (2 hours)

★ **Goat Lick**—Located on Highway 2 and marked with a highway pullout and display, a bluff through the trees provides a natural source of salt and minerals for the many mountain goats in the park. (1 hour)

FITNESS AND RECREATION

Glacier Wilderness Guides, (406) 387-5555 or (800) 521-RAFT, is the only backpacking guide service inside the park, and they do their job well. Trips range from day hikes ($50/person, four-person minimum) to three-day ($285 to $425/person), four-day ($380 per person), and six-day ($570 to $1,465/person) trips. Good food is included.

    Montana Raft Company, (406) 387-5555 or (800) 521-RAFT, offers half- or full-day white-water or scenic floats. Half-day trips are $36 for adults, $28 for children; full-day trips are $69 for adults, $44 for children. One-day hike and raft trip (highly recommended) is a hike-in, raft-out adventure for $78 per adult and $68 per child. The company also schedules one-day "ride and rapids" trips, i.e., morning horseback riding and afternoon white water for $81 per person. Two-, 2½-, and 3½-day river trips are also available from $250 through $420 for adults.

    Horseback touring is available at **Apgar Corral**, (406) 888-5522, **Lake McDonald Corral**, (406) 888-5670, and **Blackfoot Riding Stables**, (406) 732-9296, from hourlong trail rides to overnight pack trips.

© Donnie Sexton/Travel Montana

St. Mary Lake

FOOD

Like many national parks, Glacier is not especially noted for its food, but with the scenery of the park itself and the atmosphere afforded by the grand old buildings, there aren't a lot of complaints. All of the restaurants listed here are run and staffed by Glacier Park, Inc. Reservations are always recommended and can be made in the hotels.

The **Cedar Dining Room** at the Lake McDonald complex offers standard fare in a hunting-lodge-type atmosphere. Open daily June 1 through September 20. In East Glacier, the **Great Northern Steak & Rib House**, at the junction of U.S. 2 and State Highway 49, (404) 226-9311, specializes in steak and ribs as well as fresh-baked breads and a great view. Open the same dates as the Cedar Dining Room. The **Ptarmigan Dining Room**, 12 miles from Babb, is a large complex with average food but a happy singing waitstaff. Open June 10 through September 10. **Swiftcurrent Italian Gardens Ristorante**, 13 miles west of Babb, (406) 226-9311, is popular with hikers because of its location. Open daily June 10 through September 10. **Two Dog Flats Mesquite Grill**, 5 miles west of St. Mary, like all of the restaurants, has better scenery than food.

LODGING

Although we recommend spending at least one night inside the park (preferably at Many Glacier Lodge) because of the ambiance and view the structures offer, the lodgings and amenities in the gateway communities are often superior to the Glacier Park, Inc., facilities within the park. Please note that the reservation numbers for Glacier Park, Inc., lodges are the same, (406) 226-5551 (summer) or (602) 207-6000 (winter).

Called "the big tree lodge," **Glacier Park Lodge** is the first hotel in the park. The complex offers a nine-hole golf course and a huge comfortable lobby. The last time I was there I noticed General Norman Schwartzkopf sitting across from me reading a book. Rates are from $99 to $187; open Memorial Day through early September. The **Lake McDonald Lodge** was originally built in 1895 and was restored in 1915. It still has a classic hunting lodge feel, with big-game trophies staring down from the timber walls. Montana cowboy artist Charlie Russell may have designed the pictographs surrounding the lodge's fireplace. Cabins run from $55 to $61; motel rooms, $69 to

$75; and lodge rooms, from $100 up. **Many Glacier Hotel** is a 200-room Swiss-style chalet offering perhaps the best scenery in the park. Rooms run from $81 to over $106.

Apgar Village Lodge, (406) 888-5484, is located 2 miles northwest of West Glacier at Apgar and is not a Glacier Park, Inc. facility. It offers 48 rooms and rustic cabins open May 1 to September 30. Rooms range from $57 to $59 for singles, and the cabins run from $120 to $200, depending on the number of rooms. The **Swiftcurrent Motor Inn**, 13 miles west of Babb near the Many Glacier complex, and the **Rising Sun Motor Inn**, 5 miles west of St. Mary, offer budget accommodations from $61 to $75 per night.

Outside the park, in Essex, is the charming **Izaak Walton Inn**, Izaak Walton Inn Road, (406) 888-5700, a historic 33-room property (check out the fascinating restored cabooses out back) with $92 year-round rooms.

CAMPING

Glacier is a great national park for camping and offers some excellent facilities. All of the sites within the park are operated by the National Park Service, and reservations aren't accepted. There are no hookups and few pull-throughs. RVs are allowed at all camping locations except Bowman and Kintla Lakes. Most have seven-night maximums in July and August, with rates of $10 to $12 per night. Only Many Glacier, Rising Sun, and St. Mary have showers, and Apgar, Avalanche, Fish Creek, Many Glacier, Rising Sun, St. Mary, and Two Medicine have dump stations. They all share the same information number, (406) 888-5441.

Apgar, with 196 sites, is located 1 mile northwest of West Glacier on Going-to-the-Sun Road; open May 15 through October. **Avalanche**, with 87 sites, is 14 miles northeast of West Glacier on Going-to-the-Sun Road; open June 15 through August. **Bowman Lake**, with 48 sites, is 32 miles northwest of West Glacier on North Fork Road; open May 15 through September. **Fish Creek**, with 180 sites, is 4 miles northwest of West Glacier on Camas Creek Road; open May 15 through September. **Kintla Lake**, with 13 sites, is 47 miles north of West Glacier on North Fork Road; open May 15 through September. **Many Glacier**, with 112 sites, is located 13 miles west of Babb on Many Glacier Road; open June through September. **Rising Sun**, with 83 sites, is located 6 miles southwest of St. Mary on Going-to-the-Sun Road; open June through September. **St. Mary**, with 156 sites, is located on Highway 2; open June through September. **Sprague Creek**, with 25 sites, is located 10 miles northwest of West Glacier on Going-to-the-Sun Road; open June through September. **Two Medicine**, with 99 sites, is located 12 miles north of East Glacier; open June through September 6.

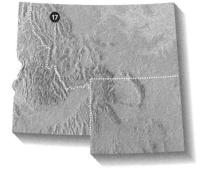

17

THE FLATHEAD VALLEY— KALISPELL/WHITEFISH

Talk about location. Imagine a lush mountain valley hard against Glacier National Park to the north, bordered by millions of acres of wilderness on the east and national forest to the west, and a 200-square-mile lake to the south. This is the Flathead Valley of Montana, home to the communities of Whitefish and Kalispell (as well as Columbia Falls, Bigfork, and Polson) and virtually limitless outdoor recreation in both summer and winter. There's not much a visitor can't do here—hike, golf, white-water raft, horseback ride, sail, or shop in the summer and fall; ski, snowmobile, snowshoe, or take a dogsled ride in the winter. Kalispell, the largest city (with a population of 12,000), is a hub and retail center for the valley. Whitefish is a mountain resort town below the Big Mountain Ski and Summer Resort. Columbia Falls is considered to be the western gateway to Glacier, and both Bigfork and Polson serve as bookmarks for massive Flathead Lake.

The area was once known only to the Salish Indians, who called it "the park between the mountains," until the Great Northern Railroad created Kalispell in the late 1890s. The railroad, called the Hi-Line, is still an integral part of the region because it brings tourists. It's ironic that the Flathead Valley bills itself as "Undiscovered Montana" because it's certainly been discovered for its recreation, mild climate, resort facilities, and pleasant attitude. Relocation to the valley is an issue of much concern, although the California pipeline seems to be slowing down a bit. ∎

KALISPELL

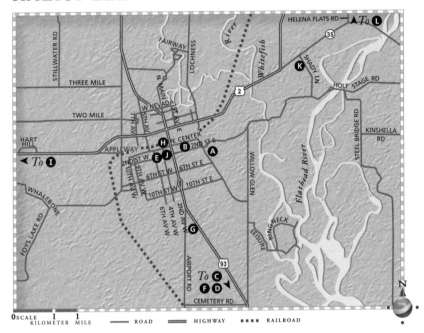

Sights

A Conrad Mansion National Historic Site Museum

B Hockaday Center for the Arts

C National Bison Range

D The People's Cultural Center

Food

E Montana Coffee Traders

F Showthyme!

Lodging

G Best Western Outlaw Inn

H Cavanaugh's

I Hargrave Guest Ranch

J Kalispell Grand Hotel

Camping

K Glacier Pines RV Park

L Rocky Mountain Hi Campground

A PERFECT DAY IN THE FLATHEAD VALLEY

On a summer day, start the morning with coffee and homemade muffins at Montana Coffee Traders in Kalispell. Then go golfing on one of the valley's seven world-class golf courses, either brand-new Northern Pines Golf Course or well-known Eagle Bend or Buffalo Hill. Follow your game with lunch and a gallery stroll in Bigfork, an artist's community. Then climb aboard a boat tour of Flathead Lake to see the horses on Wild Horse Island and its ancient petroglyphs. Wind up the evening with a horse-drawn hayride and cowboy barbecue in the mountains.

If you're visiting in winter, begin your day with a massive platter of *huevos rancheros* at the Buffalo Café in Whitefish with the locals. Then it's time to get in the car and . . . ascend. When the skies are clear, the view from the Big Mountain of the Flathead Valley and Whitefish Lake far below will take your breath away. Knock off early in the afternoon and do a snowmobile ride near the resort to see unique "snow ghosts"—pine trees packed hard with snow that resemble snowmen. End the evening with dinner and a couple of Black Star brews in town before collapsing.

SIGHTSEEING HIGHLIGHTS

Although Kalispell, Whitefish, Bigfork, and Polson each have information centers, the best way to get good valley-wide information is to contact the Flathead Convention and Visitors Association (FCVA), 15 Depot Park, Kalispell, MT 59901; (406) 756-9091 or (800) 543-3105.

★★★ **Big Mountain Ski and Summer Resort**—With more than 3,000 acres of skiable terrain only 30 miles from Glacier Park, the Big Mountain is among North America's largest and most scenic ski and summer resorts. When there is no fog (and fog can be a problem), the resort offers absolutely spectacular views of the Flathead Valley and Whitefish Lake as well as a feeling of having the huge mountain to yourself. This is the place where Olympic gold medalist Tommy Moe grew up and learned to ski fast.

In summer, activities include a scenic gondola ride, hiking, horseback riding, dinners, and music festivals in an outdoor amphitheater. Call for information on summer and winter activities and rates. Details: P.O. Box 1400, Whitefish, MT 59937; (406) 862-1900 or

(800) 858-5439; open early May through September 10 a.m. to 9:45 p.m., late November through mid-April 9 a.m. to 10 p.m. (1–8 hours)

★★★ **Flathead Lake**—The largest freshwater lake west of the Mississippi River, Flathead is a beautiful natural playground for water sports enthusiasts. Boating, fishing, sailing, and sea kayaking are a few of the activities available. Simply looking at the deep blue of the massive 200-square-mile lake is also popular. Wildlife watching is excellent, especially on Wild Horse Island, which hosts bighorn sheep, wild horses, and 75 bird species including bald eagles and osprey. The southern half of the lake lies within the boundaries of the **Flathead Indian Reservation**, home to the Confederated Salish and Kootenai tribes. For scenic boat trips on the lake, try **Classic Cruisin' Charters**, Marina Cay Resort, Bigfork, (406) 253-3585, whose 1926 56-foot wooden luxury yacht takes visitors on two-hour Flathead Lake cruises. Dinner and overnight cruises are also available. Open daily May through October, $22 per person. Also, the *Far West* **Cruise Boat**, Bigfork, (406) 857-3203, gives 90-minute

© Travel Montana

National Bison Range

cruises Sunday through Wednesday 2 p.m. to 7 p.m. Fares are $8 for adults, $5 for children.(1½ hours)

★★★ **Kalispell**—The largest community in the Flathead Valley, Kalispell is a very nice mixture of cowtown, agricultural center, retail hub, recreation center, and resort town in northwest Montana. It's certainly the focal point of the Flathead Valley in services and attitude. Outside of town the valley's mild climate allows cherries, potatoes, Christmas trees, and peppermint to grow. Details: Kalispell Area Chamber of Commerce, 15 Depot Park, Kalispell; (406) 257-2500. (3 hours)

★★★ **Whitefish**—Larger than the other Flathead Valley communities, Whitefish (population 4,500) began in the late 1800s as a fur-trading location. When railroad workers cut the first trees for the Whitefish townsite, the community was nicknamed "Stumptown." But since Big Mountain Ski Resort was established and visitors and locals engaged in the huge variety of recreation here, "Stumptown" has been known as the "Recreation Capital of Montana." Details: Whitefish Chamber of Commerce, P.O. Box 1120, Whitefish, MT 59937; (406) 862-3501. (3 hours)

★★ **Bigfork**—With a population of only 2,080, Bigfork is the smallest and most compact of the Flathead Valley communities. This is a place to stroll and poke in on the main street's art galleries, crafts stores, and other unique shops. Open all year, it's home to many artists. Details: Bigfork Area Chamber of Commerce, P.O. Box 237, Bigfork, MT 59911; (406) 837-5888. (2 hours)

★★ **Conrad Mansion National Historic Site Museum**—This 26-room Norman-style mansion was the home of C. E. Conrad, a Montana pioneer who gained his wealth as a Missouri River freighter and founder of Kalispell. All of its rooms have their original furniture. Details: 6 blocks east of Main on Fourth Street East, Kalispell; (406) 755-2166; open May 15 to June 14 10 a.m. to 5:30 p.m., June 15 to September 15 9 a.m. to 8 p.m., September 16 to October 15 10 a.m. to 5:30 p.m., special tours available daily at noon, 3 p.m., and 6 p.m. Admission: $5 adults, $1 children. (1 hour)

★★ **National Bison Range**—Established in 1908, this 18,000-acre national wildlife refuge is home to more than 500 bison. The range also maintains herds of elk, mule deer, white-tail deer, bighorn sheep, and pronghorn antelope. The 19-mile scenic drive is the best way to see it. A visitor's center offers displays and exhibits. Details: 30 miles south of Polson off U.S. 93, Moiese; (406) 644-2211; open year-round during daylight hours. Admission: $4 for vehicles with fewer than six people. (2 hours for scenic loop)

★★ **The People's Cultural Center**—This tribal center is run and operated by the Confederated Salish and Kootenai tribes and exists to share the culture. The center contains a gallery, learning center, living museum, library, gift shop, and archives for scholars. It also includes Pend Oreille tribe information and history. Interpretive guided tours on the Flathead Reservation are available through **Native Ed-Ventures**, (406) 675-0160 or (800) 883-5344. Details: 53253 U.S. 93, Pablo; (406) 675-0160; open April through September daily 9 a.m. to 7 p.m.; October through March Monday through Friday 9 a.m. to 5 p.m. Admission: $2 adults, $1 seniors and children. (1 hour)

★ **Hockaday Center for the Arts**—The "cultural center of Kalispell" offers changing visual arts exhibitions and educational programs for adults and children. Housed in a 1902 Carnegie library building, the center also sponsors performing arts and fairs throughout the valley. Call for current events and exhibitions. Details: Second Avenue East at Third Street, Kalispell; (406) 755-5268; open year-round Tuesday through Friday 10 a.m. to 4 p.m., Saturday 10 a.m. to 3 p.m. Admission: $2 adults, $1 seniors, children free. (1 hour)

FITNESS AND RECREATION

We can't talk about recreation in the Flathead Valley without first acknowledging the 700 miles of hiking trails in neighboring **Glacier National Park** as well as all of the activities covered in the previous chapter. But visitors to the valley will find plenty to do year-round.

For golfers, the valley is a Northern Rockies dream come true, with eight excellent courses. Courses include the **Buffalo Hill Golf Club**, **Northern Pines**, and **Village Greens Club** in Kalispell; **Eagle Bend Golf Club** in Bigfork; **Meadow Lake Golf** in Columbia Falls; **Mission Mountain Country Club** in Ronan; **Polson Country Club** in Polson; and **Whitefish Lake Golf Club**. Reserve tee times at any of these courses by calling (800) 392-9795.

White-water rafting trips on the Middle Fork of the Flathead River (remember *The River Wild* with Meryl Streep?) are available from **Glacier Raft Company**, (406) 883-5454 or (800) 235-6781; **Montana Raft Company**, (406) 387-5555 or (800) 521-RAFT; or **Great Northern Whitewater**, (406) 387-5340 or (800) 735-7897.

In winter there is excellent downhill skiing at the **Big Mountain Ski and Summer Resort**, P.O. Box 1400, Whitefish; (406) 862-1900 or (800) 858-5439. Snowmobiles can be rented from **Canyon Creek Cat House**, (406) 888-5109 or (800) 933-5133, or **Adventure Motorsports**, (406) 892-2752. Dog-sledding is available from **Dog Sled Adventures**, (406) 881-2275.

FOOD

If you've forgotten our definition of "resort food," please review the Jackson Hole chapter. Then proceed cautiously.

Tupelo Grille, 17 Central Avenue, Whitefish, (406) 862-6136, is one of Whitefish's finest restaurants, with pasta, chicken, seafood, and Cajun specialties in a casual setting. **Café Kandahar**, Big Mountain Resort, (406) 862-0326, is a low-key and very charming restaurant serving European dishes under the shadow of the mountain. This place has an après-ski atmosphere even in August. **Truby's**, 115 Central Avenue, Whitefish, (406) 862-4979, formerly Stumptown Station, specializes in good wood-fired gourmet pizza. Don't be scared off by the name **Showthyme!**, 548 Electric Avenue, Bigfork, (406) 837-0707—you won't be molested by singing waiters and aspiring thespians here. Instead you can enjoy an eclectic menu of Southwestern foods and fresh vegetables. Check out **Montana Coffee Traders**, 326 West Center Street, (406) 756-2326, for espresso and muffin-type breakfast fare. The place for *big* breakfasts and local color is the **Buffalo Café**, 516 Third Street East, Whitefish, (406) 862-2833.

One of my favorites is the **Great Northern Bar and Grill**, 27 Central Avenue, (406) 862-2816, with excellent pub food and Black Star, one of the best local beers in all of Montana, if not the entire region.

LODGING

Starting with the big dogs—if Kalispell is the hub of the Flathead Valley, then the **Best Western Outlaw Inn**, 1701 Highway 93, (406) 755-6100, is the hub of Kalispell. With 220 rooms, shops, and convention facilities,

WHITEFISH

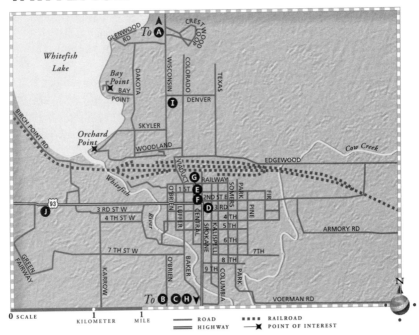

Sights

Ⓐ Big Mountain Ski and Summer Resort

Ⓑ Bigfork

Ⓒ Flathead Lake

Food

Ⓓ Buffalo Café

Ⓐ Café Kandahar

Ⓔ Great Northern Bar and Grill

Ⓕ Truby's

Ⓖ Tupelo Grille

Lodging

Ⓗ Best Western Rocky Mountain Lodge

Ⓘ Good Medicine Lodge

Ⓙ Grouse Mountain Lodge

Ⓐ Kandahar Lodge

Camping

Ⓑ Ronde Vue Park RV and Campground

Ⓑ Woods Bay Marina & RV

Note: Items with the same letter are located in the same town or area.

this property might be fading a bit, but it's still formidable. Likewise, the **Best Western Rocky Mountain Lodge**, 6510 Highway 93 South, Whitefish, (406) 862-2569, and **Cavanaugh's** at Kalispell Center, 20 North Main, Kalispell, (406) 752-6660, are large, comfortable, conventional family hotels, with rates ranging from $70 to $90 per night.

The **Kalispell Grand Hotel**, 100 Main Street, Kalispell, (406) 755-1888, has history, character, and charm, right in the middle of town. **Grouse Mountain Lodge**, 1205 Highway 93 West, Whitefish, (406) 862-3000, is a beautiful facility set on a golf course with good rates in the summer and winter off season. One of the most comfortable lodges in the valley is the **Kandahar Lodge**, Big Mountain Resort, Whitefish, (406) 862-6098, a true mountain lodge, where guests are encouraged to read good books in the lobby (but not to smoke). The **Good Medicine Lodge**, 537 Wisconsin Avenue, Whitefish, (406) 862-5488, is a charming historic house-turned-inn with a central location and $75 to $105 rates.

One of the better working guest ranches in the West is the **Hargrave Guest Ranch**, 300 Thompson River Road, Marion, (406) 858-2284, for two main reasons: hosts Leo and Ellen Hargrave. Only Ellen can say things like, "Most folks are like a barbed wire fence—they have their good points," and actually mean it.

CAMPING

There is abundant camping in and around the Flathead Valley. If you can't find a good spot, put on your glasses and look again. In addition to all of the campsites available in the Flathead National Forest, Glacier Park, Whitefish State Park, and Flathead Lake Park, there is also the **Ronde Vue Park RV & Campground**, 27202 East Lake Shore, Bigfork, (406) 837-6973, with full hookups, trees for cover, and $50 rates. The **Woods Bay Marina & RV**, 624 Yenni Point Road, Bigfork, (406) 837-6038, has a quiet lakeside location and $22 rates. **Glacier Pines RV Park**, 1850 Highway 35 East, Kalispell, has 180 sites with hookups for $16. **Rocky Mountain Hi Campground**, 825 Helena Flats Road, Kalispell, (406) 755-9573, is out of town but quiet, with a creek running through it, and $11 to $12 rates.

NIGHTLIFE

The **Bigfork Summer Playhouse**, 526 Electric Avenue, Bigfork, (406) 837-4886, is a summer-stock theater that produces Broadway musicals well-regarded by locals and tourists alike. Open late May through Labor Day Monday through Saturday at 8:30 p.m. Call for details and the playbill. **Moose's Saloon**, 173 North Main Street, Kalispell, (406) 755-2338, is a semi-legendary joint with excellent pizza and cold beer, where throwing peanut shells on the floor is not just encouraged but mandatory.

18

GREAT FALLS

I t's unfortunate that the city of Great Falls is often overlooked when visitors (or travel book writers) tick off the highlights of this region. The community and its environs have a lot to offer, much of which is Authentic Montana. Great Falls is the state's second largest city (56,000 folks, behind Billings) and, in a way, the most self-contained, given that it is so far from anywhere else of any size. It bills itself both as a gateway to Glacier National Park and just a day's drive from Yellowstone, and that is the reason many first-time visitors find themselves here.

Part of the attraction of Great Falls is its realness. It's an authentic Northern Rockies city borne of agriculture, mining, timber, and tradition that has largely escaped the imported cuteness and pretension found in some of Montana's sexier mountain towns. You can get a latte in Great Falls, but the proprietor might smile and roll her eyes a little as she serves it. The town was an important stop in 1805 for Lewis and Clark, who discovered and named the "great falls" of the Missouri River. An impressive new museum is being constructed well in advance of their visit's 200th anniversary. It was here, too, in the center of Montana's wheat and cattle country, that cowboy artist Charles M. Russell chose to live and work. The C. M. Russell Museum Complex is in itself worth a special trip to town. Outside of Great Falls are massive wheat fields, missile silos, mountains, and dams. ◼

GREAT FALLS

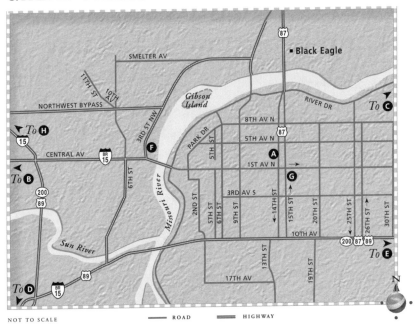

NOT TO SCALE   ▬ ROAD   ▭ HIGHWAY

Sights

Ⓐ **C. M. Russell Museum**

Ⓑ **Egg Mountain**

Ⓒ **Giant Springs Heritage State Park**

Ⓓ **Great Falls Historic Trolley**

Ⓔ **Lewis and Clark Interpretive Center**

Ⓕ **Montana Cowboys' Association Museum**

Ⓖ **Old Trail Museum and Rocky Mountain Front**

Ⓖ **Paris Gibson Square Museum of Art**

Ⓗ **Ulm Pishkun State Park**

Note: Items with the same letter are located in the same town or area.

A PERFECT DAY IN GREAT FALLS

This is as good a place as any to contemplate the amazing journey of Captains Meriwether Lewis and William Clark as they ventured across Blackfoot Country in this unmapped and unknown continent from 1804 to 1806. After breakfast, visit the falls itself, where the Corps of Discovery had to portage the white water with one eye on the river and the other on the looming mountains to the west. Visit the Ulm Pishkun buffalo jump to experience what life was like for the Indians before the expedition. In the afternoon, visit the C. M. Russell Museum, reliving the cowboy years in the real West. Wind up the evening beneath a tree on the banks of the Missouri reading *Undaunted Courage* or, if you're brave, *The Journals of Lewis and Clark* as the sun sets.

SIGHTSEEING HIGHLIGHTS

★★★ **C. M. Russell Museum**—Many historians believe the work of Charles M. Russell perfectly portrays the true "Old West." The legendary, self-taught cowboy artist spent most of his adult life in and around Great Falls. Highly personal and unique, this is one of the best collections of any artist I've ever seen. Russell created nearly 4,000 works of art during his lifetime, and the 46,000-square-foot museum owns the most complete collections of his works and personal objects in the world. The complex also features pieces by other renowned Western artists and houses the **Browning Firearms Museum**. Details: 400 13th Street, Great Falls; (406) 727-8787; open May through September Monday through Saturday 9 a.m. to 6 p.m., Sunday 1 p.m. to 5 p.m.; rest of the year Tuesday through Saturday 10 a.m. to 5 p.m., Sunday 1 p.m. to 5 p.m. Admission: $4 adults, $3 seniors and students. (2–3 hours)

★★ **Egg Mountain (Choteau)**—Remember the opening scene in *Jurassic Park*, where the scientists are at work unearthing dinosaur eggs when the helicopter arrives to whisk them away? That location was based on Egg Mountain, near Choteau, where the eggs' discovery reinvented scientific theory about dinosaur behavior. The site is run by the Museum of the Rockies in Bozeman, but tours every day at 2 p.m. during the summer months provide a fascinating trip into natural history. Two-day dig courses are also available. Details: Museum of the Rockies, Bozeman (although the site is located in

Choteau), (406) 994-2251; Old Trail Museum and Rocky Mountain Front, 823 North Main, Choteau, (406) 466-5332. Free. (3 hours)

★ **Giant Springs Heritage State Park**—This 218-acre park features several interpretive signs detailing the Lewis and Clark Expedition along the Missouri River. The park includes one of the world's largest natural springs, with a flow of 7.9 million gallons per hour, plus picnic grounds and a state fish hatchery. The 201-foot-long Roe River flows into the Missouri from Giant Springs and is the shortest river in the United States. Details: 4600 Giant Springs Road, 4 miles northeast of Great Falls; (206) 454-5840; open year-round. Admission: $3 per vehicle. (1 hour)

★ **Great Falls Historic Trolley**—Take an informative tour of Great Falls, including interpretation of the Lewis and Clark Expedition, Giant Springs State Park, C. M. Russell Museum, Paris Gibson Square, and historic buildings. The tour provides a good overview of the city and the region. Details: 156 Woodland Estates, Great Falls; (208) 452-9216; open June through August Monday through Saturday 8:30 a.m. to 8:30 p.m., Sunday noon to 5 p.m. Admission: $15 per person, also good for the C. M. Russell Museum and Giant Springs. (1½ hours)

★ **Old Trail Museum and Rocky Mountain Front**—Located in Choteau (pronounced "shoat-OH"), this recently renovated and expanded museum features not only paleontological displays but also a history of the area and the Rocky Mountain Front. Details: 823 North Main, Choteau; (406) 466-5332; open daily May 16 to September 14 9 a.m. to 6 p.m., Tuesday through Saturday 10 a.m. to 3 p.m. the rest of the year. Admission: $2 adults, 50 cents children. (1 hour)

★ **Paris Gibson Square Museum of Art**—Paris Gibson (great name!) was the man who founded and plotted Great Falls in 1883. The museum is designated a National Historic Landmark and features Montana contemporary art as well as the local **Cascade County Historical Society**. The building is constructed of sandstone quarried from the area. Details: 1400 First Avenue North, Great Falls; (406) 727-8255; open year-round Monday through Friday 10 a.m. to 5 p.m., weekends noon to 5 p.m. Free, but donations appreciated. (1 hour)

★ **Ulm Pishkun State Park**—*Pishkun* is an American Indian word for buffalo jump, a place where herds of buffalo were driven to their deaths to provide food, shelter, and tools. This milelong prehistoric bison kill-site features informative signs explaining how the Pishkun were used. It is thought to be the largest site of its kind in the United States. The center will tell the story of the buffalo jump and of the Indian culture prior to white settlement. The bluff commands a great panoramic view and features interpretive sites. Details: Take I-15 for 10 miles to the Ulm Exit, then 4 miles northwest on the county road; (406) 454-5840. Free. (1 hour)

Lewis and Clark Interpretive Center—Opening in time to capitalize on the interest brewing for the Lewis and Clark Expedition bicentennial, this 22,500-square-foot facility will focus on the Montana portion of the famous Corps of Discovery route. The center will also contain exhibits highlighting the area's natural history, the Plains Indian culture (including a living history site), and a huge theater and auditorium. Details: Great Falls Area Chamber of Commerce, River Road; (406) 761-4434; call for hours and admission fees. (1 hour)

Montana Cowboys' Association Museum—Dedicated to the real working cowboys of Montana, the museum is housed in an old log cabin with double fireplaces and hitching posts. It is filled with over 500 items, including branding irons, ox yokes, saddles, and rawhide ropes. Details: 311 Third Street, NW, Great Falls; (406) 761-9299; open daily 11 a.m. to 2 p.m. Free, but donations appreciated. (1 hour)

FITNESS AND RECREATION

In addition to the pathways and trails associated with the **Ulm Pishkun State Park** and **Giant Springs Heritage State Park**, the city of Great Falls offers the **River's Edge Trail** along the Missouri, which leads from the Tenth Avenue Bridge to Giant Springs. Golfers will enjoy the **Meadow Lark Country Club**, Country Club Boulevard, (406) 453-6531, and the **R.O. Speck Golf Course**, 29th Street and River Drive North, (406) 761-1089. **Montana Outfitters**, 2427 Old Havre Highway, (800) 800-8219, offers white-water and scenic floats on the Missouri as well as fishing excursions. Call for rates and trips.

FOOD

Great Falls offers an assortment of traditional, puzzling, and unique places to eat, starting with **Jakers Steaks, Ribs and Fish House**, 1500 Tenth Avenue South, (406) 727-1033. It features excellent big *beef* and more *beef* for the *beef* lover. **Bert 'n' Ernies**, 300 First Avenue South, (406) 453-0601, is one of Great Falls' more popular restaurants, located in historic downtown and specializing in burgers, salads, soups, steaks, and seafood.

Borries Family Restaurant, 1800 Smelter Avenue, (406) 761-0300, has both American and Italian food, with prime rib as their calling card. **3-D International Restaurant**, 1825 Smelter Avenue, (406) 453-6561, serves an eclectic—and delicious—blend of Cantonese, Szechuan, Thai, Mongolian Grill, and American entrees in an art deco setting. **Penny's Gourmet to Go**, 815 Central Avenue, (406) 453-7070, is a dandy casual restaurant featuring good soups, salads, pizza, chili, and (surprise) a quality vegetarian slate. **Candie's Soup du Jour & Specialities**, 705 Central Avenue West, (406) 727-1313, is a good place to start the day, with bagels, muffins, espresso, omelettes, and fresh bread.

LODGING

Great Falls has quite an array of quality lodging at affordable prices. The **Best Western Heritage Inn**, 1700 Fox Farm Road, (406) 761-1900, is the big dog in town and the central convention hotel, with 239 rooms, excellent indoor health facilities, and the most extensive amenities. Rates range from $68 to $80. The **Best Western Ponderosa Inn**, 220 Central Avenue, (406) 761-3410, is half the size with full service as well. Rates are $54 to $66. The **Holiday Inn of Great Falls**, 400 Tenth Avenue South, (406) 727-7200, offers 169 similar-quality rooms and amenities for $54 to $76 per night. The **Townhouse Inns of Great Falls**, 1411 Tenth Avenue, (406) 761-4600, is a Montana chain with some in-room exercise equipment and good service at $53 to $71 per night. **Fairfield Inn by Marriott**, 1000 Ninth Avenue South, (406) 454-3000, is typical of the chain, charging $49 to $59 rates. The **Triple Crown Motor Inn**, 621 Central Avenue, (406) 727-8300, is clean and affordable at $39 to $41 per night. The **Old Oak Inn Bed and Breakfast**, 709 Fourth Avenue North, (406) 727-5782, has five nice rooms for $45 to $55.

GREAT FALLS

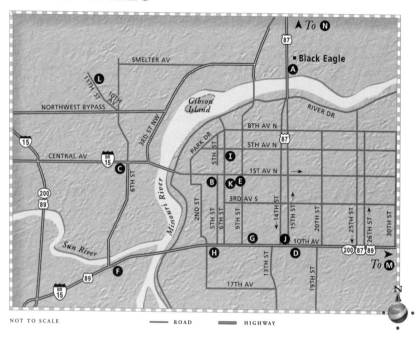

NOT TO SCALE — ROAD — HIGHWAY

Food

- **A** 3-D International Restaurant
- **B** Bert 'n' Ernies
- **A** Borries Family Restaurant
- **C** Candie's Soup du Jour & Specialties
- **D** Jakers Steaks, Ribs and Fish House
- **E** Penny's Gourmet to Go

Lodging

- **F** Best Western Heritage Inn
- **B** Best Western Ponderosa Inn

Lodging (continued)

- **G** Fairfield Inn by Marriott
- **H** Holiday Inn of Great Falls
- **I** Old Oak Inn Bed and Breakfast
- **J** Townhouse Inns of Great Falls
- **K** Triple Crown Motor Inn

Camping

- **L** Dick's RV Park
- **M** Great Falls KOA
- **N** Rocky Mountain Front National Forest Campgrounds

Note: Items with the same letter are located in the same town or area.

CAMPING

There are many public campgrounds and sites in the national forest along Kings Hill Scenic Byway and **Rocky Mountain Front National Forest Campgrounds**. For details, contact the Great Falls Area Chamber of Commerce at (406) 761-4434. In town are the **Great Falls KOA**, 1500 51st Street South, (406) 727-3191, with 126 sites, plug-ins, Kamping Kabins, and a tent village; and **Dick's RV Park**, 1403 11th Street, (406) 452-0333, with 178 sites, plug-ins, and some pull-throughs.

19
MISSOULA

No doubt about it—Missoula, Montana, is an interesting place. It's about as far away culturally and politically from conservative cities like Great Falls and Billings as you can get. In eastern Montana they consider "mi-ZOO-la" a strange and distant island filled with odd hairy people who make no sense. Missoula is a town in which University of Montana students mix with loggers, writers rub shoulders with outfitters, and local granola-heads order beers next to ex-Californians. In current politically correct terms, Missoula is "diverse."

Missoula lies at a natural crossroads and thoroughfare in the Rocky Mountains, a place where people have been encountering different cultures and attitudes since Lewis and Clark met the Blackfeet. The name *Missoula* is derived from a Salish Indian word meaning "near the cold, chilling waters." The search for gold opened up the valley to non-natives in the 1860s, and the Northern Pacific Railroad reached town in 1883. The mild climate in the valley nurtured agriculture, and the mountains produced timber. The University of Montana opened its doors in 1895 and now has 11,000 students. The city itself is home to more than 45,000, and the surrounding county brings the immediate population to 87,000. Natural and cultural attractions abound, from nearby mountains, skiing, and wilderness areas to symphonies, orchestras, and lively, controversial voices from the University of Montana.

Native author Norman Maclean wrote about Missoula, "Eventually, all things merge into one, and a river runs through it." ◼

MISSOULA

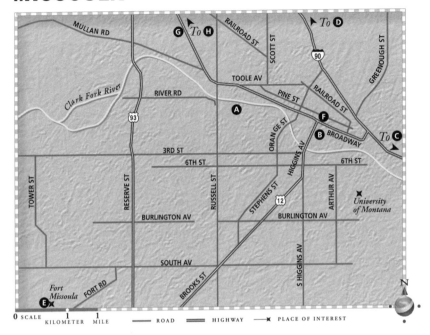

Sights

A A Carousel for Missoula

B Downtown Missoula

C Garnet Ghost Town

D Historic Ninemile Remount Depot Visitor Center

E Historical Museum at Fort Missoula

E MAVIS Summer Interpretive Programs

F Missoula Museum of the Arts

G Rocky Mountain Elk Foundation

H Smoke Jumpers Center

Note: Items with the same letter are located in the same town or area.

A PERFECT DAY IN MISSOULA

After a mountain bike ride through downtown Missoula followed by a massive egg-potato-and-sausage breakfast at the Old Town Café, visit the Smoke Jumpers Center and the Rocky Mountain Elk Foundation right next door. Stroll the shops and galleries of old downtown Missoula, stopping at a book store to buy a few novels written by local writers. Pick up a copy of *A River Runs Through It, Young Men and Fire, The Last Best Place,* or *Dancing Bear* and start reading. After dark, join the locals in a classic Missoula bar crawl, making sure to end up eventually at the Oxford Club for a traditional plate of brains and eggs.

SIGHTSEEING HIGHLIGHTS

★★★ **Smoke Jumpers Center**—Officially the "Aerial Fire Depot and Smokejumper Center," this facility is the nation's largest staging and training ground for elite smokejumpers, who are dispatched across the Rockies to fight fires in remote locations. The smokejumpers have a *Top Gun* mentality which is more than obvious when you visit the small but fascinating visitor's center. The book *Young Men and Fire,* by Norman Maclean, was written about this facility's smokejumpers who died fighting a fire in the Gates of the Mountains area near Helena. It's unfortunate that the visitor's center doesn't contain more because the topic of wildfire and the facility's history is so interesting. Details: U.S. 3, Missoula; (406) 329-4934; open Memorial Day to Labor Day 8:30 a.m. to 5 p.m. Tours are available from 10 a.m. on, except from noon to 1 p.m. Free, but donations are encouraged. (45 minutes)

★★ **A Carousel for Missoula**—The first fully hand-carved carousel to be built in the country since the 1930s, A Carousel for Missoula has a unique local story. All 38 horses and two chariots were crafted by local volunteers, and the fundraising for and organization of the project was a purely volunteer effort. Details: 1 Caras Park; (406) 549-8392; open daily Memorial Day through Labor Day 11 a.m. to 7 p.m., noon to 5:30 p.m. the rest of the year. Free. (30 minutes)

★★ **Downtown Missoula**—The best way to experience the diversity and flavor of Missoula is simply to stroll along the walks of downtown as they hug the banks of the Clark Fork River. There's no other town quite like it. In addition to hiking trails, bike trails, and parks, you can sample from the eclectic collection of restaurants, specialty shops, old-time cowboy and logger bars, art galleries, antique stores, and enough coffee and beer to float a barge. Details: Missoula Downtown Association, 101 East Main; (406) 543-4238. (2 hours)

★★ **Rocky Mountain Elk Foundation**—Funded by an international wildlife association dedicated to the propagation and hunting of elk, the foundation's visitor's center houses wildlife displays, world record elk mounts, wildlife art, and gifts. Even if you're not a hunter, it's worth a visit to catch a glimpse of the big-game hunting culture of the Northern Rockies. Details: 2291 West Broadway; (406) 523-4545; open daily Memorial Day to Labor Day 8 a.m. to 6 p.m., rest of the year 8:30 a.m. to 5 p.m. Free. (1 hour)

★★ **Historic Ninemile Remount Depot Visitor Center**—Located 25 miles west of Missoula (22 miles west on I-90, then 4 miles north at Exit 82), the center provides a historic journey to the early days of mountain firefighting. This was the "smokejumpers center" before airplanes, fire retardant chemicals, and parachutes, when firefighters had to use pack mules to get to the fires. The facility is very well-preserved. Details: 20325 Remount Road, Huson; (406) 626-5201; open Memorial Day to Labor Day 9 a.m. to 5 p.m. Free. (1 hour)

★ **Garnet Ghost Town**—While a number of ghost towns exist throughout the western Montana mountains in old mine locations, Garnet is one of the better ones because the Bureau of Land Management keeps it in good condition. Two completely outfitted cabins may be rented. Details: Call BLM for directions, (406) 329-1031. (2 hours)

★ **MAVIS Summer Interpretive Programs**—Want to see a hawk up close and personal or find out what the Missoula area looked like 10,000 years ago? The Missoula Area Visitor Information Service (MAVIS) offers programs via the Lolo National Forest. Information and talks on wildlife, geology, American Indian land use, and the history of the Missoula area are provided. Details: Building 24-A, Ft. Missoula; (406) 329-3814; talks mid-June through mid-September Thursday and Saturday 7 p.m. Free. (1 or more hours, depending on the program)

★ **Missoula Museum of the Arts**—Along with its permanent collection of historic and contemporary regional art, the museum hosts national and international exhibits. Guided tours are given by appointment; call for exhibit and tour information. Details: 335 North Pattee Street; (406) 728-0447; open Monday through Saturday noon to 5 p.m. Free. (1 hour)

★ **Historical Museum at Fort Missoula**—The museum is the hub of what was once Fort Missoula, a facility established by the U.S. Army during the fight with Chief Joseph and the Nez Percé Indians in the late 1870s. Today there are a dozen historic structures in the complex as well as displays on the history of the valley that include timber and agriculture. It's a quiet, pleasant outpost. Details: South Avenue, 1 mile west of Reserve Street; (406) 728-3476; open in summer Tuesday to Saturday 10 a.m. to 5 p.m., Sunday noon to 5 p.m.; rest of year noon to 5 p.m. Admission: $1. (1 hour)

FITNESS AND RECREATION

Like most college towns, Missoula is brimming with recreational opportunities and activities. **Feet First** is a continuous network of green

© Donnie Sexton/Travel Montana

Garnet ghost town

trailways throughout the Missoula Valley. The organization is sponsored by the city and county of Missoula, the university, Lolo National Forest, and the state of Montana. For maps and further information, call (406) 523-4762. The **Rattlesnake Wilderness Area** (sounds inviting, eh? Don't worry.), located just 4 miles north of Missoula, has trails for short hikes and cross-country ski trails. For maps and information, contact the Missoula Ranger District Office, (406) 329-3814.

Two miles southeast of town on U.S. Highway 93 South is the beginning of the **Blue Mountain Recreation Area**, with trails for hikers, runners, bicycles, horses, motorcycles, and ATVs. There's an interpretive trail at Maclay Flats for foot traffic. **Ninemile Ranger District** offers hiking, wildlife viewing (deer, elk, eagles), and self-guided trails in and around the ranger station. Tour the historic **Ninemile Remount Depot and Ranger Station** or visit **Grand Menard, Kreis Pond, Squaw Creek**, or **Petty Creek** for hiking and camping. For more information, call the ranger station at (406) 626-4201.

Six golf courses are available in Missoula, including 18-hole **Larchmont Golf Course**, 3200 Ft. Missoula Road, (406) 721-4416, and nine-hole **University Golf Course**, 515 South Avenue East, (406) 728-8629. Missoula could make a serious run at being the "Biking Capital of America" and is most certainly the bike capital of Montana. Mountain bikes can be rented from **Lewis and Clark Trail Adventures**, (406) 728-7609, and **Low Impact Mountain Bicyclist** (L.I.M.B.), (406) 329-3962. Horses can be rented anywhere from one hour to overnight. Among the better places to ride are **Lolo Hot Springs**, (406)-273-2290, and **Mountain Trail Rides**, (406) 549-7759.

In winter the **Snowbowl Ski Area**, 1700 Snowbowl Road, Missoula, (406) 549-9777, is a 20-minute drive from downtown, with a continuous drop of 2,600 feet. It's a wild place in looks, altitude, and attitude—a "local" ski area that's probably too challenging for the average downhill intermediate cruiser but is legendary among University of Montana alumni and students. Cross-country ski trails can be found throughout the area, including **Lolo Pass, Seeley Lake, Lubrecht, Garnet, Lost Trail Pass, Pattee Canyon, Rattlesnake Recreation Area, Blue Mountain Recreation Area**, and the **Bitterroot Mountains**.

FOOD

Like Missoula itself, the variety of restaurants packed into such a small community boggles the mind.

MISSOULA

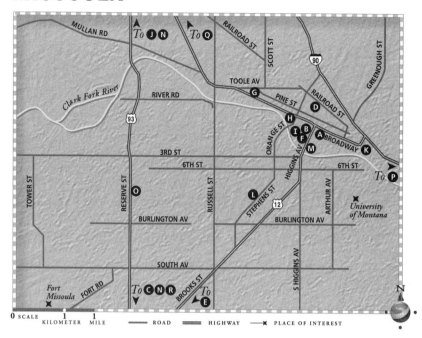

Food

- **A** Butterfly Herbs
- **B** Casa Pablo's
- **C** The Depot
- **D** Jaker's Steaks, Ribs and Fish House
- **E** Mammyth Bakery
- **F** Montana Mining Company
- **G** Muralt's Truck Plaza Café
- **H** The Mustard Seed
- **I** The Shack

Lodging

- **J** Best Western Grant Creek Inn
- **K** Goldsmith's Bed and Breakfast
- **L** Greenough Bed and Breakfast
- **M** Holiday Inn Missoula-Parkside
- **N** Homestead/4B's Inns
- **O** Ruby's Reserve Street Inn

Camping

- **P** Beavertail Hill State Park
- **Q** El Mar KOA
- **R** Lewis and Clark Campground

Breakfasts range from industrial size, like those at **Muralt's Truck Plaza Café**, 8196 Highway 93 North, (406) 728-8182, and **The Shack**, 222 West Main, (406) 549-9903, to health-conscious and ahead-of-the-trend-curve, like those at the **Mammyth Bakery**, 131 West Main, (406) 549-5542, and **Butterfly Herbs**, 232 North Higgins, (406) 728-8780.

Lunches and dinners run the gamut as well. **The Mustard Seed**, 419 West Front Street, (406) 728-7825, serves highly recommended Chinese with variations; and **The Depot**, 201 West Railroad Road, (406) 728-7007, is a classic Montana steakhouse. The **Montana Mining Company**, 1210 West Broadway, (406) 543-6192, is known for steak and seafood in a pleasant family atmosphere; and **Casa Pablo's**, 147 West Broadway, (406) 721-3854, is a comfortable American and Mexican location. **Jaker's Steak, Ribs and Fish House**, 3515 Brooks Street, (406) 721-1312, serves, not surprisingly, steak, ribs, and fish.

LODGING

There are plenty of rooms in Missoula, and new ones have been added in bunches in the last few years, which means value to travelers and headaches to hotel owners. The new **Best Western Grant Creek Inn**, 5280 Grant Creek Road, (406) 543-0700 or (800) 543-0700, is a well-run 126-room property with good management and a European breakfast buffet at rates from $65 to $85. The **Holiday Inn Missoula-Parkside**, 200 South Pattee Street, (406) 251-2665 or (800) 399-0408, is the largest convention-style property, with 200 rooms at $75 per night set in a fine location for accessing the Clark River, the parkway, and downtown. **Ruby's Reserve Street Inn**, 4825 Reserve Street, (406) 721-0990 or (800) 221-2057, is a handsome 127-room hotel with a creek and picnic area and $49 to $59 rooms. The **Homestead/4B's Inns**, south location: 3803 Brooks, (406) 251-2665 or (800) 272-9500; north location: 4953 North Reserve Street, (406) 542-7550 or (800) 272-9500, offer clean and efficient budget accommodations on each end of town from $36 to $47 per night. **Goldsmith's Bed and Breakfast**, 809 East Front, (406) 721-6732, is Missoula's original historic bed and breakfast. It sits on the Clark River with seven well-appointed rooms and $60 to $80 rates. The elegant and romantic **Greenough Bed and**

Breakfast, 631 Stephens, (406) 728-3626, has only three rooms with private baths at $80 and up.

CAMPING

Campers and RV folks travel many miles to stay overnight at the **El Mar KOA**, 3695 Tina Avenue, Missoula, (406) 549-0881, with its petting zoo, evening and weekend programs, and presentations on topics like wildlife conservation, biology, and history. If there is such a thing as an enlightened campground, this is it. El Mar offers 200 sites with hookups, and all sites are pull-through. Rates are $15 to $18 per night. This may be the best private campground in the three-state area. **Beavertail Hill State Park**, (406) 542-5500, is located 26 miles from Missoula on I-90 South and has 25 public sites on 65 acres for $9 per night. **Lewis and Clark Campground**, (406) 329-3750, is 15 miles west of Lolo and 6 miles east of the Lolo Pass Visitor Center. Lolo Hot Spring and horse rentals are nearby, and there are 17 sites at $6 per day.

NIGHTLIFE

The University of Montana stages concerts and plays throughout the year. To find out what's on, call **University of Montana Productions** at (406) 243-6661, or the UM Theater box office at (406) 243-4581. The **Garden City Ballet/Dance Works**, (406) 721-3675, and the **Missoula Symphony Orchestra**, (406) 243-6880, also stage productions well beyond the expectations of many visitors to this town of 45,000 people.

Many of the excellent local writers have noted that it's sometimes hard to concentrate on literature in Missoula because the bars are so much fun and the bartenders so darned accommodating. Hence, the exhilarating and destructive case for the Missoula pub crawl, where you can rub elbows with cowboys, loggers, writers, movie stars, students, Communists, right-wingers, and who knows who else. On your rounds, try to include the **Top Hat**, 134 West Front (406) 728-9865; **Jay's Upstairs**, 119 West Main, (406) 728-9915; **Iron Horse Brew Pub**, 100 West Railroad Avenue, (406) 728-8866; **Stockman's**, 135 West Front, (406) 549-9668; and **Rhino**, 158 Ryman Avenue, (406) 721-6061. And, if you want to feel like an official big-shot Missoulian, end the evening at the classic dive the **Oxford Club**, at North Higgins and

Pine, (406) 549-0117, and order up a plate of brains and eggs. It's been said that this meal helps replace some of the brain cells destroyed in the previous hours, but you'd be hard-pressed to prove it based on the condition of the old-timers seated around the bar.

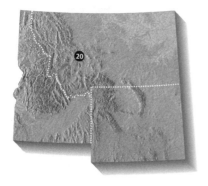

20

HELENA

OK, so it's 1864, and these four down-on-their-luck ex-Confederate soldiers are just about to give up on their dream of striking it rich in Montana. They find a creek in the middle of nowhere, declare it their "last chance," and stick their pans in the water. Yup, they find gold—lots of it! And silver as well. From there, it's history.

"Last Chance Gulch" begat Helena (pronounced "HELL-uh-nuh"), which, after a vicious political battle against Virginia City, became the capital of the Montana Territory in 1875 and later, the state capital. The precious minerals ran out, but not before Helena's wealthy citizens established the community as an architectural and cultural wonder, with Victorian buildings, a beautiful cathedral, and a stately capitol.

Today Helena has a population of nearly 25,000 people, and Last Chance Gulch is the heart of town. Helena is strategically located between Glacier and Yellowstone National Parks, a wonderful jumping-off point for summer and winter outdoor recreation. Even though it doesn't generate the buzz associated with such Montana cities as Bozeman and Missoula, Helena is one of my favorite places on this tri-state tour. It's a cheerful, historic, and even elegant place with a thriving arts and cultural community, terrific access to outdoor recreation, and a still-powerful hint of its Wild West beginnings.

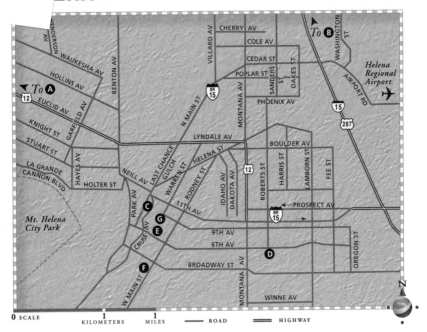

Sights

Ⓐ Archie Bray Foundation

Ⓑ Gates of the Mountains

Ⓒ Holter Museum of Art

Ⓓ Last Chance Gulch Tour

Ⓓ Montana Historical Society

Ⓔ Original Governor's Mansion

Ⓕ Reeder's Alley

Ⓖ St. Helena Cathedral

Ⓓ State Capitol

Note: Items with the same letter are located in the same town or area.

A PERFECT DAY IN HELENA

Start the morning early with a vigorous hike on Mount Helena, which overlooks town, followed by coffee and bagels downtown. Preview some major points of interest in town by riding the "Last Chancer" Tour Train. Then drive 16 miles to Hilger Landing on the Missouri River and take an excursion boat to the spectacular Gates of the Mountains area, first noted by Lewis and Clark. Return to Helena to visit the Archie Bray Foundation, the state capitol, and the St. Helena Cathedral before dinner at one of Helena's lively restaurants in historic Last Chance Gulch.

SIGHTSEEING HIGHLIGHTS

★★★ **Gates of the Mountains**—On the Missouri River in July 1805, Captains Lewis and Clark found themselves in a deep canyon with 1,200-foot-high walls that seemed to close in on them like a vice. Suddenly, as the expedition approached an apparently impenetrable wall, the mountains opened before them like a giant gate, letting them pass through. Lewis called the area the "Gates of the Mountains." Though still wild and undeveloped, it can be accessed via boat tour. Mann Gulch, the focus of Norman Maclean's *Young Men and Fire*, about the fire that killed 13 smokejumpers in 1949, is also in this area. Details: Gates of the Mountains Boat Tours, 16 miles north of Helena off I-15; (406) 458-5241; open daily Memorial Day weekend through September 21, call ahead for departure times. Fares: $7.50 adults, $6.50 seniors, $4.50 children ages 4 to 17. (3 hours)

★★ **Last Chance Gulch Tour**—Conducted in an open-air tour train, this tour offers an excellent one-hour overview of Helena sites and history. Departing from the Montana Historical Society, the train breezes by the Old Fire Tower, Last Chance Gulch, Reeder's Alley, historic homes, St. Helena Cathedral, the state capitol, and old and new governors' homes. Details: Sixth and Roberts Streets; (406) 442-1023; open daily June 1 through Labor Day hourly tours from 9 a.m. to 6 p.m.; May 15 to May 31 and Labor Day to September 30 four daily tours. Fares: $4.50 adults, $4 seniors and $3.50 children. (1 hour)

★★ **Montana Historical Society**—Across the street from the state capitol, this museum is widely considered Montana's finest—and it certainly is, as far as "things Montana" go. In addition to its changing exhibits, the museum also encompasses the **Mackay Gallery of Charles M. Russell Art, Montana Homeland Exhibit**, and the **Library and Photo Archives**. The Last Chance Gulch Tour departs from the museum (see above). Details: 225 North Roberts Street; (406) 444-2694; open Memorial Day to Labor Day Monday through Friday and weekends 8 a.m. to 6 p.m; during winter open 8 a.m. to 5 p.m. weekdays, 9 a.m. to 5 p.m. weekends. Free, but patrons are encouraged to join the Montana Historical Society. (1 hour)

★★ **State Capitol**—Built of Montana sandstone and granite, Montana's impressive capitol looks north over Helena. The dome is Butte copper, topped by a *Goddess of Liberty* statue. Inside are terrazzo tile floors and Charles M. Russell's largest painting, *Lewis and Clark Meeting the Flathead Indians at Ross' Hole*, as well as six paintings by fellow Montana artist Edgar S. Paxson. Details: Sixth and Montana Streets; (406) 444-4789; June through Labor Day guided tours depart on the hour Monday through Saturday 10 a.m. to 4 p.m., Sunday 11 a.m. to 3 p.m., by appointment the rest of the year. The building is open to the public 8 a.m. to 5 p.m. for self-guided touring; pick up a map at the information desk. Free. (30 minutes)

★★ **St. Helena Cathedral**—Visitors who expect to see nothing but Old West stuff in the region will be awestruck by this stunningly beautiful neo-Gothic cathedral in the middle of Montana. Modeled after the Votive Church of Vienna, Austria, the 1924 cathedral contains stained glass windows made in Munich. Details: Lawrence and Warren Streets; (406) 442-5825; open Monday through Friday 10 a.m. to 4 p.m., Saturday 10 a.m. to 6:30 p.m., Sunday 7 a.m. to noon. (30 minutes)

★ **Archie Bray Foundation**—This interesting complex located outside of Helena serves as a studio, workshop, classroom, and gallery for ceramic artists. The Bray family founded this site in a 100-year-old brickyard. Artists-in-residence produce unique works for sale, and visitors can tour the gallery and facilities. Details: 2915 Country Club Avenue; (406) 443-3502; open Monday through Saturday 10 a.m. to 5 p.m., Sunday 1 p.m. to 5 p.m. Free. (1 hour)

★ **Original Governor's Mansion**—Managed by the Montana Historical Society, this refurbished 20-room mansion housed nine Montana governors from 1913 to 1959. Details: 304 North Ewing

Street; (406) 444-2694; open year-round for hourly tours 9 a.m. to
5 p.m. Free. (1 hour)

★ **Reeder's Alley**—This restored collection of quaint shops and
restaurants was once one-room apartments built for itinerant workers
in 1880s boom-town Helena. The narrow alleyway and closely spaced
brick buildings comprise the town's most complete remaining block
from this era. Details: Last Chance Gulch Tours; (406) 442-1023.
Free. (1 hour)

Holter Museum of Art—The artwork at this museum ranges from
historical to modern to contemporary, with one-person and group
exhibits, plus nationally juried shows and retrospectives. The museum
also houses a permanent collection of regional art. Details: 12 East
Lawrence Street; (406) 442-6400; open June through August Tuesday
through Friday 10 a.m. to 5 p.m., Sunday noon to 5 p.m.; September
through May Tuesday through Friday 11:30 a.m. to 5 p.m., weekends
noon to 5 p.m. Free. (30 minutes)

FITNESS AND RECREATION

As described earlier in the chapter, the Helena area offers a wealth of
hiking and walking opportunities, including the hiking trails on **Mount
Helena** and the downtown walks past historic buildings and homes.
Information on both can be obtained at the Helena Area Chamber of
Commerce, 201 East Lyndale Avenue, (406) 442-4120. If you're looking for more vigorous hiking (in fact, if you feel like walking 300 miles
north to Canada), you can hop on the **Continental Divide National
Scenic Trail** west of Helena. The trail follows the spine of the Rockies
to Canada. For maps and information, contact the Forest Supervisor,
Helena National Forest, 2880 Skyway Drive, Helena, MT 59601, (406)
449-5201. **Montana ECO Treks & Tours**, P.O. Box 511, Helena,
MT 59601, (406) 442-0214 or (800) 285-8480, offers one- or two-day
outdoor treks and two- or three-week wilderness adventures, including
Watchable Wildlife Tours, llama treks, horseback trips, river floats, and
mountain biking, beginning at $29.95 per person. Call for departure
times and details. Helena contains three golf courses (state capitals
equal lobbyists equal golf courses), the **Bill Roberts Municipal Golf
Course**, (406) 442-2191; **Fox Ridge**, (406) 227-8304; and the **Green
Meadow Country Club**, (406) 442-1420.

FOOD

Just as state capitals equal lobbyists and golf courses, they also often offer excellent lunch and dinner places. Helena is no exception, and restaurant options and varieties belie its size. The **Stonehouse Restaurant**, 120 Reeder's Alley, (406) 449-2552, open for lunch and dinner, boasts good steaks in a wonderful location. The **Windbag Saloon**, 19 South Last Chance Gulch, (406) 443-9669, is open for lunch and dinner. Nodding to the nature of government with its name and logo, it serves big burgers and sandwiches. **Victor's**, 22 North Last Chance Gulch in the Park Plaza, (406) 443-2200, open for all meals, offers patio seating and an interesting menu. **Bert and Ernies Last Chance Saloon and Delicatessen**, Last Chance Gulch, (406) 443-5680, is a Montana staple featuring good burgers, sandwiches, and salads.

Helena's brand-new microbrewery is the **Brewhouse Pub and Grill**, 939 Getchell, (406) 457-9390, and it's outstanding—better-than-average pub grub and excellent beer. I recommend the sausage sampler and the Black Forest ham & swiss, chased down with a pint or two of bitter. The **Jade Garden**, 3128 North Montana Avenue, (406) 443-8899, is a highly recommended Chinese restaurant. The **Pasta Pantry**, 1220 11th Avenue, (406) 442-1074, is a commendable Italian restaurant specializing in fresh pasta and great sauces. Fine Northern Italian cuisine can be found at **On Broadway**, 106 Broadway, (406) 443-1929. Darned good!

LODGING

The **Best Western Colonial Park Inn**, 2301 Colonial Drive, (406) 443-2100, is the "unofficial" Montana capitol during the legislative session as well as Helena's largest (149 rooms) property. Located on "hotel row" on the edge of town, "The Colonial" is the place to see and be seen in Helena. Rooms range from $64 to $84. The **Park Plaza Inn**, 22 North Last Chance Gulch, (406) 443-2200, has the advantage of its downtown location as well as a good restaurant (Victor's) and rooms from $60 to $78. **Jorgenson's Holiday Motel**, 1714 11th Avenue, (406) 442-1770, remains popular, despite its early-'60s decor, for its large rooms and diner-style restaurant. Rooms are $45 to $95. The **Holiday Inn Express Hotel**, 701 Washington, (406) 449-4000, has $59 to $64 rooms.

HELENA

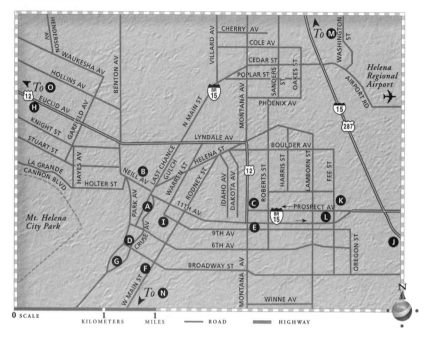

Food

- **A** Bert and Ernies Last Chance Saloon and Delicatessen
- **B** Brewhouse Pub and Grill
- **C** Jade Garden
- **D** On Broadway
- **E** Pasta Pantry
- **F** Stonehouse Restaurant
- **A** Victor's
- **G** Windbag Saloon

Lodging

- **H** Appleton Inn B&B

Lodging (continued)

- **I** Barrister B&B
- **J** Best Western Colonial Park Inn
- **K** Holiday Inn Express Hotel
- **L** Jorgenson's Holiday Motel
- **A** Park Plaza Inn
- **I** Sanders Bed and Breakfast

Camping

- **M** Helena Campground
- **N** Helena National Forest
- **O** Kim's Marina & RV Park

Note: Items with the same letter are located in the same town or area.

Helena's got several outstanding bed and breakfasts, starting with the **Sanders Bed and Breakfast**, 328 North Ewing, (406) 442-3309, a seven-room 1875 Victorian mansion a block from the original Governor's Mansion. Rooms are $70 to $98. The **Appleton Inn B&B**, 1999 Euclid Avenue, (406) 449-7492, is excellent as well, with six rooms ($60 to $85) in a beautifully restored 1890 home. The **Barrister B&B**, 416 North Ewing, (406) 443-7330, is an 1874 Victorian home with five rooms ranging from $75 to $105.

CAMPING

Kim's Marina & RV Park, on Highway 12E, 21 miles outside of Helena at Canyon Ferry, (406) 475-3723, has 100 sites. In a good location near the lake, its well-groomed sites offer plenty of amenities (baseball field, horseshoes, docks). Rates from $9 to $18 include hookups and some pull-throughs. **Helena Campground**, 5820 North Montana Avenue, (406) 458-4714, is a former KOA Kampground with hookups, some pull-throughs, a pool, and a playground just 4 miles north of town. Rates are $13 to $17. Plenty of campgrounds are available in the **Helena National Forest**, as close as 10 miles from town, for free or nominal fees. For more information, contact the NFS at (406) 449-5490.

NIGHTLIFE

Actress Myrna Loy was from the Helena area. The classy **Myrna Loy Center**, downtown at 15 North Ewing, (406) 443-0287, is a nonprofit arts organization offering American and foreign films in its theater (or for rent), plus Broadway shows; classical, jazz, folk, and blues performances; Myrna Loy historic photos and memorabilia; and more. Call to find out what's on. The **Grandstreet Theater**, 325 North Park Avenue, (406) 442-4270, features live dramatic and musical performances by local college and community theater groups. Call for a schedule and prices. After the performance, hit the new **Brewhouse Pub and Grill**, 939 Getchell, (406) 457-9390, for a refreshing microbrewed beverage and a snack.

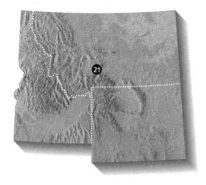

21
BOZEMAN

When John Bozeman and his wagon train fought their way north through Wyoming in 1846, encountering the Sioux and Blackfoot Indians, who detested him (and later killed him), he probably would have had a hard time imagining the attractive, prosperous community that would later bear his name. However, there could be no doubt, even then, that the Gallatin Valley was a special place—lush, green, and surrounded by towering mountains.

Although smaller in population, Bozeman rivals Missoula as the coolest city in Montana. Montana State University and its 10,000 students provide the cutting-edge feel for this town of 30,000 people, and the surrounding land and water provide its soul. The celebrities who've moved in have added some uncomfortable glitz to Bozeman and the Paradise Valley but confirm what a wonderful place it is.

For fly fishers there is probably no better base. Trout-filled blue-ribbon fisheries like the Madison, Yellowstone, and Gallatin Rivers course through the area (*A River Runs Through It* was filmed here). Recreation is year-round, with fishing, hiking, biking, camping, trekking, and horseback riding in summer and excellent downhill skiing at two fine resorts in winter. The influx of new residents to the area in recent years has altered the laid-back culture to some degree, but the last couple of hard winters have driven the worst of them back home. ◼

BOZEMAN

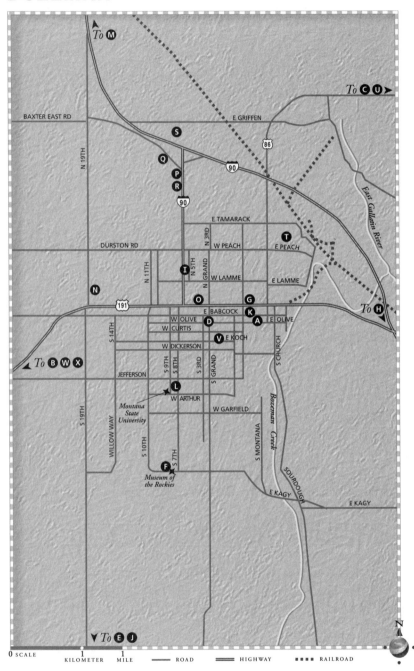

To ⓜ

To ⓒⓤ ►

BAXTER EAST RD

E GRIFFEN

N 19TH

Ⓢ

Ⓠ

Ⓟ

Ⓡ

86

90

90

East Gallatin River

E TAMARACK

N 3RD

DURSTON RD

W PEACH

E PEACH

Ⓣ

N 11TH

N 5TH

N GRAND

Ⓘ

W LAMME

E LAMME

Ⓝ

191

Ⓞ

E BABCOCK

Ⓖ

Ⓚ

To Ⓗ

W OLIVE

Ⓓ

E OLIVE

Ⓐ

S 14TH

W CURTIS

W DICKERSON

Ⓥ

E KOCH

S CHURCH

To Ⓑ Ⓦ Ⓧ

JEFFERSON

S 9TH

S 8TH

S 3RD

S GRAND

Bozeman Creek

Ⓛ

S 19TH

Montana
State
University

W ARTHUR

W GARFIELD

S MONTANA

WILLOW WAY

S 10TH

S 7TH

Ⓕ

Museum of
the Rockies

E KAGY

SOURDOUGH

E KAGY

N

▼ To Ⓔ Ⓙ

0 SCALE   1   1
   KILOMETER MILE   ━━ ROAD   ═══ HIGHWAY   ▪▪▪▪ RAILROAD

Sights

- **A** American Computer Museum
- **B** Big Sky
- **C** Bozeman Fish Technology Center
- **D** Emerson Cultural Center
- **E** Hyalite Canyon and Gallatin Canyon
- **F** Museum of the Rockies

Food

- **G** Bacchus Pub
- **H** Chico Hot Springs
- **I** Frontier Pies Restaurant and Bakery
- **J** Gallatin Gateway Inn
- **K** John Bozeman's Bistro
- **L** Pickle Barrel
- **M** Sir Scott's Oasis
- **N** Spanish Peaks Brewery
- **O** Western Café

Lodging

- **P** Best Western Grantree Inn
- **B** Best Western Buck's T-4 Lodge
- **Q** Bozeman Holiday Inn
- **R** Days Inn
- **S** Fairfield Inn by Marriott
- **J** Gallatin Gateway Inn
- **T** Lehrkind Mansion Bed and Breakfast
- **U** Silver Forest Inn
- **V** Voss Inn Bed and Breakfast

Camping

- **W** Bozeman Hot Springs KOA
- **X** Gallatin National Forest

Note: Items with the same letter are located in the same town or area.

A PERFECT DAY IN BOZEMAN

It's morning on the Yellowstone River, and you're fishing from a drift boat. Mountains dominate the horizon in all directions, and the only sound is the quiet kiss of the oars in the water. The guide has seen a huge brown trout rise, and he noses the boat across the current. This is more like hunting than fishing because you're stalking the fish. You cast and place the dry-fly upstream, letting the current take it into the pool. BOOM!—*the big fish takes it.* You eventually win the fight and hold the big colorful fish in the water, feeling his power. Then you let him go.

SIGHTSEEING HIGHLIGHTS

★★★ **Big Sky**—In 1969 then–NBC news anchor Chet Huntley and a group of investors bought what is now known as Big Sky Ski and Summer Resort in Gallatin Canyon. In the last decade the resort has really come into its own, attracting international attention for its summer and (especially) winter activities. Big Sky and the Gallatin Canyon are surrounded by more than 3 million acres of wilderness, including the Spanish Peaks Wilderness Area and Yellowstone National Park. Several mountain peaks exceed 11,000 feet. In summer, Big Sky is a base for golfers, who tee off at the 18-hole Arnold Palmer course. White-water enthusiasts enjoy rafting on the Gallatin River. Big Sky is 48 miles from Bozeman. Details: P.O. Box 160001, Big Sky, MT 59716; (800) 548-4486. (3 hours)

★★★ **Museum of the Rockies**—This Montana State University campus museum houses a planetarium, an ethnology center, and a history section, but those aren't the main reasons people visit. The real reason is dinosaurs. Museum paleontologist Jack Horner served as the model for the dinosaur hunters in the book *Jurassic Park*, and he heads a scientific movement that's redefining our understanding of how dinosaurs moved, lived, and looked. Displays include a T-Rex skull and dinosaur eggs unearthed in Montana. Details: South Seventh and Kagy Boulevard, Montana State University; (406) 994-2251; open Memorial Day through Labor Day daily 8 a.m. to 8 p.m., May through September Monday through Saturday 9 a.m. to 5 p.m., Sunday 12:30 p.m. to 5 p.m. Admission: $6 adults, $4 children ages 5 to 18. (2 hours)

★★ **Hyalite Canyon and Gallatin Canyon**—Located south of Bozeman, the 34,000-acre area includes summer and winter recreation opportunities, in such places as Hyalite Reservoir, Palisades Falls, Grotto Falls Trail, Window Rock Cabin, Blackmore Recreation Area, and Langhor Campground. Details: 7 miles from Bozeman on South 19th Avenue; contact the Gallatin National Forest for brochures and trail maps, (406) 587-6752. (3 hours)

★★ **Paradise Valley**—The Yellowstone River pours out of Yellowstone Park to Livingston through the Paradise Valley—one of the most scenic big-mountain valleys in the area. The Paradise Valley has several noteworthy attractions, like **Chico Hot Springs**. But the biggest draw is simply the view of the rolling foothills leading up to towering mountains on both sides of the highway. Although ranching still exists, the valley is now known primarily as a place where celebrities, including Randy Quaid and Meg Ryan, Peter Fonda, Tom Brokaw, and Ted Turner and Jane Fonda, have chosen to reside. Credit the state of Montana for easy fishing access to the Yellowstone throughout the

© Donnie Sexton/Travel Montana

Paradise Valley

valley. Details: 80 miles south of Livingston on U.S. Highway 85; (406) 333-4933. (2 hours)

★ **American Computer Museum**—Not every museum in the region is solely dedicated to Western history. This 6,000-square-foot facility traces the history of the computer from the abacus to the microchip. It was the 1994 winner of the Dibner Award for Excellence in Exhibits of History of Technology and Culture. Details: 234 East Babcock Street; (406) 587-7545; open daily June through August 10 a.m. to 4 p.m., September through May Tuesday, Wednesday, Friday, and Saturday noon to 4 p.m. Admission: $3 adults, $2 children. (1 hour)

★ **Bozeman Fish Technology Center**—On a tour of this center visitors see researchers studying fish culture and habitat, fish diseases, reproduction, fish-fed development and testing, broodstock diet testing, and fishery management. Center scientists help recover fish in waters nationwide and provide technical assistance to federal and state fisheries agencies. Call ahead for a tour. Details: 4050 Bridger Canyon Drive; (406) 587-9265; open daily 8 a.m. to 4 p.m. Free. (1 hour)

★ **Emerson Cultural Center**—Located in a school building listed on the National Register of Historic Places, the Emerson Center is dedicated to promoting artistic and cultural development in the community. The building includes galleries, artists' studios, and performance groups, and visitors can view and purchase local artwork and crafts. Performances vary; call for information. Details: 111 South Grand Avenue and Beall Art Center; (406) 587-9797; open Tuesday through Saturday 10 a.m. to 5:30 p.m. Free. (30 minutes)

★ **Livingston Depot Center**—This restored Northern Pacific train depot includes regional history and art exhibits on such subjects as Western history, railroad history, and art. This was the station used by early visitors to Yellowstone Park, and it's interesting to see the lavishly decorated depot exactly as they saw it. Details: 200 West Park, Livingston; (406) 222-2300; open mid-May through mid-October Monday through Saturday 9 a.m. to 5 p.m., Sunday 1 p.m. to 5 p.m. Admission: $3 adults, $2 children, $8 families. (30 minutes)

Park County Museum—Housed in a former school, this museum focuses on the history of the county, with pioneer displays, old automobiles and fire engines, and a restored home. Details: 118 West Chinook, Livingston; (406) 222-4184; open daily June 1 through Labor Day noon to 5 p.m. and 7 p.m. to 9 p.m. Admission: $3 adults, $2 children. (30 minutes)

FITNESS AND RECREATION

As I've indicated, Bozeman is a great place to fly fish. I recommend a guided float, even if you're an expert. Dave Kumlien of **Montana Troutfitters**, 1716 West Main Street, (406) 587-4707 or (800) 64-ORVIS, is an excellent outfitter offering expert instruction and guide service on several local rivers. In Livingston, visit **Dan Bailey's Fly Shop** for tackle, guide service, and tips on what's working where. For a fly fisher, Dan Bailey's is a dream come true.

Golfers can enjoy three public 18-hole courses in the vicinity, including **Big Sky Resort Golf Course**, Big Sky, (406) 995-4706; **Cottonwood Hills Golf Course**, River Road, Bozeman, (406) 587-1118; and **Bridger Creek Golf Course**, 2500 Springhill Road, Bozeman, (406) 586-2333.

The **Gallatin National Forest** offers dozens of great trails within easy access of Bozeman, including Bridger Foothills National Recreation Trail (20.8 miles), Fairly Lake Campground and Sacagawea Peak Trail (2 miles), Hidden Lake Trail (3 miles), Golden Trout Lakes Trail (2.5 miles), Garnet Mountain Lookout Trail (4 miles), History Rock Trail (1.2 miles), Palisades Falls National Recreation Trail (.6 mile), and Hyalite Peak Trail (7.2 miles). For trail maps and details, contact the Bozeman Ranger District of the Gallatin National Forest, 3710 Fallon Street, Bozeman, (406) 587-9784.

White-water rafting is available on both the Madison and Gallatin Rivers. I recommend riding the Gallatin with **Yellowstone Raft Company**, Big Sky, (406) 995-4613, which features half-day trips and full-day rafting, and guided fishing trips.

WINTER IN BOZEMAN

Downhill skiers will find Bozeman an excellent base for world-class and specialty skiing. **Big Sky Ski and Summer Resort**, (800) 548-4486, is considered an up-and-comer, launched into the big time by the recent completion of Lone Peak Tram, which carries skiers to the 11,150-foot Lone Mountain Peak. The tram opened up 1,200 additional acres of terrain in addition to the 2,300 acres already in place. Big Sky averages 400 inches of powder snow per year. Lift tickets are $46 for a full-day pass; they drop with multiday packages.

Only 16 miles away, **Bridger Bowl Ski Area**, 15795 Bridger Canyon Road, (800) 223-9609, is owned by the city of Bozeman and is immensely popular with locals for its easy access, cheap lift tickets, and incredible bowl and chute skiing. Bridger features 1,200 acres of terrain and a comfortable, real-people atmosphere. Because Bozeman is a genuine town and not an ersatz resort, skiers can access Big Sky and Bridger while staying in town at reasonable rates. There may not be a better ski bargain around. Bridger lift rates are $28 for a full-day pass; multiday packages are also a bargain.

Bozeman offers six excellent cross-country ski trails, including **Lindley Trail** and **East Gallatin Park** within the city limits, and nearby **Bozeman Creek to Mystic Lake** (10 miles), **New World Gulch to Mystic Lake** (5½ miles), **Hyalite Ski Loop** (14 miles), and **Hyalite Reservoir Ski Loop** (4 miles). For trail maps and information, contact the Bozeman Chamber of Commerce, (406) 586-5421 or (800) 228-4224. **Lone Mountain Guest Ranch** (see below) is perhaps the only one in the Rockies that caters almost exclusively to cross-country skiers. The ranch provides 65 kilometers of groomed trails, with terrain for every level of skier. **Bohart Ranch**, Highway 86, 16.6 miles northeast of Bozeman, (406) 586-9070, also offers a complete slate of cross-country skiing throughout the winter.

FOOD

Bozeman is a great place to eat. For breakfast, do the **Western Café**, 443 East Main Street, (406) 587-0436, for massive pancakes or biscuits and gravy in a loud, local, crowded environment. **Spanish Peaks Brewery**, 120 North 19th, (406) 585-2296, is my favorite local venue for drinking beer and eating interesting Italian food. Black Dog Ale, the specialty micro brand from Spanish Peaks, is, in my humble opinion, *the best beer* brewed in Wyoming, Montana, and Idaho. The **Pickle Barrel**, 809 West College, (406) 587-2411, is considered by many the best sandwich shop in town. Pickles come with every order. The **Gallatin Gateway Inn**, Highway 1919 South, (406) 763-4672, is a true fine dining experience—elegant food and wine served in a beautifully restored depot. The **Bacchus Pub**, 105 East Main Street, (406) 586-1314, is popular not only for its burgers, but also for its location in the

LIVINGSTON

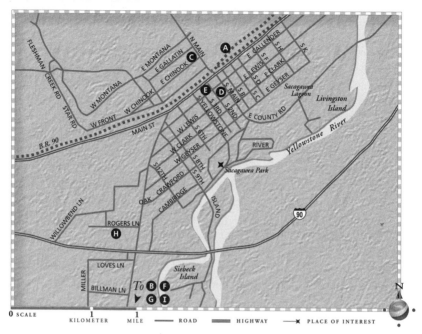

Sights

- Ⓐ Livingston Depot Center
- Ⓑ Paradise Valley
- Ⓒ Park County Museum

Food

- Ⓓ The Sport
- Ⓔ Winchester Café

Lodging

- Ⓕ Chico Hot Springs Lodge and Resort
- Ⓖ Mountain Sky Guest Ranch
- Ⓔ Murray Hotel

Camping

- Ⓗ Paradise Livingston Campground
- Ⓘ Paradise Valley KOA

Note: Items with the same letter are located in the same town or area.

old Baxter Hotel lobby. **Frontier Pies Restaurant and Bakery**, 302 North Seventh Avenue, (406) 586-5555, specializes in hearty, family-style cooking, including 29 different pies. **John Bozeman's Bistro**, 242 East Main Street, (406) 587-4100, has good homemade breads and soups and is not shy about delivering quantities of each.

The **Winchester Café**, 201 West Park Street, in Livingston's Murray Hotel, (406) 222-1350, is an excellent choice for food and atmosphere, serving terrific lamb, trout, and beef. **The Sport**, 114 South Main, Livingston, (406) 222-3533, is a great burger place with a wall full of trophies and cold beer. In our endless search for even bigger slabs of meat, add **Sir Scott's Oasis**, in Manhattan (15 miles west of Bozeman across the tracks), for truly mind-boggling steaks served in a wonderfully tacky steakhouse with sassy waitresses and pool tables in the back. **Chico Hot Springs**, in Pray, (406) 333-4933, is good for everything, and that includes excellent dining. Folks will travel hours—and some even fly in on the private airstrip—just for dinner. The buffalo steak and black bean soup are to die for.

LODGING

Most visitors passing through Bozeman stay at one of the larger chain properties (good rates and inclusive amenities, including airport shuttles) located at I-90 Exit 306. These include the **Best Western Grantree Inn**, 1325 North Seventh, (406) 587-5261, with singles' rates from $56 to $78; the **Bozeman Holiday Inn**, 5 Baxter Lane, (406) 587-4561, with $59 to $87 rates; the **Days Inn**, 1321 North Seventh Avenue, (406) 587-5251, $45 to $62; or the **Fairfield Inn by Marriott**, 828 Wheat Drive, (406) 587-2222, $44 to $65.

The **Gallatin Gateway Inn**, Highway 1919, 15 miles from Bozeman, (406) 763-4672, is a magnificently restored historic railroad hotel with high ceilings, a terrific restaurant, and landscaped grounds. Rooms are cozy but well-appointed, at $60 to $85. The **Silver Forest Inn**, 15325 Bridger Canyon Road, (406) 586-1882, is located near Bridger Bowl and features a comfortable log-cabin atmosphere at $55 to $85 per night. The **Voss Inn Bed and Breakfast**, 319 South Willson, (406) 587-0982, sits on a quiet wooded side street in residential Bozeman. As with the best bed-and-breakfasts, the owners and their unbridled hospitality make every stay a pleasant experience. The **Lehrkind Mansion Bed and Breakfast**, 719 North Wallace Avenue, Bozeman, (406) 585-6932, is a fully restored Victorian mansion listed on the National Register of Historic Places. Its four rooms range from $65 to $155.

With apologies to the many nice properties within the village of Big Sky, the **Best Western Buck's T-4**, 46625 Gallatin Road, (406) 995-4111, is *the* place to stay in Big Sky. Located just off the highway, Buck's has atmosphere, food, and rates that make you feel good ($62 to $87 per single depending on the season). In Livingston, the **Murray Hotel**, 201 West Park Street, (406) 222-1350, across from the depot, has become legendary for the characters who have stayed there. Among them is eccentric film director Sam Peckinpah, who is blamed for the bullet holes in the ceiling. Rates are reasonable, from $49 to $150 per night.

Chico Hot Springs Lodge and Resort, in Pray, (406) 333-4933, is a very special part of the Paradise Valley, with natural mineral pools, fine dining, horse activities, an excellent restaurant, and a variety of accommodations. The telephone number alone, (800) HOT-WADA, suggests the funky attitude of the place, and owner Mike Art somehow balances cowboy funk with hospitality, history, and celebrity (the last time I was there Dennis Quaid and his son were playing checkers in the lobby). The accommodations in the new addition are excellent, but the rooms in the main lodge and behind the barn are small and spare.

The **Mountain Sky Guest Ranch**, Big Creek Road, Emigrant, (406) 333-4911, is an excellent, extremely well-run, full-fledged dude ranch resort in the summer months, with seven-day stays costing upwards of $2,000 per person. If that's out of reach, consider daily rates (with a three-night minimum) prior to and after the summer rush.

CAMPING

The Bozeman Ranger District of the **Gallatin National Forest** maintains 12 public campgrounds, ranging from 68-site Red Cliff to three-site Spanish Creek. Fees range from free to $8. For a complete listing and map, contact the Bozeman Ranger District, 3710 Fallon, Box C, Bozeman, MT 59715, (406) 587-6920.

The **Bozeman Hot Springs KOA**, 81123 Gallatin Road, (406) 587-3030, offers 145 sites in a shaded location with a hot spring (admission charged) and a "stream running through it" for $14 to $18 per night. The **Paradise Livingston Campground**, Rogers Lane, Livingston, (406) 222-1122, has 32 sites with hookups and $14 rates.

The **Paradise Valley KOA**, 163 Pine Creek Road, Livingston, (406) 222-0992, has 78 sites in an 11-acre wooded location with hookups for $14 per night.

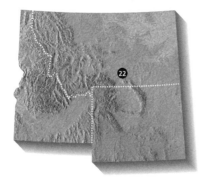

22
BILLINGS

Billings is the second largest city (population 110,000) in the tri-state region, behind Boise. It bridges green and mountainous western Montana and stark and rural eastern Montana. Growing up in Wyoming, I thought Billings was bigger than Denver or Salt Lake City because its reach extends far beyond the city limits or state line. Billings is the banking, service, cattle shipping, and retail center not only for Montana, but also for much of Wyoming, western North Dakota, and northwestern South Dakota. To hear western Montanans talk about it (often in disparaging terms), you realize that the city *needs* the support it gets from the rest of the region. Billings has, by necessity, developed a thick skin.

Nestled into the Yellowstone River Valley north of the Crow Indian Reservation and shielded by the steep Rimrocks, Billings was established in 1882 with the founding of the Northern Pacific Railroad. It was boosted several years later when the Chicago, Burlington, and Quincy Railroads arrived, soon afterward becoming the regional shipping center for cattle and other agricultural products. Today Billings boasts an interesting downtown, a busy airport, a 12,000-seat events center, and a vibrant economy and nightlife. It doesn't take very long to realize that it's a fun, boisterous place—a little cowtown that has become a big cowtown and is darned proud of it. ∎

BILLINGS

To C H

To C

COBURN RD

MONTANA AV

River

Yellowstone

87

A

N 10TH ST

3RD AV N

1ST AV N

S 25TH ST

S 28TH ST

N 23RD ST

S 31ST ST

RIVERSIDE RD

N 25TH ST

S 35TH ST

J

K

N 28TH ST

KING AV E

N 31ST ST

D

N 32ND ST

212

ORCHARD LN

MOUNTAIN VIEW RD

5TH ST W

3

F

PARKHILL DR

90

B

To

BILLINGS BLVD

MOORE LN

CENTRAL AV

RIMROCK RD

15TH ST W

18TH ST W

MONAD RD

GRAND AV

To L

To E I

To

N

Sights

- **Ⓐ** Black Otter Trail and Boot Hill Cemetery
- **Ⓑ** Chief Plenty Coups State Park
- **Ⓒ** Little Bighorn Battlefield National Monument
- **Ⓓ** Moss Mansion
- **Ⓔ** Oscar's Dreamland
- **Ⓕ** Peter Yegan Jr. Yellowstone County Museum
- **Ⓖ** Pictograph Cave State Park
- **Ⓗ** Pompeys Pillar
- **Ⓘ** Red Lodge
- **Ⓙ** Western Heritage Center
- **Ⓚ** Yellowstone Art Center
- **Ⓛ** ZooMontana

A PERFECT DAY IN BILLINGS

After a ranch breakfast at the Radisson Northern Hotel among area businessmen and cattle buyers, drive I-25 South to experience the Little Bighorn Battlefield National Monument, where Custer was whipped by Chief Sitting Bull and Crazy Horse. Order an Indian taco and meet Pug and his Crow Indian staff at the Custer Battlefield Trading Post and Café adjacent to the monument entrance. Return and tour the Moss Mansion in the Pictograph Cave State Park as the sun sets among the Rimrocks. Finish the evening with a big steak at the Rex, followed by hot blues at Casey's Golden Pheasant.

SIGHTSEEING HIGHLIGHTS

★★★ **Little Bighorn Battlefield National Monument**—In 1876, a strutting Lt. Col. George Armstrong Custer (he wasn't officially a general) led an ill-advised charge against the largest American Indian encampment of Lakota Sioux and Cheyenne ever gathered. He was obliterated, losing 260 Seventh Cavalry men in the process. It was the Indians' greatest victory, but Chief Sitting Bull and Crazy Horse soon realized that it would be the last.

The battle still rages on the Little Bighorn River, only now it's a battle over political correctness, among traditionalists who view Custer as a flawed hero, American Indian and other activists who consider the site a monument to the folly of western expansion, and historians trying to define what really happened. The site lies within the Crow Indian Reservation. The battlefield and cemetery have been managed by the National Park Service since 1940, and rangers are on duty year-round to help visitors understand and interpret. I strongly recommend touring the site with former park superintendent Jim Court of Custer Battlefield Tours, 416 North Cody Avenue, Hardin, (406) 665-1580 or (800) 331-1580. Details: P.O. Box 39, Crow Agency, MT 59022; (406) 638-2621; open summer 8 a.m. to 8 p.m., and winter 8 a.m. to 4:30 p.m. Admission: $4 per vehicle. (1–3 hours)

★★★ **Red Lodge**—Red Lodge deserves its own section for pure charm alone. Nestled in the foothills of the Beartooth Mountains, this alpine town boasts a high-quality ski area at Red Lodge Mountain, with a 2,016-foot vertical drop and bargain $24 lift tickets. This resort and ranching community of 2,000 has a colorful coal-mining past and a quaint, historic downtown. At one time, "Liver Eatin'" Jeremiah Johnson was the town sheriff. In summer, Red Lodge is the jumping-off point for the **Beartooth Highway**, which runs to Cooke City and the northeast gate of Yellowstone Park. This route has been called "the most scenic highway in America" by Charles Kuralt, and it rivals anything in the Rockies for spectacular mountain vistas—Beartooth Pass has an elevation of nearly 11,000 feet—and unpredictable weather. The highway is closed in winter, which can come as early as mid-October. Details: Red Lodge lies 60 miles southwest of Billings on U.S. 212. For more information, contact the Red Lodge Chamber of Commerce, Box 998, Red Lodge, MT 59068; (406) 446-1718. (4 hours)

★★ **Pictograph Cave State Park**—Located 3 miles from Billings in the sandstone outcroppings of the Bitter Creek Valley, this state park preserves the remains of a 5,000-year-old prehistoric culture. Ancient paintings found on the back walls are remarkably well-preserved, despite inevitable vandalism by spray-paint goons. Interestingly, the spray paint has faded, but the original artwork hasn't. Details: 2300 Lake Elmo Drive, Lockwood; (406) 247-2940; open April 15 through October 15 8 a.m. to 8 p.m. Admission: $3 per vehicle. (1 hour)

★ **Black Otter Trail and Boot Hill Cemetery**—The rugged entrance of the Rimrocks surrounding Billings has branded this area since time began. Chief Black Otter was a Crow war chief killed in a battle with the Sioux. His grave and that of Yellowstone Kelly, a famous Indian scout, trapper, and Governor of the Philippines (really), are two points of interest along the drive. Billings' history unfolds along this winding sandstone skyline. Beginning at U.S. 10, seven mountain ranges can be seen including Pryor, Big Horn, Bull, Snowy, Crazy, Absaroka, and Beartooth. (30 minutes)

★ **Chief Plenty Coups State Park**—The park is homesite of Chief Plenty Coups (1848–1932), who was the last chief of the Crow Tribe. Chief Plenty Coups led scouts under General Crook and was named to represent all of the Plains Indian nations (whether they wanted to be represented by him or not) in Washington, D.C. The Eastern press tagged him "Chief of Chiefs." After he willed his 1880s log home and property as a park for all people, the Chief Plenty Coups Museum was developed to archive Crow artifacts. The park is located 40 miles south of Billings at the base of the Pryor Mountains and Castle Rocks, which are considered sacred. Details: West of Pryor; (406) 252-1289; open daily May through September 8 a.m. to 8 p.m.; museum open 10 a.m. to 5 p.m. Admission: $3 per vehicle. (1 hour)

★ **Moss Mansion**—The mansion captures life around the turn of the century, when the Preston Boyd Moss family lived in this 1903 red sandstone structure. The mansion has been almost perfectly preserved, with loving details such as original draperies, fixtures, furniture, Persian carpets, wall coverings, and artifacts. Its architect was Henry Janeway Hardenbergh, who also designed the Waldorf-Astoria and Plaza Hotels in New York City. Details: 914 Division Street, Billings; (406) 256-5100; open June 15 to Labor Day Monday through Saturday 10 a.m. to 4 p.m., Sunday 1 p.m. to 3 p.m., rest of the year daily 1 p.m. to 3 p.m. Guided tours are available on the hour in the summer. Admission: $5 adults, $4 seniors, and $3 children. (1 hour)

★ **Pompeys Pillar**—Lewis and Clark named this Ayers Rock–like outcropping "Pompeys Pillar" after Sacajawea's baby, who was nicknamed "Pomp," or "little chief." The formation became a landmark along the Lewis and Clark Trail. Although the site might not interest all visitors, it is an important physical icon to Lewis and Clark scholars because it remains virtually unchanged from the days of the 1805 expedition. Details: 25 miles east of Billings off I-94; open June through September Monday through Friday 10:30 a.m. to 5 p.m., Sunday 2 p.m. to 5 p.m. Free. (30 minutes)

★ **Western Heritage Center**—Displays include a walk through the Yellowstone River Valley's infancy period. Places, people, and images of the valley from 1880 to 1940 are showcased in this interactive museum. Details: 2822 Montana Avenue, Billings; (406) 256-6809; open year-round Tuesday through Saturday 10 a.m. to 5 p.m., Sunday 1 p.m. to 5 p.m. Free. (30 minutes)

★ **Yellowstone Art Center**—The center reopened in the fall of 1997, doubling its space for more than 20 changing exhibitions of regional artists. "The Montana Collection" is a permanent exhibit featuring contemporary Western art. Details: 401 North 27th Street, Billings; (406) 356-6804; open Tuesday through Friday 11 a.m to 5 p.m., Saturday noon to 4 p.m. Free. (30 minutes)

Oscar's Dreamland—Billed as one of the largest collections of self-propelled farm machinery in the world, Oscar's has more than 500 steam and gasoline tractors. Details: Wise Lane, Billings; (406) 656-0966; open daily May through September 9 a.m. to 6 p.m. Admission: $5 adults, $1.50–$2.50 for children. (20 minutes)

Peter Yegan Jr. Yellowstone County Museum—This jumble of cowboy and Indian artifacts is located in a two-floor log building on the outskirts of the airport. Details: Logan International Airport, Billings; (406) 256-6811; open Monday through Friday 10:30 a.m. to 5 p.m., Sunday 2 p.m. to 5 p.m. Free. (1 hour)

ZooMontana—Located on 70 acres and still in progress, this is Montana's only zoo. Displays are dedicated to regional wildlife, botanical gardens, and such native and exotic animals as Siberian tigers and river otters. Details: 2100 South Shiloh Road, Billings; (406) 652-8100; open April 15 through October 15 10 a.m. to 5 p.m. Admission: $4 adult, $2 children. (1 hour)

FITNESS AND RECREATION

Trails for feet, hooves, and tires entwine Billings. **Riverfront Park** (South Billings Boulevard) features trails with views of the Yellowstone River. Fishing, camping, hiking, and biking are available in and around the city at **Lake Elmo State Park** in Billings Heights. Intrepid fly fishers will want to take the two-hour journey to the **Big**

Horn River, which, along with the Madison, Yellowstone, and Gallatin, is considered one of the top five fly-fishing trout rivers in the country. For information on the Big Horn River as well as **Rock Creek, Stillwater, Boulder, Musselshell**, and **Yellowstone Rivers**, contact the Montana Department of Fish, Wildlife, and Parks at (406) 252-4654.

Billings offers six public golf courses, including **Circle Inn Golf Links**, (406) 248-4201; **Lake Hills Golf Club**, (406) 252-9244; **Par 3 Exchange City Golf Course**, (406) 652-2553; **Peter Yegan Jr. Golf Club**, (406) 656-8099; **Briarwood**, (406) 248-2702; and **Pryor Creek**, (406) 256-0626.

In winter, **Red Lodge Mountain**, (800) 444-8977, features more than 30 downhill ski runs, 2,000-plus vertical feet, value lift tickets at $24, and a comfortable cowboy-town atmosphere.

FOOD

Billings is one of the better cities around for great big juicy steaks served with aplomb. This cattle shipping center keeps a few, and residents and visiting ranchers demand the best beef in large quantities. **The Rex**, 2401 Montana Avenue, Billings, (406) 245-7477, is located in Billing's old historic district and is beautifully renovated. You'll feel like a visiting rancher when the big steaks arrive. **Jakes of Billings**, First Avenue North, (406) 259-9375, serves big beef as well as lighter fare. It's a popular local date restaurant because the lounge is always hopping. The **Golden Belle Restaurant**, 19 North 28th Street, (406) 245-2232, is part of the Radisson Northern. Many a business deal has been conducted over the delicious lamb, seafood, and beef dishes. **George Henry's Restaurant**, 404 North 30th, (406) 245-2232, slings those big steaks in a renovated historic home.

Walkers Grill, 301 North 27th Street, (406) 245-9291, is well-known locally for fine pizza and Italian food. The **Montana Brewing Company Brew Pub**, 113 North Broadway, (406) 252-9200, serves good ales and pub food. Billboards for the **Great Wall of China Restaurant**, 13th and Grand Avenue, (406) 245-8601, say it's "the best Chinese Restaurant in Montana," and there are those who agree. **Miyajima Gardens**, 5364 Midland Road, (406) 245-8240, offers traditional Japanese cuisine (this might be the best Japanese restaurant in Montana), with brazier cooking and private tatami rooms.

BILLINGS

N

COBURN RD

MONTANA AV

87

90

Yellowstone River

N 10TH ST

D

3RD AV N

1ST AV N

S

T

G

I

S 25TH ST

S 28TH ST

N 23RD ST

Q

H

N

B

M

S 31ST ST

RIVERSIDE RD

N 25TH ST

F

S 35TH ST

N 28TH ST

A

K

212

KING AV E

N 31ST ST

N 32ND ST

MOUNTAIN VIEW RD

3

5TH ST W

ORCHARD LN

PARKHILL DR

90

R

BILLINGS BLVD

E

MOORE LN

CENTRAL AV

J

RIMROCK RD

C

15TH ST W

MONAD RD

GRAND AV

18TH ST W

To L

O

P

HIGHWAY

ROAD

0 SCALE

KILOMETER MILE

1

1

Food

Ⓐ George Henry's Restaurant

Ⓑ Golden Belle Restaurant

Ⓒ Great Wall of China
Restaurant

Ⓓ Jakes of Billings

Ⓔ Miyajima Gardens

Ⓕ Montana Brewing
Company Brew Pub

Ⓖ The Rex

Ⓗ Walkers Grill

Lodging

Ⓘ Best Western Ponderosa

Ⓙ Holiday Inn Billings Plaza

Lodging *(continued)*

Ⓚ Josephine Bed and Breakfast

Ⓛ Lonesome Spur Ranch

Ⓜ Pollard Hotel

Ⓝ Radisson Northern

Ⓞ Rock Creek Resort

Ⓟ Sanderson Inn
Bed and Breakfast

Ⓠ Sheraton Billings Hotel

Camping

Ⓡ Big Sky Campground

Ⓢ Billings Metro KOA

Ⓣ Garden Avenue RV Park
and Campground

LODGING

There are plenty of generally affordable places to stay in Billings. But since this is a convention town, call ahead to check availability. The historic **Radisson Northern**, 19 North 28th Street, (406) 245-5121 or (800) 333-3333, has changed in the past few decades but still resonates with the cowtown-boomtown. The Northern (as it's known locally, despite the more recent Radisson affiliation) has 160 rooms ranging from $80 to $95. Ask for one of the restored old rooms, and if you can, stay for Sunday brunch. The **Best Western Ponderosa**, 2511 First Avenue North, (406) 259-5511, is newly redecorated with spacious, affordable ($50 to $70) rooms. The **Holiday Inn Billings Plaza**, 5500 Midland Road, (406) 248-7701, is a massive 315-room convention hotel near the interstate with lots of amenities and $60 to $80 rooms. The **Sheraton Billings Hotel**, 27 North 27th Street, (406) 252-7020 or (800) 588-ROOM, with 282 rooms in a 23-story highrise, seems out of place but offers big $60 to $80 rooms and good service.

The **Josephine Bed and Breakfast**, 514 North 29th Street, (406) 248-5898, has a choice location near downtown, with rooms ranging from $50 to $60. The **Sanderson Inn Bed and Breakfast**, 2038 South 56th Street, (406) 656-3388, sits between Billings and Laurel, featuring three nice rooms ($40 to $60) and a resident herd of about 20 sheep.

In Red Lodge it's a tussle to decide whether to stay at the historic and well-appointed **Pollard Hotel**, 2 North Broadway, (406) 446-0001, for $75 to $175 per night, or the beautifully situated, log-constructed **Rock Creek Resort**, U.S. 212, (406) 446-1111, for $65 to $88 per night.

Although there are plenty of good guest and dude ranches around Billings, the **Lonesome Spur Ranch**, RR 1, Bridger, (406) 662-3460, is exceptional because of Darleen Schwinn's wonderful hospitality and the fact that it *really is* a working ranch that hosts a few guests. Stays can be a night or two or weeks on end, and you can help on the ranch if you wish.

CAMPING

KOA Kampgrounds' corporate headquarters are located in Billings, so yes, there are campgrounds here. The **Billings Metro KOA**, 547 Garden Avenue, (406) 252-3104, is a large 180-site facility on 47 acres near the river. It provides lots of activities and amenities, including a restaurant, for $14 to $20 per night, depending on the season. **Big Sky Campground**, 5516 Laurel Road, (406) 259-4110, has 99 sites on 7 acres, with hookups and pull-throughs, for $10 per night. Call for directions. **Garden Avenue RV Park and Campground**, 309 Garden Avenue, (406) 259-0878, offers 87 sites with hookups and pull-through sites for $19 per night, April through September.

NIGHTLIFE

Always a good sports town, the **Billings Mustangs** are a Pioneer League minor-league baseball club and part of the Cincinnati Reds farm team. They have a big local following and cool baseball caps. For a schedule of home games, contact the Billings Area Chamber CVB at (406) 245-4111 or (800) 711-2630. In the winter the minor-league **Billings Bulls** hockey club occupies the ice at MetraPark. For a schedule and ticket details, call (406) 256-2400.

The **Alberta Bair Theater**, Broadway and Third Avenue North, (406) 256-6052, hosts Broadway musicals, ballet, the **Billings**

Symphony, and celebrity musicians on tour. It's billed as the largest performing arts theater between Minneapolis and Spokane. Call for what's playing.

The Western, 2712 Minnesota Avenue, (406) 252-7383, is a full-fledged country honky-tonk that's a good place to find a date . . . or a fight. Billings has a surprisingly good local blues scene, which can be viewed in full plumage at **Casey's Golden Pheasant**, 109 North Broadway (enter through the alley), (406) 256-5200, over a cigarette and a pint of black-and-tan.

Scenic Route: Beartooth Highway

In the summer months, **Red Lodge** is the jumping-off point for the Beartooth Highway, or Highway 212, which runs through **Beartooth Pass** to **Cooke City** and the northeast gate of Yellowstone Park. The Beartooth Highway was called "the most scenic highway in America" by Charles Kuralt, and it rivals anything in the Rockies for spectacular mountain vistas—Beartooth Pass has an elevation of nearly 11,000 feet—and unpredictable weather. This 68-mile stretch of highway climbs **Rock Creek Canyon** and crosses the Wyoming border, reaching a 10,350-foot elevation at the twin summits. Several of the mountain vistas afforded from pullouts and parking areas are simply stunning; you feel literally on top of the world. Glaciers can be seen at any time of the year, and the snowpack is such that the U.S. Ski Team trains here in summer months. I once got into a snowball fight in late July. The highway is closed in winter, which can occur as early as mid-October. ◣

BEARTOOTH HIGHWAY

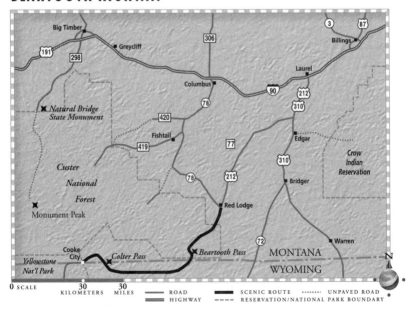

APPENDIX

METRIC CONVERSION CHART

1 U.S. gallon = approximately 4 liters
1 liter = about 1 quart
1 Canadian gallon = approximately 4.5 liters

1 pound = approximately $\frac{1}{2}$ kilogram
1 kilogram = about 2 pounds

1 foot = approximately $\frac{1}{3}$ meter
1 meter = about 1 yard
1 yard = a little less than a meter
1 mile = approximately 1.6 kilometers
1 kilometer = about $\frac{2}{3}$ mile

90°F = about 30°C
20°C = approximately 70°F

Planning Map: Montana, Wyoming & Idaho

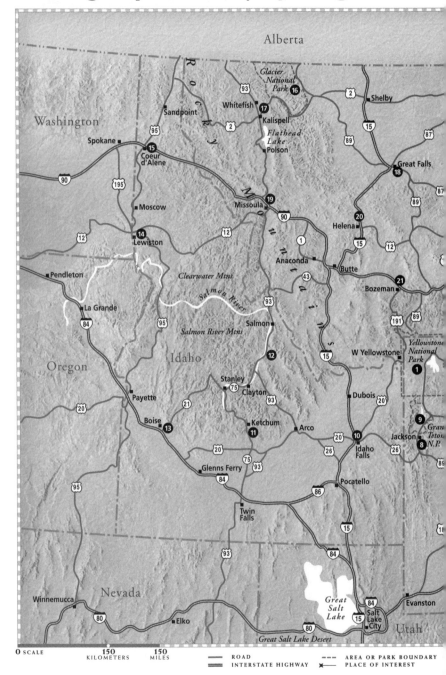

Alberta

Washington

Glacier National Park 16
Whitefish 17
Sandpoint
Kalispell
Shelby
Spokane
Coeur d'Alene
Flathead Lake
Polson
Great Falls 18
Moscow
Missoula 19
Helena 20
Lewiston 14
Anaconda
Butte
Pendleton
Clearwater Mtns
Bozeman 21
La Grande
Salmon River
Salmon
Salmon River Mtns
W Yellowstone
Yellowstone National Park 1
Oregon
Idaho
Stanley 75
Clayton
Payette
Boise 13
Ketchum 11
Arco
Dubois
Jackson
Gran Teton N.P. 9 8
Idaho Falls 10
Glenns Ferry
Pocatello
Twin Falls
Winnemucca
Nevada
Great Salt Lake
Salt Lake City
Evanston
Utah
Elko
Great Salt Lake Desert

O SCALE
150 KILOMETERS
150 MILES

ROAD
INTERSTATE HIGHWAY
AREA OR PARK BOUNDARY
PLACE OF INTEREST

INDEX

MAP INDEX